# THE LAST UNENCRYPTED MESSAGE

Trust the wrong device, and it will kill you.

*Bill Johns*

*Peninsula Network Security, LLC*

*2025*

# DEDICATION

To my daughter, Catherine—

Not because she is technical (she's not), but because, from an early age, she has always understood the intrigue, the stakes, and the human stories hidden beneath the surface of this work.

For every time she listened with curiosity, asked the hard questions, and saw that cybersecurity is not just about machines or code, but about trust, failure, and the quiet battles fought in invisible places.

She understood the intrigue and the human aspects — the heroes and the antiheroes, the ironies and the accomplishments — and she recognized that behind every signal and every breach, there are people, choices, and consequences.

Her ability to find meaning in the unseen, and significance in the overlooked gave these stories a second life beyond the technical details.

This book, and the lessons it carries, are for her.

—B.J.

# TABLE OF CONTENTS

## About the Author

*They trusted the air.*
*They trusted the silence.*
*They trusted until it killed them.*

# FOREWORD

Some warnings are gentle. This one was not.

When the pagers started exploding—loud, synchronized, unmistakable—it didn't feel like a glitch. It felt like a message. Not in Morse code or whispered signals, but in the universal language of violence: *you have been heard. You are not safe.*

The Last Unencrypted Message is not about a quiet failure. It is about a spectacular, public collapse of technological trust. It is about how systems designed for speed and convenience, trusted out of habit, became broadcasting stations for the enemy. It is about how a device so small it barely warranted a second thought ended up detonating operational security in front of everyone's eyes.

Bill Johns doesn't ask you to imagine this failure. He takes you there. To the moment when the old assumptions about wireless safety—assumptions built on complexity, on obscurity, on wishful thinking—died in the fire of real-world exploitation. He shows how a small, forgotten system—the pager—became the ignition point for a far larger collapse. Not because it was glamorous. Not because it was new. But precisely because it was assumed to be too insignificant to matter.

This was not a battle between symmetric forces alone. It was a battle where enemies who could not match you tank for tank or drone for drone could still break you by exploiting the seams you refused to defend. And it was a battle where enemies who *could* match you—and outgun you—pressed the advantage by attacking the blind spots that your own architecture made inevitable.

The explosions of the pagers were not an accident of history.

They were the first audible proof that the battlefield had expanded: into the air, into the spectrum, into every quiet assumption layered invisibly into operational life.

No signal is peripheral.
No channel is exempt.
No trust survives unchallenged.

This book is not just a technical autopsy of failure. It is a study in the physics of modern vulnerability: how complex systems rot from the edges inward, and how in the crucible of real-world conflict, enemies will always find—and strike—the places you least want them to see.

The last unencrypted message you ever receive might come on your pager — right before it kills you.

# INTRODUCTION — A WORLD BEFORE ENCRYPTION

There was a time when the air itself was trusted. It feels almost alien now, a historical artifact as distant as iron armor or flintlock rifles. Yet for most of the twentieth century, and well into the twenty-first, the idea of wireless communication carried a peculiar faith: if something was difficult to intercept, or simply unfamiliar to outsiders, it was considered safe. Secure by obscurity, protected by indifference, and defended only by the limits of technology itself. Not encrypted. Not hardened. Just there, humming invisibly through the atmosphere, a secret whispered in a crowded room with the naive confidence that no one else was listening.

This trust was not born of malice or laziness. It was born of a world where the cost of listening was high, and the technical skill to do so even higher. Radios, early telegraphs, the first transatlantic cables, all operated under the implicit assumption that while messages could theoretically be intercepted, few had the means, the resources, or the interest to do so. The signals were public in the strictest technical sense—flashing, beeping, vibrating through open mediums—but private in practice. Like letters dropped in a vast unmarked field, they were visible only to those who knew where to look, and few did.

By the late twentieth century, this invisible trust had hardened into quiet doctrine across militaries, hospitals, corporations, and governments. It was not written into law or formally taught in universities. It was simply understood. If a message was transmitted out-of-band—meaning outside the normal channels of voice or written communication—then it was safer by default. Out-of-band systems were seen as auxiliary, supplemental, almost disposable. They were the backup lines, the logistical fillers, the routing notes and paging calls that kept institutions functioning beneath the visible layer of critical operations. And because they were seen as peripheral, they were treated with a corresponding carelessness.

No technology embodied this cultural blind spot more perfectly than the pager. The humble beeper, once the symbol of prestige and urgency, had quietly evolved from a doctor's indispensable lifeline into a ubiquitous but overlooked infrastructure supporting hospitals, emergency services, industrial operations, and even military deployments. By the 1990s, pagers were cheap, reliable, and omnipresent. And despite their wireless nature, they were almost never encrypted. Their transmissions blared openly across publicly known frequencies, encoded in simple, standardized protocols designed for efficiency, not security. In a world obsessed with speed and coverage, privacy was an afterthought at best.

The protocols themselves told the story. POCSAG, developed in the late 1970s, was a marvel of engineering simplicity—a way to encode messages efficiently for low-power, wide-area transmission. FLEX, its successor in the 1990s, improved on speed and error correction but still made no serious attempt at protecting the content. Messages were blasted into the ether, addressable to specific receivers but perfectly visible to anyone else inclined to listen. No keys, no authentication, no expectation of confidentiality. After all, who would bother?

Within this environment of invisible vulnerability, two assumptions calcified into operational practice. The first was that low-level communications—logistics updates, medical alerts, administrative orders—were not sensitive enough to warrant protection. The second was that even if they were, the technical barrier to interception was sufficiently high to deter most adversaries. These assumptions would prove catastrophically wrong, but at the time, they made perfect sense to the institutions that relied on pagers and other unencrypted wireless systems.

In the Israeli Defense Forces, these assumptions were doubly entrenched. A military built on technological innovation and strategic agility, Israel prided itself on maintaining an edge over its adversaries in almost every domain. Encryption was a priority for radio communications between command centers and frontline units. Tactical data links and secure phones were deployed for operational planning. But paging systems, used for everything from personnel recalls to medical logistics, were considered peripheral. Useful, yes. Critical, sometimes. But sensitive? Unlikely. The messages were short, procedural, easily buried in the noise of a modern battlefield. They were, in the calculus of operational security, invisible enough.

The IDF was not alone in this miscalculation. Across the world, pager traffic coursed openly through hospitals, police departments, fire stations, and government offices. In New York City, a terrorist monitoring an SDR receiver in the 1990s could have passively collected emergency services pages with minimal effort. In London, researchers demonstrated how hospital patient data could be intercepted from the air with a laptop and a modest antenna. In Tokyo, corporate espionage experts quietly harvested insider information from pager broadcasts at financial institutions. But because the technical barrier was still nontrivial—because doing so required a certain expertise and equipment—the broader world remained oblivious. Risk, as always, was measured not in theoretical terms, but in practical ones. And practically speaking, few had the means or motive to listen.

The Middle East, however, was changing the equation. Long before "cyberwar" became a buzzword, long before sophisticated malware and AI-enabled surveillance reshaped the contours of conflict, there were organizations that understood the power of interception. Hezbollah was among the first non-state actors to weaponize it seriously. A political party, a militant group, a regional actor backed by Iranian funding and training, Hezbollah had learned from its own vulnerabilities in previous conflicts. It had learned that technology could be both a weakness and a weapon. And by the early 2000s, it had begun to invest in the kind of low-cost, high-impact capabilities that would exploit the blind spots of a complacent enemy.

In the run-up to the 2006 Lebanon War, Hezbollah quietly expanded its electronic warfare capabilities. Borrowing from Soviet doctrine, acquiring Iranian hardware, and cultivating local technical expertise, the group assembled mobile listening posts capable of intercepting a wide array of wireless communications. These units operated out of vans, apartments, and hilltop positions, blending into civilian infrastructure while sweeping the airwaves for exploitable signals. Their targets were obvious: Israeli radio transmissions, mobile phone chatter, military coordination channels. But alongside these high-priority intercepts, they discovered a hidden goldmine—pager traffic.

Israe Israeli pager broadcasts were rich with information: logistics updates about troop movements, medical alerts hinting at casualties, personnel assignments and call-ups revealing deployment structures, tactical orders cloaked in bureaucratic language but exposing patterns when pieced together. Hezbollah did not need to break sophisticated encryption or compromise hardened networks. It simply needed to listen, correlate, and act.

What followed was a quiet revolution in asymmetric warfare. While tanks rumbled across the border and fighter jets screamed overhead, an invisible battle was unfolding in the airwaves. Hezbollah used intercepted pager messages to anticipate Israeli operations, prepare ambushes, target artillery, and manipulate its own deployments to maximum advantage. For the first time, a non-state actor had achieved a degree of real-time electronic situational awareness against a modern military power. And it had done so not with billion-dollar satellites or nation-state espionage networks, but with ingenuity, patience, and a ruthless understanding of its enemy's technological arrogance.

The 2006 war was supposed to be a conventional conflict. It was supposed to be fought with armor and infantry, missiles and drones. Instead, it became, in part, a war of signals—a war in which the humble pager, the forgotten infrastructure of a bygone technological era, became both a weapon and a weakness. And it revealed something far more profound than a tactical vulnerability. It revealed that the assumptions underpinning modern communication security—the assumptions that peripheral systems could be ignored, that obscurity was protection, that technical barriers were deterrents—were dangerously obsolete.

In the years that followed, militaries and intelligence agencies around the world would scramble to harden their communications, to encrypt their out-of-band systems, to inventory and secure their invisible infrastructure. But the lesson, once learned, was indelible. Every signal, every transmission, every faint whisper of data in the air was a potential target. And in the silent spaces between tanks and missiles, between visible battles and formal declarations of war, a new kind of conflict had begun to unfold—one where victory would belong not just to those who fought hardest, but to those who listened best.

This is the story of how the air itself became a battlefield. How assumptions collapsed. How low-cost interception reshaped the calculus of war. It begins with pagers. It ends with a warning: In an interconnected world, there are no peripheral systems. Every channel matters. Every signal carries risk. And the most dangerous vulnerabilities are often the ones no one sees coming.

The weakness was not hidden in some obscure corner of the architecture; it was the very design itself. Pagers were engineered to be loud and public by nature. In cities across the globe, massive base stations hurled their signals out into the air without discrimination, covering miles of territory with powerful broadcasts intended for anyone carrying a tiny, passive receiver. The addresses of those receivers—the cap codes that identified individual pagers—were no secret either. They were assigned methodically, predictably, often with little regard for operational secrecy. And because the pager was primarily a tool for convenience, the idea that someone might sit quietly with an antenna and a decoding rig, harvesting every message passing through a city or a battlefield, simply did not factor into the system's risk model.

When the first pagers were deployed in military settings, they were treated as administrative aids. They freed commanders from being tethered to radios or landlines, allowing quick, discrete notifications without the formality of a call. As conflicts grew more mobile, as operations became more distributed, pagers found new life in coordinating complex logistics—resupplies, medevac requests, personnel movements. And in all of these roles, their fundamental insecurity remained unseen because it was so deeply normalized.

Even among those who understood the theoretical risks, the practicalities of war had a way of overriding caution. Encryption, where available, introduced delays. Authentication protocols, still in their infancy for wireless systems, added complexity that often clashed with the brutal tempo of frontline operations. It was far easier to believe that the enemy was too unsophisticated, too distant, or too busy to bother with intercepting secondary communications. Operational security was a resource, like fuel or ammunition, and commanders spent it carefully. For the humble pager, the cost of securing it seemed greater than the benefit.

This cognitive bias, the prioritization of visible threats over invisible ones, is an ancient flaw in human conflict. Armies through history have fortified walls while leaving the wells unguarded, have armored the chest while leaving the joints exposed. In the digital age, the same flaw persisted, and nowhere was it more apparent than in the unexamined spaces of wireless communication.

By the turn of the millennium, the technical barriers that once protected pager traffic through obscurity were crumbling. What once required expensive, specialized receivers and deep technical expertise could now be accomplished with off-the-shelf components and open-source software. The advent of Software Defined Radio (SDR) technology brought the cost of wideband interception down dramatically. A hobbyist with a laptop and a few hundred dollars' worth of equipment could scan vast swaths of radio spectrum, decode pager transmissions in real-time, and reconstruct the information as easily as reading an email. The only thing lagging behind was awareness. The vulnerability was no longer theoretical. It was practical. But because few had publicly exploited it at scale, the institutions relying on pagers remained in a kind of operational sleepwalk, secure in a safety that no longer existed.

In Lebanon, Hezbollah was wide awake.

Their approach was methodical. Training cadres specializing in signal collection, equipping them with a mix of Soviet-surplus intercept gear and newer Iranian-built receivers, positioning them along likely avenues of Israeli advance. They were listening to radios, cell phones, military repeaters —and now, to the pager broadcasts humming freely through the contested airspace. It was an ecosystem of surveillance, patient and voracious, one that treated every unsecured transmission as a potential source of advantage. Using a combination of scavenged Soviet-era receivers, Iranian-supplied equipment, and increasingly sophisticated scanning techniques, Hezbollah's teams mapped Israeli pager networks with a precision few anticipated.

What Hezbollah understood, and what their adversaries did not fully grasp until it was too late, was that in asymmetric warfare, the value of information could outweigh the value of firepower. A single intercepted message, properly understood, could reposition troops, redirect artillery, or foil an ambush. A sequence of routine logistical updates could sketch the outline of an entire operation. And once mapped, once modeled, the enemy's movements could be anticipated, their plans unraveled, their initiative stolen.

It did not require breaking into encrypted systems. It did not require defeating hardened networks. It required only listening where no one thought to defend.

The Israeli Defense Forces entered the 2006 Lebanon War with superior equipment, superior training, and superior firepower. They had electronic warfare units, cyber defenses, sophisticated intelligence networks. But in their reliance on a patchwork of communication systems, they had unknowingly left a backdoor ajar. The pagers, chirping faithfully across their coverage zones, were one such backdoor. They whispered secrets into an uncaring sky, and Hezbollah, diligent and attentive, caught those whispers and turned them into weapons.

The exploitation of pager traffic during the war was not, by itself, decisive. Wars are complex, sprawling events, influenced by thousands of factors large and small. But it mattered. It mattered tactically, in battles where foreknowledge allowed Hezbollah to ambush Israeli units or preempt airstrikes. It mattered operationally, in how the IDF had to adapt mid-campaign to the realization that their communication channels were not as private as believed. And it mattered strategically, in how it signaled a shift in the nature of conflict—an early warning that the traditional separation between kinetic warfare and cyber-electronic warfare was dissolving.

After the war, there were inquiries, reports, reforms.

Communications security policies were revised. Encryption was mandated more aggressively, even for seemingly peripheral systems. New training emphasized the vulnerability of all wireless transmissions, no matter how trivial they might seem. But the damage had been done, and the lessons learned at cost. An enemy had weaponized the overlooked and the obsolete, and in doing so, had illuminated a permanent truth of modern conflict: no signal is too small to matter. No communication is beneath notice. In a world where everything talks, everything can be overheard. And what is overheard can be used.

The pager war, as it came to be known among a small circle of specialists, was not a grand cyber campaign like those that would dominate headlines a decade later. It was not Stuxnet, with its precision-engineered sabotage of Iranian centrifuges. It was not NotPetya, unleashing catastrophic economic disruption across continents. It was something quieter, older, and in some ways more unsettling. It was a reminder that technological sophistication is no substitute for operational vigilance. That even the simplest systems, left exposed, can become the lever by which a larger machine is moved.

It is tempting, in retrospect, to view the interception of pager traffic as an inevitable consequence of technological advancement. To imagine that as SDRs became cheaper, as hacking tools became more available, someone was bound to notice the vulnerability and exploit it. But this narrative misses the human element—the deliberate choices made, the discipline exercised, the patience required. Hezbollah's exploitation was not just a technological feat; it was a human one. It required the will to listen, the discipline to wait, the skill to interpret, and the audacity to act. It was not inevitable. It was earned.

The lessons of that conflict reverberate today, far beyond the hills of southern Lebanon. As wireless systems proliferate —from IoT devices chattering over unlicensed spectrum, to industrial control systems broadcasting telemetry across factory floors—the surface area for interception and exploitation has exploded. Yet the mindset that allowed the pager vulnerability to exist endures. Convenience still trumps security. Assumptions still go unchallenged. Out-of-band communications are still, too often, treated as afterthoughts rather than attack surfaces.

The air remains full of secrets. And the ears that listen have only grown sharper.

This book tells the story of the pager wars: the rise of wireless vulnerability, the fall of institutional complacency, and the birth of a new understanding of the invisible battlefield. It is a story of technological innocence lost, of invisible signals made deadly, and of a world that woke up—too late—to the risks it had long ignored.

Wireless technology, for all its marvels, was built on principles that inherently resisted secrecy. The earliest radio pioneers were not concerned with hiding information; they were concerned with transmitting it over distance, with overcoming the constraints of wire, terrain, and atmosphere. Marconi's first transatlantic signal in 1901 was an act of raw communication power, not subtlety. The entire ethos of wireless transmission was expansive: cast wide, reach far, overcome obstacles. Privacy was a secondary concern, if it was considered at all.

The protocols that evolved from these early efforts carried the same DNA. They were designed for coverage, for efficiency, for low power consumption and maximum reach. Even when digital encoding replaced analog waves, the fundamental paradigm remained. Broadcast to many. Assume only the intended recipient will pay attention. Ignore the rest.

By the late twentieth century, the limitations of this model were clear to security specialists, but their warnings often went unheeded. Encryption technologies existed—strong ones, mathematically sound and proven in academic and military contexts. But applying them to every communication channel was expensive, both in terms of computational load and logistical overhead. Encrypting voice channels required new radios, new key distribution systems, new training. Encrypting pager messages demanded an overhaul of receiver firmware, transmitter architecture, and carrier practices. In a world still operating under the momentum of physical warfare, where tanks and aircraft commanded budgets and mindshare, securing the pager network was a low priority.

Moreover, the early culture of wireless communication bred a false sense of compartmentalization. Military planners, corporate security officers, and emergency managers viewed their different communication modes as isolated streams. Secure radios for command and control. Cellular phones for convenience. Pagers for alerts and administrative tasks. Each stream was treated separately, its security assessed in a vacuum, without fully appreciating how even an unclassified administrative message could, when pieced together with others, form an actionable intelligence mosaic.

It was not just the content of the messages that mattered; it was the patterns they revealed. Timing, frequency, repetition, correlation with known events—these could transform the most banal logistics note into a window onto operational tempo, force composition, or strategic intention. The intelligence value of the pager network did not lie in any one message, but in the aggregation of thousands, the slow accumulation of context that allowed a skilled analyst to read between the lines.

This kind of pattern-based analysis was not new. It had been practiced by signals intelligence agencies for decades, famously exemplified by the codebreakers of Bletchley Park during World War II, who could infer German military movements not only from decrypted Enigma messages, but from traffic analysis alone—the who, when, and where of transmissions, even without knowing the what. But in the supposedly low-risk world of civilian and auxiliary communications, such methods were largely forgotten or ignored. The pager, humming busily across urban landscapes and military staging areas alike, was seen as noise, not signal.

Hezbollah saw it differently.

To them, every fragment of information was valuable. Every intercepted page, every unguarded radio call, every observable pattern was a step toward understanding, predicting, and ultimately countering the movements of a superior enemy. Their analytical discipline reflected a broader truth of asymmetric warfare: when you cannot match your adversary's firepower, you must outmatch their situational awareness. You must know them better than they know you.

In practice, this meant that Hezbollah's electronic warfare units operated less like traditional SIGINT teams and more like hunters. They did not have vast centralized databases, satellite constellations, or massive decryption farms. They had mobile receivers, field notebooks, human analysts. They listened, they observed, they cross-referenced, they hypothesized. A series of personnel pages calling up medical units could suggest an impending operation. A surge of maintenance requests might indicate logistical strain. A sudden silence, the absence of routine traffic, could itself be a warning of a coming strike.

The Israeli pager traffic, unencrypted and prolific, offered them a running commentary on the invisible gears of the war machine. Not the polished statements of commanders, but the raw, unfiltered metadata of military life. It was, in a sense, the shadow language of conflict—the background noise that, when carefully interpreted, spoke volumes.

And yet even as Hezbollah exploited these signals, the broader doctrine of wireless security remained stubbornly unchanged in many parts of the world. The pager persisted into the 2010s, quietly supporting critical infrastructure across hospitals, emergency services, and even some governmental operations. In hospitals, where HIPAA regulations mandated strict patient data protections, pager traffic continued to broadcast unencrypted patient names, diagnoses, room numbers, and emergency codes over publicly interceptable frequencies. In public safety, fire dispatches and police coordination still leaked sensitive information into the open air.

Research groups periodically demonstrated the ease with which such traffic could be captured. In one infamous study, a team used $20 SDR receivers and free software to intercept thousands of pager messages from major metropolitan areas, uncovering everything from law enforcement tactical updates to insider corporate communications. Their warnings echoed the lessons of the 2006 conflict: the air is not a safe place. The invisible is not the invulnerable.

Despite these warnings, despite the accumulating evidence, a kind of technological inertia persisted. Systems that had always operated in the clear continued to do so, buffered by a combination of habit, budgetary constraints, and the lingering belief that risk equated to visibility—that unless a breach was visible and catastrophic, it was not worth the cost of preemption. In this way, the pager vulnerability became less a technical failing than a cultural one, emblematic of a broader human tendency to discount invisible threats until they manifest in undeniable, often irreversible ways.

It is easy, from a modern vantage point, to look back and assign blame. To wonder how decision-makers could have been so blind, so careless. But such judgments ignore the complex realities of technological evolution. Systems are built not in isolation but atop layers of earlier assumptions, earlier priorities. Risk models lag behind capability shifts. Organizational awareness lags behind technological possibility. And often, the most dangerous vulnerabilities are those that feel too small to see, too marginal to matter, until suddenly they don't.

The story of the pager wars is not just a cautionary tale about one specific technology. It is a microcosm of a larger phenomenon—the perpetual arms race between communication and interception, between convenience and security, between what we choose to defend and what we leave exposed. It is about the blind spots that every system develops, and the adversaries who learn to see through them.

The war that would come in the summer of 2006 was, on the surface, a conventional conflict. It was fought with rockets and tanks, drones and infantry. It was visible on television screens, mapped in news reports, parsed through political analyses. But beneath that visible layer, a quieter war unfolded —one of signals and counter-signals, of intercepted messages and inferred movements, of an enemy listening patiently to an adversary who did not realize they were speaking too loudly into the void.

It is this quieter war—the war before encryption—that this book seeks to illuminate.

The quiet exploitation of Israeli pager traffic in the 2006 Lebanon War was not the product of luck. It was the culmination of years of adaptation by Hezbollah, a group that had studied its adversary with the cold patience of an insurgency that knew it could not outgun its enemy, but could outthink him. To Hezbollah's operational planners, every dimension of Israeli military behavior was a data source. Not merely battlefield movements or air sorties, but supply lines, medical evacuation patterns, even the timing of shift rotations among support personnel. Where traditional armies sought decisive battles, Hezbollah sought informational advantage.

The pagers provided exactly that. They were the unintentional heartbeat of an entire logistical ecosystem, pulsing silently through the background noise of war. Each message a fragment; each fragment a clue. Standing alone, the information might seem insignificant—an alert to a medic, a scheduling update, a request for additional supplies. But patterns emerge quickly to those who are looking. Multiple medical alerts from a specific unit hinted at casualty rates. Frequent resupply requests in a zone suggested a buildup of forces, or prolonged engagements. Mobilization notices for particular reserve units signaled areas of strategic concern.

The brilliance of Hezbollah's exploitation lay in their ability to collate, correlate, and act. Their electronic warfare teams did not merely intercept pager traffic; they harvested it systematically, cataloging transmissions, mapping them to locations, creating timelines. Over days and weeks, a portrait of Israeli operations would slowly resolve, as distinct as if it had been painted by an insider. In a war where mobility was essential, where rapid response was supposed to be a key Israeli advantage, Hezbollah used these insights to blunt and bleed their opponent.

Israeli commanders, for their part, realized too late that their communications had been compromised. When they did understand, the initial reaction was disbelief, followed by a frantic push to secure what could still be secured. Orders were revised to limit pager use. Alternative communication channels were emphasized. But adaptation under fire is a poor substitute for preparation. The damage had already been done. Hezbollah's early access to unguarded communications had given them a strategic elasticity—allowing them to avoid engagements they could not win, to mass fire where it would do the most harm, and to conserve their forces for a longer war than Israel had anticipated.

What is perhaps most striking, in retrospect, is how preventable this vulnerability was. The technical means to secure pager communications existed. Encrypted paging systems, though more complex and costly, had been developed for specific industries where confidentiality was a higher concern. But widespread adoption lagged, hampered by budgetary inertia and a pervasive underestimation of the threat. Encryption was seen as necessary for radios carrying live voice commands. For battlefield data links controlling drones and targeting systems. For political communications passing between senior leaders. Pagers, meanwhile, were relegated to the background, classified as administrative convenience rather than operational necessity.

This misclassification speaks to a broader failure of imagination. Security measures are too often applied according to hierarchical visibility—what is perceived as critical, urgent, or dangerous—rather than a true systemic understanding of interdependencies. The pager system was invisible not because it was unimportant, but because it worked silently, reliably, without demanding attention. In human systems, as in complex machinery, it is often the quietest components whose failure proves catastrophic.

The 2006 Lebanon War marked a painful transition point, not just for Israel, but for the global understanding of electronic vulnerabilities. It was a proof-of-concept that sophisticated interception no longer required the resources of a superpower. That wireless infrastructure, even outside the traditional boundaries of "cyber" targets, could yield battlefield advantage to a patient adversary. And that asymmetric forces, once seen primarily as tactically agile but technologically inferior, were rapidly evolving into information-age hunters.

The ripple effects of this realization were profound. In the years following the conflict, militaries around the world initiated sweeping reviews of their wireless communication practices. Pager systems in defense environments were either phased out, encrypted, or heavily restricted. Training programs were revised to emphasize emission control not just for radios, but for every wireless device in use, from tactical routers to personal cell phones. New doctrines began to treat the electromagnetic spectrum as a contested battlespace in its own right, rather than a mere enabler of conventional operations.

Yet even as these reforms took root, the vulnerabilities did not vanish. Legacy systems lingered, embedded in the infrastructure of public health, emergency services, utilities, and transportation. Paging networks continued to relay unencrypted messages across major cities well into the 2010s. In hospitals, doctors' pagers still carried patient information in the clear, exposing sensitive medical data to anyone with the means and motive to intercept it. In corporate environments, IT alerts, security incident notices, and even internal crisis communications sometimes rode on the aging backbone of unsecured wireless paging systems.

The pager had become a technological ghost—obsolete in public consciousness, yet still operational, still vulnerable. And in that ghostly persistence lay a broader truth about security failures: they are rarely about technology alone. They are about culture, about inertia, about the stories organizations tell themselves to justify why change is unnecessary. They are about who gets heard when risks are raised, and who gets dismissed.

The 2006 Lebanon War forced some of these stories to change. But it did not erase the underlying patterns that created them. The invisible trust in out-of-band communication had been broken, but new forms of invisible trust arose in its place. Trust that mobile apps, cloud systems, or IoT devices would somehow be secure by default. Trust that if a system had not yet been attacked publicly, it was safe enough. Trust that obscurity, once again, could substitute for protection.

It is in this sense that the story of the pager wars is not merely a historical episode, but an ongoing parable. The same dynamics that allowed Hezbollah to turn cheap radios into strategic advantage still operate today, albeit in more complex technological forms. Attackers still seek the edges of systems, the forgotten channels, the paths of least resistance. They still exploit the belief that if a system is peripheral, it can be neglected.

The difference now is one of scale. Where once the risk was a few kilobytes of unencrypted pager messages, today it is terabytes of unsecured IoT telemetry, orphaned cloud databases, and side-channel emissions from critical infrastructure. The air is even more crowded, the stakes even higher, and the ears even sharper.

The battlefield has expanded, but the lessons remain the same.

The practice of exploiting ambient, unsecured signals to gain strategic advantage is not new. Long before wireless pagers became vulnerable arteries on the battlefield, armies and intelligence services learned the power of what could be gathered without direct confrontation. During the Second World War, before the Allied codebreakers of Bletchley Park ever cracked a single Enigma cipher, they made crucial use of traffic analysis—the study of who was sending messages to whom, when, and how often. Even encrypted communications revealed patterns, and those patterns exposed command structures, hinted at operations, and allowed strategic deductions to be drawn from otherwise inaccessible information.

Similarly, in the Cold War, both the United States and the Soviet Union invested heavily in signals intelligence infrastructures designed not merely to decrypt enemy communications, but to **listen to everything**, map the electromagnetic environment, and pull insights from noise. The great listening posts, like Menwith Hill in the UK or Lourdes in Cuba, absorbed millions of transmissions daily, sweeping up voice, telemetry, radar emissions, and passive signals that filled the global spectrum. It was understood that in a world increasingly saturated by signals, the side that could hear best, and correlate fastest, would possess a decisive edge.

What Hezbollah achieved in 2006, though much smaller in scale, was an application of the same ancient principle in a new, asymmetric context. It was a proof that the informational advantage historically wielded by state powers could be inverted, if the vulnerabilities were there and if the will to exploit them was strong enough.

Their success was not simply a matter of intercepting data; it was about interpretation, correlation, and operationalization. In this, Hezbollah mirrored the techniques used by major intelligence agencies. They did not need to read every message in isolation. They needed only to listen carefully enough, long enough, to understand the patterns—the rhythm of logistics, the pulse of mobilizations, the gaps in defenses.

In traditional warfare, knowledge of the enemy's intentions is a luxury. In asymmetric warfare, it is a necessity. Hezbollah understood that it could not match Israel tank for tank, aircraft for aircraft. But if it could anticipate Israeli actions, shape the battlefield with superior information, and maneuver faster than its opponent's decision-making cycle, it could blunt Israel's technological and kinetic advantages. The interception of pager traffic, humble though it may have seemed to outsiders, was an integral part of this strategy.

It is important to remember that wireless exploitation was only one facet of Hezbollah's broader approach. They invested in hardened communications of their own—fiber optic lines buried underground, decentralized command structures that minimized the impact of any single point of failure, and redundant systems that could survive electronic warfare attacks. They studied Israeli tactics and technology, and adapted in ways that Western analysts often failed to predict. Their doctrine emphasized resilience, local initiative, and informational asymmetry, all of which were amplified by their ability to tap into the invisible veins of their enemy's communication networks.

In this sense, the pager interception was not a standalone phenomenon; it was a symptom of a deeper shift in the nature of conflict. A shift where information, once the province of spies and satellites, became accessible through far cheaper, more distributed means. A shift where operational security failures at the edges of a system could have cascading effects at the center. And a shift where asymmetric actors, long dismissed as technologically backward, demonstrated a sophistication that belied their perceived status.

The 2006 war was a glimpse into the future—a future where wars would be fought as much with electrons and algorithms as with bullets and bombs. Where the battlefield would include not just territory, but spectrum. Where dominance in the electromagnetic environment could translate into dominance on the ground. Where every communication, however small, would have to be treated as a potential vector of vulnerability.

Israel, for all its military strength, found itself forced into a reactive posture against an enemy that had, in some critical respects, seized the informational initiative. This was not a total victory for Hezbollah, nor was it a decisive defeat for Israel. But it was a demonstration—a sharp, unforgettable lesson—that would reverberate through military doctrine worldwide.

In the aftermath, as inquiries dissected the war's failures and successes, one theme recurred with uncomfortable frequency: the vulnerabilities were not new. They had been known. They had been acknowledged in abstract terms, buried in reports and technical assessments. But they had not been prioritized. Other concerns—operational tempo, cost savings, legacy system support—had taken precedence. The pager system had remained unsecured because no one had demanded otherwise with sufficient urgency.

And this, perhaps, is the most enduring lesson. Vulnerabilities are not always hidden. Sometimes they are known, tolerated, rationalized away. They become part of the background noise of an organization's risk landscape, present but unaddressed, until a motivated adversary weaponizes them. At that moment, the familiar transforms into the catastrophic.

Hezbollah did not defeat Israel in 2006. But they demonstrated that technological advantage could be eroded, even reversed, by those willing to exploit the seams, the oversights, the places where complexity and complacency intersected. They showed that security is not just a function of hardware and software, but of mindset. Of discipline. Of respect for the hidden costs of convenience.

As modern militaries, corporations, and governments race to secure their new digital perimeters—building firewalls, encrypting data, deploying AI-driven defenses—the same old vulnerabilities persist. Forgotten devices. Legacy protocols. Channels of communication deemed too minor to matter. The lessons of the pager wars whisper through these systems, for those willing to listen.

In the air around us, every day, signals still fly. Emergency alerts. Infrastructure telemetry. Industrial control commands. Personal health data. Some encrypted. Some not. Some protected by best practices. Some by nothing at all. The battlefield has expanded into the very fabric of our daily lives, and the enemies who once sat in vans with simple receivers have grown more sophisticated, more numerous, more patient.

Yet at the heart of it, the principle remains unchanged: what is broadcast can be heard. What is heard can be understood. What is understood can be used.

And what is used can change everything.

By the early months of 2006, the air between Israel and southern Lebanon was thick with a kind of invisible tension. Patrols edged along uneasy borders. Intelligence reports whispered of stockpiled rockets, fortified villages, and an enemy that had grown not only in arsenal, but in discipline. Hezbollah had evolved in ways that were not immediately visible. To the outside world, they remained a militia, a political movement armed with weapons smuggled from Tehran and Damascus. But beneath the surface, they had been quietly constructing a new kind of operational sophistication —one built not merely on firepower, but on knowledge.

The Israelis prepared for the conflict they believed was coming. Their command and control systems were robust. Their air force, lethal and responsive. Their ground forces, battle-tested and confident. Years of technological dominance had bred a doctrine that assumed superiority not only in weaponry, but in information. Secure radios, encrypted satellite feeds, battlefield data links—these were the arteries through which the war machine pulsed. And because these channels were fortified, the IDF believed its operational intent would remain obscured, its movements unpredictable.

But the fortress had a forgotten side door. Pagers, relaying logistics orders, personnel callups, emergency notifications, status reports. Not encrypted. Not monitored. Not even considered, in most operational threat models, as an intelligence source worth defending. They were administrative tools, part of the background hum of a modern military bureaucracy, unglamorous and thus invisible.

Hezbollah's analysts, however, were not blinded by such assumptions. They had been listening, long before the war began, mapping the patterns of this forgotten channel. They knew that while encrypted radios carried orders, pagers carried the habits, the schedules, the necessities of sustaining an army in the field. They knew that no military could move without its logistics, and that logistics spoke constantly, thoughtlessly, into the ether.

When hostilities erupted, it was these whispers—these unsecured, unnoticed transmissions—that gave Hezbollah an informational edge. In the opening weeks of the conflict, as Israeli forces mobilized, Hezbollah's EW units intercepted a flood of pager messages. Some carried obvious information: medical alerts for wounded soldiers, requests for engineering support. Others required more careful reading, more patient correlation. But taken together, they formed a latticework of insight. They revealed where units were massing, where supply lines were strained, where reinforcement patterns suggested impending offensives.

Hezbollah did not need to hack Israel's command systems. It did not need to decrypt high-level orders or break into secure networks. It needed only to listen to what was already being given away freely. In doing so, they turned Israeli operational rhythms into predictable patterns—and predictable patterns, in warfare, are fatal.

The pager traffic was a seam, a crack in the armor, and Hezbollah drove a wedge into it. Their forces maneuvered to avoid concentrations of Israeli power. They prepared ambushes against resupply convoys. They shifted artillery and rocket teams based on inferred vulnerabilities. They engaged selectively, choosing battles that attrited Israeli forces without overcommitting their own. In an environment where every physical confrontation carried enormous risks, the ability to anticipate even a fraction of the enemy's intent was transformative.

Israeli commanders, when they realized the breach, were stunned. The idea that a lowly administrative system could provide such operational advantage to the enemy challenged deeply held assumptions about information security. Reactions ranged from disbelief to quiet rage. Orders were issued to clamp down on pager use, but in the chaos of war, enforcement lagged. Some units adapted quickly; others continued to bleed information into the sky, unaware that every signal might be their own undoing.

The tragedy of the pager vulnerability was not just its technical simplicity. It was that it illustrated how the hierarchies of technological trust could be so fatally misaligned with operational reality. What an organization views as peripheral may, to an adversary, be central. What a planner dismisses as noise may, to a patient listener, become symphony. In the complex web of modern conflict, there are no small communications. There are only signals unexamined.

Looking back, the interception of pager traffic in the 2006 Lebanon War seems almost inevitable. The conditions were perfect: a reliance on legacy systems, a failure to account for low-cost adversary intelligence capabilities, a cultural blind spot around auxiliary communications. But inevitability is a dangerous illusion. It suggests passivity. In reality, the exploitation was the result of deliberate choices—both by those who left vulnerabilities exposed, and by those who sought, relentlessly, to exploit them.

Hezbollah chose to invest in signal interception when it could have prioritized other domains. It chose to train operators, to acquire equipment, to develop analytical capacity. It chose to listen when others assumed they would not. These were not passive consequences of technological evolution; they were acts of will.

Similarly, Israel's vulnerabilities were not random accidents. They were the cumulative product of decisions—decisions to defer encryption upgrades, to prioritize other communications security concerns, to allow certain legacy systems to persist out of expediency or cost-effectiveness. Risk was weighed, and in the absence of a visible, active threat, discounted. It is a pattern as old as warfare itself, but made newly dangerous by the democratization of interception technology.

The broader world would take time to catch up to these lessons. In the years that followed, major militaries began to regard the electromagnetic spectrum with new caution.

Secure voice was no longer sufficient; emissions control, signal hygiene, and spectrum monitoring became core components of operational planning. Even low-bandwidth, administrative systems were brought into the security perimeter, encrypted, authenticated, hardened against exploitation.

But outside the defense sector, the awakening was slower. Hospitals continued to broadcast unencrypted patient data. Emergency services continued to coordinate over open channels. Industrial sites transmitted telemetry over unprotected wireless links. Legacy systems, hidden from daily view, hummed on quietly, waiting for the next adversary patient enough, clever enough, or desperate enough to weaponize them.

This book tells the story of how it happened first. How a non-state actor, using inexpensive equipment and determined analysis, turned overlooked signals into operational advantage against one of the most technologically advanced militaries in the world. How an invisible battlefield—stretching across frequencies and protocols no one thought important—became a decisive arena of modern conflict.

It begins not with malware, not with hacking, not with shadowy cyber-espionage units deploying bespoke exploits. It begins with something simpler. Something older. A whisper in the air, a signal unguarded, a message not meant for enemy ears, but captured all the same.

It begins with a pager.

And it reminds us that in a world saturated with signals, saturated with data, saturated with communication, the greatest risks are often not the ones we anticipate, but the ones we forget.

Trust in technology does not collapse with explosions or sirens. It erodes quietly, grain by grain, until the structure that once seemed unshakable simply crumbles under its own weight. In the aftermath of the 2006 Lebanon War, as investigators pored over the wreckage of operations compromised and opportunities missed, it became clear that something profound had shifted. The trust once placed in the invisible layers of communication—the signals no one saw, the systems no one questioned—had been broken, and it could not easily be rebuilt.

It was not simply that a non-state actor had managed to intercept messages. It was that they had done so with such ease, with such devastating effectiveness, that it forced a reckoning with assumptions too long left unchallenged. If a pager could betray an army, what else could? What other silent pathways, what other overlooked systems, carried the seeds of operational ruin within them?

The answer, though unspoken at the time, was everything.

The pager exploitation was not an anomaly. It was a symptom. It revealed that the connective tissues of modern operations —logistics, administration, maintenance, even personal communications—were riddled with vulnerabilities. Not because of malice. Not because of incompetence. But because human systems, when stretched across complexity and time, inevitably accumulate risk at their margins. Because the drive for efficiency, for ease, for speed, will always find ways to outpace the slower, heavier burden of securing every edge.

In the years that followed, new tools would be developed to secure communications. Encryption would become cheaper, faster, more ubiquitous. Spectrum monitoring would grow more sophisticated. But the fundamental tension between convenience and security would not vanish. It would simply migrate, appearing in new forms—unpatched IoT devices, orphaned cloud services, shadow IT infrastructures sprawling beyond the reach of formal governance.

The lesson of the pager wars was not that technology fails us. It was that we fail ourselves, again and again, by mistaking invisibility for safety, by assuming that what we cannot see cannot hurt us. The pagers whispered into the void because no one thought it mattered. The signals hung in the air because no one believed anyone would listen. And the enemy listened, patiently, relentlessly, until they could see what the system itself refused to admit.

That patience, that discipline, that ruthless understanding of human complacency, would become the hallmark of a new era in conflict. An era where battles would not only be fought over territory, but over data. Over patterns. Over the subtle rhythms of communication and control. An era where the electromagnetic spectrum would be as contested as the land and the sea. Where the smallest signal, the quietest whisper, might tip the balance.

The 2006 Lebanon War was, in this sense, an early skirmish in a much larger, still-unfolding war. A war where every device that speaks, every channel that connects, every unseen protocol that pulses in the background of our lives, is part of the battlefield.

It is a war fought not only with firewalls and malware, with drones and cyber-espionage. It is a war fought with the hidden architecture of trust, with the assumptions we make every time we connect, every time we transmit, every time we choose not to look too closely at the systems we depend on.

The story that follows is not just about Hezbollah, or Israel, or a single summer of conflict. It is about the architecture of vulnerability itself. About how it is built, how it is ignored, and how it is finally, inevitably, exploited.

It is a story that begins, improbably, with a technology already consigned to the past—a simple pager, humming quietly in the pocket of a soldier, a medic, a supply officer.

It is a story of how the future of warfare, and the future of security, was foretold not in secret bunkers or cutting-edge laboratories, but in the neglected patterns pulsing unseen across the sky.

It is a story of how trust dies.

And how, once lost, it never returns in quite the same way. Yet history would not leave the balance untouched. The same airwaves that once betrayed Israel would, in time, become weapons in Israeli hands.

War is never static, and neither are the lessons it teaches. In the years that followed, Israel did not merely rebuild its defenses; it reimagined the battlefield itself. The same vulnerabilities that had been exploited against it would, with time, be studied, inverted, and turned outward. New generations of Israeli cyber and electronic warfare teams would learn to listen just as patiently, just as ruthlessly. They would find ways to penetrate Hezbollah's own communications, to exploit the channels Hezbollah believed safe, to weaponize trust in systems once considered peripheral. The page would turn. The air would become a battlefield not for one side, but for all sides. And in that invisible war, no signal, no message, no system would ever again be truly safe.

# CHAPTER 1 — BEEPERS, BROADCASTS, AND THE ILLUSION OF PRIVACY

The story of wireless vulnerability does not begin with smartphones or satellites. It begins with a beep. A simple, piercing beep that cut through the air and summoned doctors from their beds, engineers from their lunches, and later, soldiers from their rest. Before wireless networks blanketed the earth, before mobile phones became extensions of the human body, there was the pager: a humble device, modest in appearance and purpose, but profound in its implications. The pager was the first true mass-market personal wireless device, and its quiet ubiquity would leave an invisible mark on the architecture of communication, and the assumptions about its security.

Pagers emerged in the mid-twentieth century as a technological response to a very human need: the need to reach people who were in motion. The hospital was their first major domain. Physicians, long accustomed to being tied to phones or couriers, found in the pager a liberation of movement without a loss of availability. Early systems were crude by today's standards—a simple tone alert with no message attached, requiring the recipient to find a telephone and call in for details—but they represented a new concept: that a signal could find you wherever you were, carried invisibly through space.

The idea caught on quickly. By the 1970s, pagers had moved beyond hospital hallways into industries where mobility and responsiveness were valued. Utilities workers, airline crews, police officers, and corporate executives began to carry them clipped to belts and tucked into briefcases. Each beep was a summons, a demand for attention across distance, a small triumph over the constraints of physical separation. The device shrank as technology advanced, evolving from bulky, radio-receiver-based units into sleek, battery-powered companions with tiny displays capable of showing short numeric or alphanumeric messages. And with each step of technical refinement, the pager insinuated itself deeper into daily life.

By the 1980s and early 1990s, paging networks had grown into vast, invisible infrastructures layered atop cities and rural landscapes alike. High-powered base stations transmitted signals that could cover entire metropolitan areas, while satellite links and nationwide systems enabled communication across thousands of miles. A doctor in San Francisco could be paged from New York. An engineer in Tokyo could receive an urgent alert from Paris. Mobility had become not just a convenience, but an expectation. The pager had helped create a world where presence was optional but responsiveness was mandatory.

Technically, the underlying operation of pagers was elegant in its simplicity. A central dispatch system would encode a brief message, assign it to a unique address corresponding to an individual device, and broadcast it through a transmitter. The pager, constantly listening for its address, would chirp to life when summoned, displaying the incoming message or merely sounding a tone to prompt a callback. Early systems were largely analog, but as the demand for capacity and reliability grew, digital paging protocols emerged.

Among these, two standards came to dominate: POCSAG and FLEX. POCSAG, named for the British Post Office Code Standardization Advisory Group that developed it in the late 1970s, became the first widespread digital paging protocol. It employed a simple binary encoding scheme, transmitting batches of data at relatively low speeds. A POCSAG transmission consisted of a preamble to alert devices, a series of address and message codewords, and finally, synchronization bits to help pagers stay locked onto the signal. FLEX, introduced by Motorola in the early 1990s, refined the concept. It offered faster data rates, better error correction, and improved spectral efficiency, allowing networks to handle more messages with greater reliability.

Both protocols, however, shared a crucial trait: they were broadcast in the clear. There was no encryption, no authentication, no attempt to disguise the content of the messages or the identity of the recipient. A FLEX or POCSAG transmission was a radio signal like any other—propagating outward from its transmitter to be received by any device tuned to the appropriate frequency and able to recognize the simple format. The intended secrecy lay not in the structure of the protocol, but in the assumption that no one else was listening, or that if they were, they would not bother to decode what they heard.

At the time, this was a reasonable belief. Capturing and decoding pager traffic required specialized radio receivers, knowledge of the network parameters, and access to equipment that was expensive and technically challenging to operate. The barriers to casual interception were high enough that few considered it a practical threat. Moreover, the content of most pager messages seemed unworthy of espionage. Appointment reminders, equipment failures, shift schedules—these were the mundane details of operational life, important to their recipients but seemingly useless to outsiders. There was no apparent incentive to invest in the effort required to intercept them.

This trust, however, was not born of technical robustness. It was born of cost, convenience, and a certain arrogance of perspective. Encrypting pager traffic would have added complexity and expense to systems designed for maximum coverage and minimal operational overhead. It would have required pagers to have decryption capabilities, keys to be managed and distributed, and encryption modules to be certified and integrated into network infrastructure. All of this would have increased costs, reduced battery life, and complicated the engineering simplicity that made paging so attractive.

And so, instead of building security into the foundation of wireless paging, it was excluded by design. Not by oversight, but by a deliberate choice to prioritize reach, reliability, and simplicity over confidentiality. In this, pagers mirrored the larger trajectory of early wireless communication technologies, where the primary problem to be solved was connectivity, not secrecy. When radios were first deployed on battlefields, they too broadcast openly. When mobile phones were introduced, their early analog systems were laughably easy to intercept with scanners. In each case, the assumption was that the technical barrier to interception would protect users until better systems could be devised—and that in the meantime, the risk was acceptable.

The pager thus became a silent carrier of two intertwined illusions: the illusion of privacy, and the illusion of insignificance. Users believed their messages were private because no one had yet exploited them publicly. Organizations believed the messages were insignificant because they rarely contained state secrets or high-level strategic plans. In reality, both beliefs were dangerously wrong. Privacy is not a function of obscurity, and significance is not measured by the drama of a single message, but by the aggregation of many small facts into patterns.

Had the users of pagers considered the full implications of broadcasting their logistical arteries into the open air, they might have demanded better security. Had network operators considered the strategic potential of their transmissions to an adversary patient enough to collect and correlate them, they might have built encryption into the system from the outset. But they did not. Convenience won. Cost concerns won. And so the pager, for all its benefits, became an invisible liability woven into the infrastructure of modern life.

In time, the barriers to interception would fall. The specialized receivers would be replaced by software-defined radios—cheap, flexible, powerful devices that could capture wide swaths of the radio spectrum and decode pager traffic with ease. Open-source software would emerge, turning laptops into decoding stations. Tutorials would proliferate online, teaching hobbyists and researchers how to pluck messages from the air, reconstruct data streams, and reveal the hidden traffic once thought safe by virtue of complexity. What had once required deep technical expertise would become a matter of following instructions.

By the late 1990s and early 2000s, academic researchers and security enthusiasts began to sound warnings. Pager traffic, they showed, could be trivially intercepted. Sensitive information—patient names and diagnoses, corporate communications, even government alerts—was flying through the air unprotected. The risk was not theoretical. It was real, and it was growing. But as so often happens in the world of security, the inertia of existing systems, the costs of transition, and the absence of visible catastrophic breaches conspired to delay action.

Pagers remained embedded in critical infrastructure well into the twenty-first century. Hospitals continued to rely on them for internal alerts. Emergency services used them to coordinate dispatches. Military units deployed them for logistics and personnel notifications. Even as mobile phones became ubiquitous, even as encrypted communications grew more common, the pager persisted—quiet, cheap, and trusted.

This persistence was not merely a matter of habit. It was a reflection of a deeper truth about technology adoption: systems that work tend to endure, even when their underlying assumptions have been invalidated. The pager worked. It delivered messages reliably, across wide areas, with minimal cost. Its weaknesses were invisible until exploited, and by then, the dependencies it supported were too entrenched to unwind easily.

It was into this environment of quiet, unexamined trust that the first targeted exploitation of pager systems in modern conflict emerged—not from a superpower, but from a non-state actor willing to look where others did not. Hezbollah's realization that pager traffic was both accessible and valuable was not a product of advanced technology. It was a product of mindset. They did not need billion-dollar satellites or top-secret decryption programs. They needed only to listen, to correlate, and to act.

The era of silent vulnerabilities had begun, and the pager was its first, humble herald.

The technical anatomy of pager transmissions made them an easy target for anyone willing to assemble the right tools. POCSAG and FLEX, while marvels of efficiency in their day, were never designed with adversarial environments in mind. Their very structure assumed trust—that the radio spectrum was a neutral medium, that messages would reach their recipients without interception, that no one would bother to listen to the silent conversations moving through the air.

POCSAG's architecture was almost minimalist in its transparency. It transmitted at relatively low speeds, often 512, 1200, or 2400 bits per second, with a preamble of alternating ones and zeros to help receiving devices synchronize with the transmission. Following the preamble, batches of data were sent containing address information, frame synchronization, and the actual payload of the message. Each pager on the network was assigned a specific cap code—essentially a unique numerical address. When a pager recognized its cap code within an incoming transmission, it would activate and display or signal the corresponding message.

There was no challenge-response mechanism. No authentication that a given message truly originated from a legitimate source. No encryption to obscure the content even if someone intercepted it. It was a passive reception system, relying entirely on environmental difficulty—the challenges of capturing, demodulating, and interpreting RF transmissions—as a de facto form of protection.

FLEX, while an improvement in efficiency and capacity, did little to enhance security. Introduced in the early 1990s to handle higher paging traffic volumes, FLEX used four-level frequency shift keying (4FSK) modulation to pack more data into the available bandwidth. It supported higher data rates—typically 1600, 3200, or 6400 bits per second—and allowed for more robust error correction. But at its core, FLEX still broadcast messages in the clear. It still relied on addressable cap codes without authentication. It still assumed that intercepting and decoding the transmission was sufficiently difficult to serve as its own defense.

For most of the twentieth century, that assumption held true. Building a system capable of capturing POCSAG or FLEX traffic required specialized pagers configured in monitor mode, or purpose-built radio receivers tuned to the specific network frequencies. The interceptors needed to understand modulation schemes, error correction algorithms, and have the patience to assemble streams of fragmented data into coherent messages. It was not impossible—but it was enough of a barrier to limit the pool of potential eavesdroppers to well-funded intelligence agencies and obsessive hobbyists.

But the world was changing. By the late 1990s, the arrival of software-defined radios began to undermine the environmental assumptions that had shielded pager networks for decades. SDRs abstracted the radio hardware into software, allowing a single device to monitor, capture, and demodulate a wide range of frequencies and modulation types. Instead of needing a dedicated POCSAG receiver, a hacker or researcher could use an inexpensive SDR dongle, connected to a laptop, and sweep broad sections of the RF spectrum with relative ease.

Once the raw signals were captured, decoding them was trivial. Open-source tools proliferated—software packages that could automatically detect POCSAG preambles, extract cap codes, and reconstruct the text of messages. FLEX decoders followed, bringing the once-daunting task of pager interception within reach of anyone willing to download the right utilities and spend a few hours learning basic radio concepts. What had once required expensive equipment and deep expertise became, effectively, a matter of curiosity.

The shift was profound, but it went largely unnoticed outside niche technical communities. Pager networks, by then, had faded from public consciousness, overshadowed by the explosive growth of mobile phones, text messaging, and internet communications. But in the infrastructure of hospitals, emergency services, industrial facilities, and government agencies, pagers remained. They persisted not out of nostalgia, but out of necessity. Their reliability, simplicity, and resilience in environments where cellular coverage was spotty or overloaded kept them alive.

And because they remained invisible to the broader conversation about emerging cyber threats, their vulnerabilities were rarely addressed. Risk assessments focused on new technologies—smartphones, web applications, cloud systems—while legacy wireless systems like pagers were left out of scope. Their very ordinariness shielded them. Their oldness made them seem irrelevant. No one wanted to fight budget battles over securing a communications backbone that most executives barely remembered existed.

Even within industries that depended on pager traffic, security was an afterthought. Hospitals relied on pagers to route critical alerts between emergency departments, operating rooms, and on-call physicians. A cardiac arrest code, a surgical request, a neonatal distress call—these life-and-death communications raced across unsecured airwaves without a second thought. Corporate security teams, when they considered pagers at all, viewed them as low-risk systems carrying low-sensitivity data. IT departments, overloaded with the demands of modern networks, deferred upgrades to paging infrastructure year after year, allocating scarce resources to more visible threats.

This collective blind spot endured even as researchers demonstrated how trivial it had become to intercept pager traffic. Public presentations at security conferences in the early 2000s showed live captures of hospital alerts, police dispatches, industrial control warnings, and internal corporate messages. In some cases, the data included personally identifiable information, patient records, or sensitive operational details. The demonstrations were often met with polite interest, even alarm, but rarely with action.

Part of the problem was psychological. The pager belonged to a mental model of the past. It was associated with an era of rotary phones, floppy disks, and primitive internet connections. It felt quaint. Obsolete. Surely, if something was that old, it could not be a serious modern threat. Surely, if an attacker had the resources to build an interception system, they would target more lucrative, more modern systems. Pager traffic was assumed to be not only technically obscure, but strategically unimportant.

But information value is not measured solely by its sensitivity in isolation. In the hands of a skilled adversary, even seemingly innocuous data can be transformed into a weapon. A pattern of hospital alerts can reveal the location of mass casualty events before news outlets report them. A series of industrial maintenance pages can hint at systemic vulnerabilities in critical infrastructure. A stream of corporate pages can map the skeleton of internal operations, shift changes, supply chain rhythms, and emergent crises.

For an adversary willing to listen carefully, pager traffic offered a slow, steady drip of contextual intelligence—a mosaic assembled not from dramatic leaks or explosive hacks, but from the quiet accumulation of ordinary messages. It was an intelligence stream hiding in plain sight, waiting for someone to recognize its value.

And someone eventually would.

The willingness to dismiss pager traffic as harmless stemmed from a broader human flaw in assessing technological risk. We tend to anchor our fears to the visible, the novel, and the catastrophic. We worry about the dramatic breach, the cinematic hack, the glamorous vulnerabilities that attract headlines. Quiet, persistent, low-level threats are harder for the mind to grasp. They lack a singular event to rally against. They are slow poisons, not sudden strikes.

In the case of pagers, this blindness was magnified by familiarity. The devices had been present for so long, had performed so reliably, that they became part of the background hum of daily life. Like the pipes carrying water or the wiring carrying electricity, they were noticed only in failure. And because they rarely failed, because they chirped and beeped on schedule, they earned an undeserved aura of reliability that extended to assumptions about their security.

Even those who knew better often struggled to act. Risk management is, at its core, a competition of priorities. In any organization, securing known active systems—critical servers, user workstations, external-facing applications—takes precedence over remediating invisible legacy risks. Pager networks, especially in large institutions like hospitals and emergency services, fell into a liminal space: operationally important but administratively neglected. No one wanted to own the cost of upgrading or replacing them. No one wanted to champion a risk that had not yet produced a visible incident.

This inertia persisted even as the technical capability to exploit pager traffic became democratized. Enthusiasts demonstrated real-time interception at security conferences. Researchers published papers mapping entire hospital paging ecosystems from public streets. Hobbyists posted tutorials online explaining how to decode FLEX and POCSAG signals with cheap equipment. Each revelation chipped away at the illusion of obscurity that had protected pagers for so long, but still, systemic change was rare.

Occasionally, local incidents broke through the surface. In one case, a university hospital discovered that its pager system was leaking patient information, leading to internal reviews and rushed attempts to encrypt some messaging. In another, a corporate security audit found that internal alerts about network outages and security incidents were being broadcast over unencrypted pagers, available to anyone listening nearby. These cases, while alarming, rarely triggered widespread reforms. They were treated as isolated anomalies rather than indicators of a systemic vulnerability.

Meanwhile, in other parts of the world, actors with fewer resources but greater motivation were paying close attention. For groups like Hezbollah, whose operational survival depended on neutralizing the technological advantages of state militaries, vulnerabilities like unencrypted pager traffic were golden opportunities. They did not dismiss low-level information. They understood that in asymmetric warfare, where direct confrontation was suicidal, information itself became a force multiplier.

By the early 2000s, Hezbollah had begun assembling a quiet arsenal of electronic warfare capabilities. Some of it came through Iranian training and equipment transfers.

Some through the acquisition of surplus Soviet technology from collapsing Eastern European states. And some through their own disciplined internal development. Their operational doctrine emphasized patience, redundancy, and adaptability—traits that made them particularly suited to exploiting slow, low-bandwidth intelligence streams like pager traffic.

Their approach was not to build a technological panopticon overnight. It was to listen methodically, catalog what they heard, and slowly build patterns of inference. A supply request here, a personnel callup there, a maintenance alert somewhere else. Each piece individually insignificant, but when correlated over days, weeks, and months, capable of revealing operational rhythms, force compositions, and vulnerabilities.

Pager interception fit this model perfectly. It required no active intrusion, no exposure to counterintelligence measures. It could be conducted passively, from safe distances, using mobile or semi-fixed listening posts. And because no encryption or authentication protected the traffic, the only real technical challenges were tuning to the correct frequencies, capturing a sufficiently clean signal, and assembling the messages into usable formats.

None of these challenges were beyond Hezbollah's capabilities. Their electronic warfare teams trained in spectrum monitoring, signal demodulation, and basic traffic analysis. They equipped themselves with modified civilian receivers, scavenged military gear, and increasingly, commercial off-the-shelf components adapted for their purposes. By the time Israel crossed into southern Lebanon in the summer of 2006, Hezbollah's SIGINT units were already well-positioned to intercept not only traditional military radio traffic, but also the pager messages that formed the invisible connective tissue of Israeli operational logistics.

The irony was bitter. Israel, a nation renowned for its technological sophistication, had invested heavily in securing its primary communications channels. Tactical radios were encrypted. Command data links were hardened. Satellite feeds were protected. But the pagers—those humble, utilitarian relics of an earlier era—had slipped beneath the security perimeter. They were administrative, not operational. Peripheral, not critical. Or so it was believed.

In truth, the pager messages carried the blood and sinew of operational capacity. Casualty reports. Supply requests. Maintenance schedules. Unit reassignments. Medical emergencies. Each one a thread, and when woven together, a tapestry. Hezbollah's intercept teams were not looking for a single decisive message. They were looking for the patterns, the breathing of the machine.

And they found it.

The exploitation of pager traffic would become one of the quiet, pivotal factors in the 2006 Lebanon War. While Israeli tanks rumbled across contested ground and jets roared overhead, Hezbollah's analysts sat in shadowed rooms and listened. They listened with ruthless discipline, harvesting what others had discarded into the open air. They mapped the invisible movements of forces who never realized their footsteps echoed across the radio spectrum.

It was not the first time that underestimating an old, familiar technology had led to strategic miscalculation. Nor would it be the last. The pager, for all its humble appearance, had become an unintentional spy—a silent traitor embedded in the operational bloodstream of modern conflict.

And it had done so not because of its strength, but because of the very assumptions that had made it seem harmless.

The mechanics of interception were deceptively simple once understood. At their core, pager transmissions were little more than structured bursts of radio waves, broadcasting brief packets of information on predictable frequencies using predictable modulation schemes. Capturing them required only the right antenna, a receiver capable of tuning to the necessary band, and a way to interpret the digital pulses embedded in the signal.

In the early days of pager interception, specialized hardware was required. Modified scanners, commercial radio receivers configured for data modes, and occasionally even surplus military equipment were pressed into service by those curious or motivated enough to try. The process was tedious, demanding precise tuning, patient listening, and a deep understanding of signal behaviors in a noisy spectrum.

But by the early 2000s, the barriers had fallen dramatically. Software-defined radios shrank the once expensive and cumbersome equipment into small, affordable devices that could be plugged into any laptop. Coupled with open-source decoding software, these tools allowed even amateur hobbyists to capture, decode, and archive pager traffic from the comfort of their homes. An antenna taped to a window, a few clicks on a screen, and the invisible chatter of hospitals, corporations, and infrastructure systems spilled out into view.

Public demonstrations of this capability began appearing at security conferences. Researchers showed live captures of sensitive medical pages from major urban hospitals—alerts naming patients, describing diagnoses, even revealing treatment instructions. Others intercepted law enforcement coordination traffic, noting tactical deployments, officer call signs, and incident details. In industrial sectors, intercepted pager traffic disclosed maintenance schedules, control system warnings, and emergency shutdown notices.

Each demonstration peeled back another layer of the illusion that pagers were obscure, low-value targets. They revealed a hidden topography of communication beneath the visible internet, a world of wireless logistics and management that had been built without thought to adversarial environments. And still, for the most part, the larger institutions that relied on pagers remained inert.

The reasons for this inertia were complex, but they boiled down to a familiar triad: cost, complexity, and culture. Replacing or securing pager infrastructure meant incurring real expenses—not just in hardware upgrades, but in retraining personnel, redesigning workflows, and potentially sacrificing the simplicity and coverage that made pagers attractive in the first place. Secure paging systems existed, but they were more expensive, more finicky, and less widely supported.

Adding encryption to paging protocols would have required fundamental architectural changes. Pagers would need to store decryption keys securely, and transmitters would need to support key management at scale. In environments like hospitals or field logistics, where coverage and battery life were paramount, adding computational overhead was a hard sell. Vendors were reluctant to invest heavily in retrofitting security onto systems nearing the end of their commercial lifecycle. Customers were reluctant to push for expensive changes to infrastructure that seemed, by all external measures, to be working fine.

And then there was culture. Pagers were old. In a world obsessed with the newest threats—zero-day exploits, sophisticated malware, social engineering attacks—the idea of worrying about a decades-old technology seemed almost embarrassing. Decision-makers focused their attention on visible crises: ransomware attacks, data breaches, insider threats. Few wanted to champion a battle against a vulnerability that had not yet produced a scandal big enough to force action.

This cultural blindness was not limited to civilian institutions. In military and intelligence circles, too, the tendency was to prioritize securing primary systems—encrypted tactical radios, hardened command networks, classified data links—

while administrative and logistical communications remained secondary concerns. The operational risk assessments conducted prior to major deployments often weighted threats based on the sensitivity of the information being transmitted, not on the cumulative intelligence value of operational patterns leaking from secondary systems.

It was this cumulative value that Hezbollah recognized and exploited. In asymmetric warfare, where every advantage is precious, the slow harvest of logistical details could be more valuable than the unlikely jackpot of intercepting a major strategic order. In conventional warfare, precision strikes can win battles. In asymmetric warfare, precision information can prevent battles altogether—or shape them before the first shot is fired.

The methods Hezbollah used to exploit pager traffic were variations on techniques long known to state intelligence services. Passive interception of unencrypted signals. Correlation of message patterns to operational events. Mapping of transmission volumes and timing to infer troop movements, resupply efforts, or force concentrations. In many ways, it was traffic analysis in its purest form: the extraction of intelligence not from the content of a few secret communications, but from the mass observation of everyday logistics.

Building an operational picture from pager traffic required patience, discipline, and analytical skill. Each intercepted page was a small datum—a location, a name, a time stamp, a code. Few, if any, were immediately actionable on their own. But accumulated over time, cross-referenced with known events and behaviors, they revealed the heartbeat of an organization. Supply lines ebbed and flowed. Units rotated through areas of operation. Maintenance surges hinted at preparations for offensives. Medical traffic spiked in the aftermath of clashes. Every beep in the night was a whisper of operational truth, if one had the ears and the will to hear it.

The challenge for Hezbollah was not merely technical. It was organizational. Building a capability to capture, archive, and analyze pager traffic required more than gear. It required training, discipline, and analytical frameworks. Reports from the 2006 conflict suggest that Hezbollah's SIGINT teams operated with surprising sophistication—using mobile listening posts to stay close to the action without exposing themselves, rotating frequencies to avoid detection, and compiling intercepted data into usable intelligence products for operational commanders.

In this, they demonstrated a principle that would become increasingly important in cyber and electronic warfare: sophistication is not a function of budget. It is a function of mindset. A million-dollar encrypted radio system is worth little if a ten-dollar pager leaks its logistical underbelly. An army's secrets are only as strong as its weakest transmission. And often, that weakest link is not the one proudly displayed on the parade ground, but the one forgotten at the edges, carrying the messages no one thinks are dangerous.

The 2006 Lebanon War would be a proving ground for these ideas, a conflict where the power of passive interception, patient analysis, and infrastructural exploitation would be demonstrated not by a superpower, but by a non-state actor willing to listen carefully and act decisively. It was a glimpse into the future of conflict, a future where signals, not just soldiers, would be the primary targets. And it all began with the humble pager—a relic of another technological era, still carrying secrets into the open air.

In the final calculus of conflict, the smallest informational advantages often weigh as heavily as the largest guns. In southern Lebanon, as Israeli forces advanced into contested terrain, the assumptions that had underpinned the security of their logistical communications began to erode under pressure. Hezbollah's intercept teams, quiet and patient, had no need to break into classified networks or jam encrypted radio channels. They needed only to continue listening to the quiet hum of administrative transmissions bleeding invisibly across the hills.

The operational impact of this exploitation was subtle but profound. Hezbollah did not necessarily intercept grand strategic orders or uncover master plans through pager traffic. What they harvested instead was a constant flow of operational context—hints about where reinforcements were moving, where logistical strains were developing, where medical evacuations suggested heavy fighting. These insights allowed them to anticipate Israeli movements, prepare ambushes, reposition rocket teams, and avoid concentrations of overwhelming force.

In asymmetric warfare, where mobility and deception are life itself, such intelligence is priceless. It allows a weaker force to extend the fight, to choose the timing and location of engagements, to impose costs disproportionate to their numbers or equipment. It allows survival. It allows attrition. It turns every piece of logistical information into a weapon aimed at the assumptions of the stronger power.

For Israel, accustomed to technological superiority, the realization came slowly and painfully. As the conflict dragged on, commanders noticed that Hezbollah's forces seemed uncannily adept at avoiding direct clashes, at repositioning rocket teams just ahead of Israeli advances, at exploiting seams in operational deployments. Some of this was attributed to human intelligence—informants among Lebanese civilians, spotters hidden in the rubble of villages. But gradually, attention turned toward the possibility of signals exploitation. Toward the quiet channels no one had thought to protect.

The discovery was not immediate. In war, the noise of battle can drown out the faint signals of exploitation. Failures are attributed to chance, to enemy skill, to the fog of war itself. Only later, in the cold clarity of post-conflict analysis, did the pattern emerge with undeniable sharpness. The vulnerabilities of the pager systems—left unexamined, unencrypted, underestimated—had been weaponized against them.

It was not the kind of failure that announces itself with a single catastrophic event. No single intercepted message tipped a battle or toppled a brigade. It was a death by a thousand whispers, each small leak of information compounding into a strategic bleed. The pager network had become a fountain of operational metadata, freely available to anyone who knew how to listen, and Hezbollah had listened with ruthless discipline.

The arrogance that had shielded pagers from scrutiny for so long—the belief that obscurity was protection, that low-level logistics were beneath notice, that environmental difficulty would shield the system—had finally met an adversary willing to exploit the seam. And the consequences rippled far beyond the immediate battlefield.

In the aftermath of the war, as inquiries were conducted and lessons were drawn, the vulnerabilities of wireless systems—especially legacy systems like pagers—moved abruptly from the periphery to the center of operational security planning. No longer could secondary communications be dismissed as harmless. No longer could the environment be trusted to obscure flaws from the determined adversary.

Encryption mandates were expanded. Emission control protocols were tightened. Electronic warfare units were tasked not just with defending primary communications, but with monitoring and suppressing unsecured channels that could betray operational movements. The pager, once an unremarkable tool of convenience, became a symbol of how invisible infrastructure could become a decisive liability.

Yet even with these reforms, the deeper lesson was harder to internalize. It is easy to mandate encryption. It is harder to change the culture of trust that allows invisible risks to persist. It is easy to patch known vulnerabilities. It is harder to recognize the next overlooked system, the next legacy protocol, the next quiet channel bleeding information into the air.

The story of pagers in modern conflict is not just a story of technological failure. It is a story of human complacency, of organizational inertia, of the long, slow decay of security assumptions left unchallenged. It is a story that plays out again and again, in every era, wherever systems are built without a true reckoning of their place in the adversarial landscape.

And it is a story that continues today.

The humble pager, once a marvel of wireless connectivity, became a silent witness to the evolution of conflict from the visible to the invisible, from the kinetic to the informational. It revealed that the battlefield is not bounded by the lines drawn on maps or the roar of artillery, but extends into the invisible architectures of communication, trust, and assumption.

As the signals floated through the sky, unnoticed by those who sent them but not by those who listened, a new kind of warfare began to unfold—one that would define the conflicts of the twenty-first century not by who held the most territory, but by who held the most truth.

And that truth, as it turned out, was not hidden in vaults or guarded behind firewalls. It was humming quietly in the pocket of every soldier, every medic, every logistician. It was written in the open, for anyone with the patience and the will to read.

It was always there.

Waiting.

The echoes of the pager vulnerabilities uncovered during the 2006 Lebanon War did not end with the cessation of hostilities. They radiated outward, like invisible shockwaves, through every industry and sector that had come to rely on wireless communication without ever truly questioning its foundations. The battlefield had merely been the first place where the blind spots were weaponized. But the same blind spots existed elsewhere, waiting only for an adversary—or accident—to expose them.

Hospitals were among the most heavily dependent. Long after mobile phones became ubiquitous, pagers remained the backbone of critical alerting systems in emergency departments, surgical theaters, and intensive care units. Their resilience in poor reception areas, their long battery life, their simplicity—they made them ideal for environments where lives could turn on seconds. But the same trust that had protected them for decades continued to shield them from critical examination. The broadcasts continued, unencrypted, across hospital campuses and cities alike. Patient names. Diagnoses. Room numbers. Emergency codes. A digital pulse of life and death, fluttering across the public airwaves without protection.

Academic researchers, security professionals, and even casual hackers demonstrated the ease with which this traffic could be intercepted. In one case, a simple antenna taped to a hospital window and a $20 SDR device captured hundreds of sensitive pages per day. In another, a researcher driving through a city center intercepted emergency room trauma codes, revealing the locations and severity of incoming casualties. The vulnerabilities were not theoretical. They were immediate, tangible, alive.

And yet, change was slow. Hospitals, operating under budgetary constraints and the crushing pressures of daily operations, found it difficult to replace entrenched paging systems. Vendors offered encrypted paging solutions, but adoption lagged, hampered by cost, compatibility issues, and the cultural inertia of systems that had simply always worked.

Even when regulatory agencies began raising concerns about wireless data privacy, enforcement was spotty, fragmented, reactive rather than proactive.

Emergency services faced similar challenges. Police departments, fire brigades, and ambulance services had woven pagers into their dispatch and coordination systems for decades. Calls for backup, notifications of incidents, logistical updates about equipment and personnel—all flowed through networks that assumed, by design, that no hostile listener stood nearby with an antenna and patience. In most jurisdictions, interception remained a theoretical threat, rarely encountered in the field. But the exposure was real, and those with the motive and technical means had a quiet, unguarded window into operational realities.

Industrial systems, too, were not immune. Critical infrastructure sectors—electric utilities, water treatment facilities, transportation networks—often relied on pagers for maintenance alerts, fault notifications, and urgent system warnings. As late as the mid-2010s, researchers found evidence of unencrypted pager traffic carrying messages about grid failures, pipeline leaks, and system reboots. In one documented case, a compromised pager network provided real-time insights into the health of a regional power grid, including which substations were under maintenance and when backup generators were failing.

The risks were cumulative. In isolation, a maintenance page about a broken valve might seem trivial. A fire department callout for a routine inspection might seem mundane. A patient notification might seem limited in scope. But in aggregation, these fragments formed detailed mosaics of operational vulnerabilities, patterns of response, and institutional blind spots. They provided adversaries—whether criminal, terrorist, or nation-state—not only with intelligence, but with targeting options.

In a world increasingly defined by connectivity, the pager represented a holdover from a time when the air was trusted by default. It was a bridge between eras—a technology born in the age of analog simplicity, surviving into the digital complexity of the twenty-first century, carrying with it assumptions that no longer held.

The exploitation of pagers by Hezbollah in 2006 had been a tactical innovation born of necessity. But it was also a harbinger. It revealed that trust in the invisibility of signals was a liability, that passive collection could be just as decisive as active attack, and that technological arrogance was itself a fertile ground for operational failure.

The same patterns were poised to repeat elsewhere. Wherever legacy systems persisted, wherever wireless communication remained unexamined, wherever convenience had outpaced security, the battlefield extended. It stretched beyond Lebanon, beyond the Middle East, beyond conventional warfare, into the everyday operations of civilian life.

This realization reframed the understanding of communication risk. No longer could security be bounded by the apparent sensitivity of a channel or the visibility of a system. Every device that spoke into the air, every transmission that pulsed beyond a wire's end, became part of the contested domain. The electromagnetic spectrum was no longer neutral. It was weaponized by default.

The pager had been the canary in the coal mine, and most had not heard its song.

As new technologies rose—Bluetooth, Wi-Fi, LoRa, satellite IoT—the lessons of the pager were often forgotten or willfully ignored. New systems rushed to market with poor default security, trusting in the same invisibility that had once shielded pagers. And in the background, the threat actors—whether insurgents in warzones or hackers in basements—continued to listen, patient and tireless, waiting for the next signal to betray its sender.

This chapter closes not with the death of the pager, but with its quiet legacy: a reminder that every communication, however humble, however routine, carries risk. That every assumption of obscurity is an opportunity for exploitation. And that in the invisible spaces between devices and systems, in the silent territories of the air, the future battles for security and information would be fought.

What began as a simple beep in a doctor's pocket would echo through the fabric of a connected world, long after the last pager fell silent.

In the immediate aftermath of the 2006 Lebanon War, the lessons learned about wireless vulnerability moved from the realm of after-action reports into the bloodstream of operational doctrine. In Israel, where the failures were personal and acute, there was little choice but to adapt. The realization that unsecured administrative signals had contributed to strategic friction left deep marks on military planners. Reforms followed, some rapid, others gradual, but all pointed toward the same underlying principle: no communication could be treated as peripheral again.

It began with emissions control. Units were retrained to minimize unnecessary wireless chatter. Administrative networks that had once been ignored were scrutinized for leaks. Encryption became not just a checkbox for classified systems, but a standard expectation across every layer of communications, even those considered mundane. Pager networks were either retired, encrypted where possible, or tightly geofenced to limit their exposure. The concept of spectrum hygiene entered operational vocabulary—a new kind of battlefield awareness, not of enemy troop positions, but of one's own informational emissions into the contested air.

Other militaries took note as well. Allied forces operating

in active theaters like Iraq and Afghanistan initiated audits of their own wireless dependencies. Hospitals supporting coalition forces were instructed to review pager usage, with some shifting to encrypted SMS solutions or secured paging overlays. Tactical doctrine evolved to include passive signals intelligence as a constant threat, not just from advanced state actors, but from local insurgent groups growing more technologically adept with each passing year.

But institutional changes alone could not fully erase the underlying fragility that the pager era had exposed. The culture of assuming that low-level systems were beneath notice had been built over decades, and while training and policy could address the most glaring vulnerabilities, the deeper habits of thought would prove harder to reform. In every conflict, on every network, new generations of overlooked systems continued to emerge. Unsecured Wi-Fi hotspots in forward operating bases. Improvised messaging apps used for logistical coordination. Personal devices carried into operational theaters and broadcasting metadata without regard for emission discipline.

The lesson was clear, but its full implications were harder to live by. Total communications security in a modern, highly mobile force was an aspiration more than a reality. Operational pressures, logistical friction, and the relentless drive for convenience meant that compromises would always be made. The only question was whether those compromises were made consciously, with a clear-eyed assessment of the risks, or blindly, in the same spirit of invisible trust that had once allowed pagers to whisper operational secrets into the night air.

In civilian sectors, the pace of change was even slower. Healthcare facilities struggled with the economics of upgrading paging infrastructure. Emergency services balanced the operational necessity of reliable alerts against the cost and complexity of moving to encrypted systems.

Critical infrastructure operators evaluated the threat but often deferred action until regulatory pressures or public exposures forced change.

And so the echoes of the pager vulnerabilities continued into the broader fabric of a connected world. They became part of the unseen architecture of risk that surrounded every wireless device, every remote sensor, every out-of-band notification. The battlefield of signals remained active, even as the specific technologies evolved.

The pager story closed one chapter, but it opened a new one —a chapter in which information dominance would no longer be secured solely through strong encryption and network defenses, but through an unrelenting discipline over the invisible emissions of operational life. A chapter in which attackers would learn to listen with increasing sophistication, and defenders would have to fight not only to encrypt, but to silence, to obscure, to deny.

The first signals of this new war had been faint, easy to miss. A beep in a hospital corridor. A flicker of data across a hilltop in southern Lebanon. A message, brief and administrative, sent without a thought for who else might be listening. Each one a small surrender, a tiny broadcast of trust into a world that had already become adversarial.

The next chapters would not be about pagers alone. They would be about how that same structural vulnerability—trust in the invisibility of signals—persisted into every new generation of wireless technology, and how the battles fought over them would shape the conflicts of a century.

And so the air, once trusted, once taken for granted, became contested ground.
A battlefield without borders.
A domain where silence was survival.

Long before militaries began reevaluating their wireless security posture, small cracks had already appeared in the civilian world—early warnings for anyone willing to pay attention. They came not in the form of dramatic breaches or public scandals, but in quiet demonstrations of what was already possible with little more than curiosity and a few hundred dollars' worth of equipment.

In one city, a group of university researchers decided to map the pager ecosystem surrounding a major hospital complex. Armed with a modest software-defined radio and an omnidirectional antenna, they set up in a university laboratory overlooking the urban skyline. Within minutes, they began capturing streams of pager messages, thousands of them per day. Sorting through the traffic, they reconstructed the internal life of the hospital in staggering detail.

Patient alerts arrived in clear text, naming individuals, describing conditions, flagging critical emergencies. Shift schedules were broadcast, revealing both movement patterns and the availability of key personnel. Maintenance notices detailed equipment failures, backup generator activations, and even security alerts about broken door locks. From these fragments, the researchers built a live operational map of the hospital's daily pulse, one that updated itself automatically with every intercepted message.

They could track patterns of patient inflows during flu season, predict staff shortages before public announcements, and infer internal crises hours before they became public knowledge. It was not hacking in the traditional sense. It required no passwords, no exploit chains, no malware. It was pure passive collection—listening to what was already being said, what had always been said, only now with the tools and patience to hear it.

Elsewhere, in a quieter industrial corner of the country, an independent security consultant decided to test the resilience of infrastructure communications. Parking near a cluster of utility substations late one evening, he tuned his equipment to the known frequencies used for maintenance alerts. It did not take long for the data to begin flowing.

The messages were dry, technical, routine—and devastatingly revealing. Alerts about transformer overheating. Notifications of line maintenance schedules. Warnings about backup systems failing under load. Each page, individually, was a minor operational artifact. Together, they formed a real-time vulnerability map of a regional power grid. In the hands of a malicious actor, this information could have allowed precise timing of physical attacks, overload attempts, or simply long-term intelligence gathering about critical system weaknesses.

The consultant reported his findings to the relevant utility authority. Meetings were held. Acknowledgements were made. Promises of future upgrades were issued. But months later, on returning to the same spot, he found the air still thick with unencrypted pager traffic, humming steadily into the night.

These incidents were not isolated anomalies. They reflected a systemic pattern—an ingrained assumption that signals invisible to the casual observer were signals safe from exploitation. The fact that no catastrophe had yet unfolded was treated as evidence that no catastrophe could unfold. Risk was measured not by technical vulnerability, but by historical absence of disaster.

This mindset, more than any particular technical flaw, was the real inheritance of the pager era. It was not simply that systems were vulnerable. It was that organizations, across sectors and disciplines, had internalized a deep cultural resistance to confronting those vulnerabilities unless forced to by visible crisis. It was the triumph of the seen over the unseen, the known over the possible.

For every pager network still broadcasting medical alerts, there was a corresponding administrative decision made to defer upgrades. For every maintenance notice intercepted in the open, there was a budget meeting where cybersecurity investments were reallocated to more politically salient threats. For every unsecured dispatch call, there was a policy document asserting compliance with frameworks that never imagined an adversary patiently harvesting low-bandwidth signals from a parked van or a nearby apartment window.

The tools that enabled these passive interceptions grew sharper each year. Receivers became more sensitive. Software became more user-friendly. Online communities shared scripts, tutorials, pre-built virtual machines loaded with decoders and mapping utilities. What had once required deep expertise now required only intent.

And as the cost of interception fell, the risk calculus should have shifted. But risk perception, slow and stubborn, lagged behind. The same dynamic that once allowed insurgents in southern Lebanon to outmaneuver a modern army continued to echo through civilian infrastructure, hospitals, and emergency services worldwide.

Even when critical flaws were acknowledged, remediation often came slowly, piecemeal, constrained by competing priorities and the inertia of sunk costs. Secure messaging systems introduced latency. New devices required user retraining. Transition plans introduced operational risks of their own. In many cases, institutions judged—sometimes consciously, sometimes not—that the risks of change outweighed the risks of persistence.

It was an understandable decision. It was also, increasingly, a dangerous one.

In asymmetric warfare, the value of operational patterns is not measured by their classification level but by their ability to inform and predict. A maintenance log, a shift schedule, a list of urgent dispatches—they are all pieces of a living map of an organization's vulnerabilities and strengths. They allow an adversary to model behavior, to anticipate responses, to shape attacks not blindly, but with surgical precision.

In 2006, Hezbollah weaponized these principles on the battlefield, leveraging pager traffic to anticipate and frustrate the operations of a technologically superior foe.

In the civilian world, the same vulnerabilities lay dormant, waiting only for adversaries disciplined enough to gather what routine communication revealed.

The pager era was ending. But the era of passive interception, of ambient intelligence collection, was only just beginning.

In every city skyline, invisible to the casual observer, countless signals still drifted outward.
Some secured, some forgotten, many simply unguarded by habit.
Each one a potential whisper into the ears of those who chose to hear.
Each one a reminder that in the contest for information, silence is never accidental—it must be earned, guarded, maintained against the patience of those who listen longer than we plan.

# CHAPTER 2 — THE SECOND LEBANON WAR: CONTEXT AND CHAOS

The war that would come to define the vulnerabilities of modern wireless communication did not begin with signals or strategies. It began, as wars often do, with politics, perception, and a deep undercurrent of unresolved conflict. The summer of 2006 found Israel and Hezbollah locked in a tense and dangerous stalemate along the Blue Line, the demarcation separating Israel from southern Lebanon. To outsiders, it was a tenuous peace. To those living in its shadow, it was a slow-burning confrontation, waiting for the smallest spark.

The withdrawal of Israeli forces from southern Lebanon in 2000 had ended an eighteen-year occupation, but it had not ended the war. Hezbollah, emboldened by what it viewed as a victory through resistance, had entrenched itself deeper into the fabric of southern Lebanon, simultaneously a political movement, a social services provider, and a guerrilla army. Its arsenal grew steadily, bolstered by Iranian support and Syrian facilitation, until its missile stockpiles numbered in the thousands. Its fighters, once lightly armed irregulars, became a hybrid force—trained, disciplined, and increasingly sophisticated in their understanding of modern warfare.

Inside Israel, the perception was different. The withdrawal was seen as both a strategic necessity and a calculated risk, a gamble that removing the occupation would reduce Hezbollah's casus belli and stabilize the northern frontier. For a time, it appeared to work. The early 2000s brought relative quiet to the northern border, even as the Second Intifada raged elsewhere. But the quiet was deceptive. Beneath the surface, Hezbollah prepared for the next phase of conflict, studying Israeli tactics, refining its own, and weaving an increasingly dense network of fortifications, supply caches, and communication systems across southern Lebanon.

By 2006, Israel remained the region's preeminent military power by any conventional measure. Its air force dominated the skies with precision munitions and unmatched strike capability. Its ground forces were technologically advanced, heavily armored, and deeply experienced. Its intelligence apparatus was among the most formidable in the world, penetrating networks, intercepting communications, and mapping threats with clinical precision. In any open contest of force, the outcome seemed assured.

But dominance can breed blindness, and the asymmetries of modern conflict do not yield to sheer firepower alone. Hezbollah did not intend to confront Israel symmetrically. It had no illusions about winning in the traditional sense. Its goals were more subtle, more patient: to inflict casualties, to resist occupation, to undermine Israeli morale, and to survive. Survival itself, against overwhelming odds, would constitute victory.

On July 12, 2006, Hezbollah fighters crossed the border and ambushed an Israeli patrol, killing three soldiers and capturing two. The response was swift and overwhelming. Israeli airstrikes hammered southern Lebanon, targeting Hezbollah positions, infrastructure, and Beirut's airport. Ground incursions followed, seeking to root out entrenched fighters and destroy rocket-launching cells. The war expanded rapidly, engulfing southern Lebanon and northern Israel in a storm of violence, displacement, and destruction.

From the outset, Israel sought to leverage its technological advantages. Air dominance was used to interdict supply lines and strike command centers. Electronic warfare units attempted to jam Hezbollah communications. Intelligence units monitored radio traffic, trying to map the guerrilla network hidden among the hills and villages. Israeli forces moved with the expectation that their superior speed, precision, and firepower would quickly overwhelm Hezbollah's resistance.

But the battlefield had changed.

Hezbollah had spent the previous six years transforming southern Lebanon into a fortified battlespace. Anti-tank guided missiles awaited Israeli armor in prepared kill zones. Rocket teams operated from underground bunkers and pre-surveyed firing positions, popping up to fire salvos before melting back into the labyrinth below. Civilian infrastructure masked military assets, complicating targeting decisions and slowing operational tempo. And, perhaps most critically, Hezbollah had invested in an asymmetric approach to signals intelligence and electronic warfare.

While Israel encrypted its primary battlefield communications and secured its high-value data links, not every channel was treated with equal care. Logistical networks, administrative paging systems, and secondary coordination tools remained exposed in ways that seemed trivial until exploited. Hezbollah, recognizing the opportunity, deployed listening teams to capture, correlate, and interpret Israeli signals—not by breaking into secure systems, but by harvesting what was already floating through the air.

It was a patient, methodical effort. Mobile intercept stations, often mounted on civilian vehicles or hidden in urban environments, recorded hours of Israeli signal traffic. Analysts, trained to spot patterns in the noise, sifted through medical evacuations, resupply requests, and maintenance reports, assembling a live picture of Israeli operational movements. No single message revealed a grand plan. No single interception turned the tide of a battle. But over days and weeks, the accumulation of context allowed Hezbollah to anticipate Israeli thrusts, prepare ambushes, and avoid overwhelming concentrations of force.

The irony was acute. Israel's high-end capabilities remained intact—its fighter jets struck with devastating precision, its drones patrolled the skies unchallenged, its cyber units defended critical networks with vigor. But at the edges, where low-level signals leaked unnoticed, Hezbollah found the seams and pried them open. It was a study in the vulnerabilities that arise not from technical weakness, but from assumptions about what is worth defending.

As the conflict dragged on, it became clear that Israel's initial operational expectations would not be fulfilled. Hezbollah's rocket attacks continued, hammering northern Israeli towns and cities despite intensive air campaigns. Israeli ground forces met fierce, determined resistance in villages that had been transformed into kill zones. Casualties mounted. International pressure grew. The dream of a swift, decisive victory faded into a grinding, costly campaign with ambiguous political outcomes.

Inside Hezbollah, the conflict was seen as validation. Their survival against Israeli assault reinforced their narrative of resistance and emboldened their position within Lebanese politics and the broader regional struggle against Israel. The ability to withstand and adapt to the technological superiority of a modern military, using a combination of hardened tactics and electronic savvy, became a blueprint for future conflicts.

The Second Lebanon War was not just a clash of armies or a battle over territory. It was a collision between conventional military power and the evolving realities of asymmetric warfare. It revealed that dominance in firepower, intelligence, and technology does not guarantee dominance in outcome. It exposed how the vulnerabilities of an interconnected battlefield—especially the invisible architecture of communication—could be weaponized by adversaries willing to listen where others assumed safety.

It was a war fought in the rubble of towns and cities, but also in the unseen spaces between radios, pagers, and antennas. It was a war where a captured page, a recorded signal, a misunderstood logistic request could echo louder than an airstrike. It was a war where perception, adaptation, and patience proved as critical as armor, munitions, and airframes.

The lessons of the 2006 conflict would ripple far beyond the hills of southern Lebanon. They would shape how militaries conceived of information warfare, how they prioritized communications security, and how they understood the operational risks posed by legacy systems left unsecured. They would inform the doctrines of insurgent groups, terrorist organizations, and nation-states alike, each drawing their own conclusions about how to fight, how to resist, and how to exploit.

The chaos of the Second Lebanon War was not merely the product of unexpected tactical resistance. It was the result of a deeper, structural shift in the nature of conflict itself—a shift that had been building quietly for years, hidden behind assumptions, traditions, and technological arrogance. The wireless world, once trusted, had become a battlefield. And in that battlefield, superiority was no longer measured solely in tanks, planes, or missiles, but in who could control, obscure, or exploit the invisible flow of information.

The old hierarchies of power were crumbling at the edges. Guerrilla fighters with scavenged radios and commercial gear could undermine the operational tempo of the most sophisticated armies. Asymmetric electronic warfare was no longer the exclusive domain of superpowers. It was democratized, improvised, and dangerously effective.

In the long, grim accounting of war, it was not the presence of high technology that proved decisive, but the discipline of its application, the vigilance of its protection, and the willingness to see every channel, every signal, every invisible emission as part of the contested space.

Israel, for all its strength, had entered the Second Lebanon War with a deep trust in the architecture of its communication. Hezbollah had entered it with a deep suspicion of that same architecture—and the tools to exploit its flaws.

That difference in mindset would shape the war's outcomes in ways neither side fully understood until it was too late.

Beneath the outward machinery of Israel's military dominance, vulnerabilities had quietly taken root. They were not the vulnerabilities of weakness, but of strength left unquestioned for too long. In a world where overwhelming force had so often delivered results, there was little incentive to examine the fine-grain mechanics of communications that supported it. The battlefield was envisioned in clear terms: encrypted radios, classified data links, secure voice channels. But war is rarely as orderly as its doctrines, and it was in the messy, overlooked spaces—the administrative channels, the logistical alerts, the maintenance schedules—that Hezbollah found its foothold.

The Israeli Defense Forces relied on an intricate web of communications to coordinate their movements. Strategic orders flowed downward through secure systems, but the day-to-day realities of keeping an army operational—resupplying ammunition, coordinating medical evacuations, tracking vehicle repairs—moved through a patchwork of systems, some new and hardened, others inherited from older eras. Among these were paging systems that had once been cutting-edge but were now relics running parallel to the encrypted backbone, trusted because they had always worked.

The paging networks had not been designed with modern electronic warfare threats in mind. They were efficient, widespread, and simple, but they lacked authentication, encryption, or concealment. Every page transmitted from a command post to a field hospital, from a maintenance depot to a frontline unit, flew through the air for any receiver tuned to the right frequency to hear. It was not that commanders did not value operational security; it was that the scope of what needed securing had outpaced the systems in place to protect it.

In peacetime exercises and low-intensity operations, the risk seemed tolerable. During major mobilization, when every logistical artery was pulsing at full capacity, the exposure grew exponentially. Pagers relayed urgent requests for fuel and parts, locations for emergency medical extractions, changes in troop staging areas. Each message was small, operationally routine, easily dismissed as administrative noise. But aggregated and analyzed with discipline, they revealed the real rhythm of war—the flow of men and machines, the pulse of supply chains, the vulnerabilities of force deployments.

Hezbollah had prepared for exactly this opportunity. Throughout the early 2000s, they invested heavily in building a hybrid communications network designed to survive Israeli attacks and capitalize on Israeli weaknesses. Fiber optic lines were laid underground to connect command nodes immune to radio jamming and signal interception. Civilian infrastructure was repurposed to hide command posts and transmission equipment. Redundant, decentralized control allowed local units to operate semi-independently even when higher-level communications were severed.

But just as importantly, Hezbollah did not seek merely to defend its own communications. It sought to exploit its enemy's. Iranian advisors and operational experience from previous clashes had taught Hezbollah's leadership that asymmetric advantage lay not only in launching rockets and ambushes but in knowing when, where, and how the enemy would respond.

Hezbollah's electronic warfare teams were structured to be agile, mobile, and highly focused on passive collection. They deployed a blend of commercial off-the-shelf equipment and customized receivers, leveraging advances in software-defined radio to scan and record vast swathes of the Israeli electromagnetic spectrum. Their operators were trained to recognize not only formal military broadcasts but also the more subtle indicators hidden within secondary traffic—the administrative chatter that exposed the hidden muscles moving beneath the skin of the IDF's operations.

From the first days of the war, Hezbollah's intercept teams went into action. Mobile collection units stationed near the front lines began sweeping for signals, prioritizing the frequencies associated with known Israeli communications patterns. They recorded pager traffic, logistical coordination calls, and unencrypted bursts of data from secondary field networks. Analysts, often working in secure underground facilities, processed the incoming flood of information, searching for patterns—repetitions, timing, correlation with observed troop movements on the ground.

They were not looking for secrets in the traditional sense. They were looking for predictability. Which units were rotating in and out of combat? Which areas were seeing increased resupply activity? Where were medical evacuation requests clustering? Each answered question added another piece to the mosaic, allowing Hezbollah commanders to predict Israeli behavior with growing confidence.

Intercepted maintenance pages revealed urgent shortages of fuel and water at forward staging areas, while medical pages disclosed evacuation routes for wounded soldiers, mapping vulnerabilities invisible to traditional reconnaissance.

The process was not infallible. Electronic warfare, like all forms of intelligence, operated in a fog of partial information and uncertainty. Not every intercepted message was clear. Not every inference was correct. But Hezbollah's strength lay in its ability to integrate imperfect data into flexible, resilient tactics. They did not need perfect knowledge. They needed enough to shape the battlefield to their advantage.

The results became increasingly visible as the war ground on. Israeli ground advances, expected to be overwhelming, met with fierce ambushes in areas Hezbollah had reinforced in anticipation. Rocket teams relocated dynamically, staying one step ahead of airstrikes that should have pinned them down. Supply convoys found themselves targeted not by coincidence, but by adversaries who seemed to know when and where logistical lifelines were exposed. Even the timing of counterattacks appeared calibrated to Israeli rhythms, exploiting moments when unit rotations or resupply operations left defensive postures temporarily weakened.

Inside Israeli command circles, frustration mounted. Why was Hezbollah so often in the right place at the right time? Why were efforts to suppress rocket fire proving so elusive? Traditional explanations—superior human intelligence networks, civilian cover, hardened bunkers—were all valid, but incomplete. Gradually, a more unsettling possibility gained traction: that Israel's own communications, long trusted as secure or at least obscure, were bleeding operational secrets into the air.

The realization came too late to reverse the tide. Mid-conflict adjustments were made—restricting pager use, shifting certain logistical communications onto encrypted networks—but the initial damage had been done. Hezbollah had shaped the tempo of the war in its critical opening phases, blunting Israeli momentum and forcing a prolonged, grinding campaign that cost Israel politically, militarily, and diplomatically.

The hidden vulnerabilities in Israel's communications architecture were not born of negligence. They were the product of systemic assumptions that had outlived the environments that once justified them. A belief that secondary systems were inherently low-risk. A faith that technical obscurity was sufficient defense against opportunistic interception. An operational tempo that prized speed and efficiency over the hard, costly work of securing every channel.

Hezbollah's rise in asymmetric electronic warfare was not a miracle of technology. It was a triumph of mindset—a willingness to listen where others assumed silence, to harvest intelligence where others saw only noise, to adapt to the complex realities of modern conflict faster than their adversaries adapted to them.

The story unfolding in southern Lebanon was not just a story of rockets and raids, of tanks clashing with bunkers. It was a story about who controlled the invisible terrain—the terrain of information. It was a story about who could see first, decide faster, and strike more precisely. And it was a story that would not end in 2006, but would echo forward into every future battlefield shaped by wireless communication, asymmetric warfare, and the patient, tireless search for signals in the noise.

The longer the war ground on, the more the informational imbalance began to show its teeth. Israeli commanders found themselves grappling with an enemy that refused to behave according to the traditional models. Hezbollah did not hold ground conventionally, did not present massed forces for annihilation, did not collapse under aerial bombardment. Instead, they shifted, fragmented, reconstituted. They waited until Israeli movements committed too far, then struck at vulnerable flanks, at logistical tails, at isolated units thrown out ahead of their supply lines. The precision of these strikes could not be explained by local observation alone. Somewhere, it seemed, Hezbollah was seeing the outlines of Israeli operations before they fully emerged.

Efforts to adapt mid-conflict ran into the hard realities of military inertia. Changing operational communications protocols under fire was no simple task. Units operating in complex, overlapping battlespaces depended on established procedures to avoid fratricide, to coordinate resupply, to manage the chaotic ebb and flow of frontline engagements. Ripping out trusted, if vulnerable, systems risked creating gaps in operational tempo even more dangerous than the leaks themselves.

And so the situation became a grim calculation. Certain vulnerabilities were tolerated because the cost of immediate remediation was deemed greater than the risk of continued exposure. Some pager systems were shut down or restricted to critical use. Certain logistical coordination was pushed onto hardened channels where possible. But the sheer scale of the war—tens of thousands of troops moving across hundreds of square kilometers, sustained by intricate logistical networks—meant that total emission control was impossible. Even as reforms were implemented, the informational bleed continued, slower but not stopped.

Meanwhile, Hezbollah continued to evolve in real time. Captured Israeli communications were not simply archived for later analysis. They were fed into operational decision-making cycles, shaping where to defend, when to withdraw, where to concentrate ambushes. Hezbollah commanders operating in the field received processed intelligence distilled from signal captures, allowing them to maneuver with an agility that belied their relatively modest technological base.

This dynamic created a sense of chaos within Israeli forces that had little to do with raw combat power. Units found themselves moving into kill zones more often than expected. Rocket launchers that should have been suppressed reappeared after supposed clearances. Civilian structures thought abandoned revealed hidden fighting positions, prepped for defense. Every tactical assumption—about the predictability of guerrilla movements, about the vulnerability of fixed positions, about the timelines of enemy resupply—

began to fray under the pressure of an adversary that seemed perpetually one step ahead.

Frustration grew. Confidence eroded. Operational momentum, so vital in Israel's doctrine of rapid, overwhelming force, became bogged in uncertainty, hesitation, and reaction. Each tactical victory came at higher cost. Each forward movement invited more carefully prepared countermeasures. The sense that the enemy was everywhere and nowhere at once, that he anticipated movements without visible surveillance assets, created a psychological drag that compounded the physical toll.

Inside Israeli intelligence units, quiet internal investigations accelerated. Patterns of compromise were identified. Wireless emissions surveys were conducted. Traffic analysis of Israeli systems confirmed what some had suspected since the early stages of the war: secondary and tertiary communications channels, especially in the logistical and medical domains, had been leaking critical operational metadata. Pager traffic, minor field radios, even unguarded administrative relays—signals considered too trivial to encrypt or replace—had provided Hezbollah with a living, breathing map of the battlefield.

The recognition was bitter. It was one thing to be bested by superior tactics or overwhelming numbers. It was another to realize that operational friction had been exacerbated by one's own informational negligence. To understand that vulnerability had not been forced by enemy brilliance, but volunteered through oversight. The knowledge that soldiers had died because logistical paging systems, relics of a bygone era, had whispered their positions into the night was a heavy burden, one not easily shouldered or quickly forgotten.

Hezbollah, for its part, understood the value of the informational space it had seized. Their fighters, hardened through years of underground preparation and ideological indoctrination, were quick to adapt to battlefield realities.

They knew not to depend on any one node of communication, any single command post, any solitary channel. Redundancy, decentralization, and improvisation were built into their operational DNA.

Their exploitation of Israeli vulnerabilities was methodical, not opportunistic. Passive intercept units operated in coordination with field units, sharing intelligence through hardwired communications when possible, minimizing their own exposure to counter-surveillance. The lessons of earlier conflicts—where open radio chatter had betrayed guerrilla movements—had been learned well. Now it was Hezbollah, not Israel, who managed the electromagnetic terrain with greater discipline.

It was not that Hezbollah possessed superior technology. Their receivers were often modified civilian devices, their analysis tools built from scavenged and improvised components. Their strength lay in mindset—in the understanding that in modern conflict, every emission is a risk, every signal an opportunity, and that victory belongs not merely to those who can fire faster or farther, but to those who can hear more, see clearer, and decide quicker.

The battlefield was saturated not just with kinetic violence, but with invisible contests over information. Each side maneuvered tanks, artillery, infantry—but also signals, patterns, whispers across the spectrum. In this hidden dimension of war, Hezbollah achieved a parity that force-on-force combat alone could never have delivered. It was an asymmetry of awareness, a battlefield advantage forged not through overwhelming strength, but through better hearing in the fog of war.

As the war entered its later stages, both sides recognized that the conflict was grinding toward a political rather than a military conclusion. International pressure mounted for a ceasefire. Strategic objectives became constrained not by capabilities, but by the diplomatic clock. Yet the lessons learned about the evolving nature of modern conflict—about the centrality of signals, about the fragility of assumed security, about the lethality of small leaks—would not be lost on the militaries, insurgencies, and policymakers watching the war unfold.

The Second Lebanon War had begun as a conventional response to a conventional provocation. It ended as a harbinger of a future where the invisible battles—over signals, metadata, emissions—would be as decisive as the visible ones. And it had revealed, for any who cared to see, that the invisible battlefield was already alive and contested, whether or not its commanders had chosen to recognize it.

As the summer dragged into August, the tempo of the war shifted from fevered escalation to grinding attrition. Israeli forces pressed deeper into southern Lebanon, encountering ever more sophisticated resistance. Each kilometer gained was bought with casualties and strategic ambiguity. Hezbollah's command and control structure, though battered, remained intact enough to continue launching rockets into northern Israel. Civilian displacement, already catastrophic, grew worse. International outrage mounted. The strategic goals that had seemed clear at the outset—cripple Hezbollah, secure the northern frontier—became murkier with each passing day.

Inside Israel, doubts sharpened. Political leaders and military commanders found themselves navigating a landscape where public support was eroding alongside operational momentum. The expectation had been for a swift, overwhelming campaign, demonstrating Israel's ability to project power and deter future provocations. Instead, the nation faced images of burning forests, damaged cities, and funerals for soldiers lost in battles over anonymous hilltops and fortified villages. Questions about preparedness, about doctrine, about assumptions baked into the very structure of military operations grew louder.

Nowhere were these questions more urgent than in the realm of communications. What had begun as an unexamined trust in operational systems had evolved into a hard reckoning with the cost of informational leakage. The internal investigations running parallel to frontline operations confirmed what many field commanders had suspected: Hezbollah's uncanny ability to anticipate Israeli actions was not the result of divine insight or supernatural guerrilla instinct. It was the result of disciplined signals interception, methodical traffic analysis, and the exploitation of legacy vulnerabilities that no one had thought urgent enough to fix before the shooting started.

The pager systems, once merely a background tool of administrative efficiency, had become conduits for operational metadata. Maintenance logs, medevac requests, resupply coordination—all broadcast in the clear, all offering a mosaic of battlefield dynamics to anyone patient enough to assemble it. Supplemented by the chatter of secondary radios and unsecured administrative relays, the picture Hezbollah constructed was never perfect, but it was good enough. Good enough to anticipate offensives. Good enough to reposition assets. Good enough to stretch the war far beyond its intended scope.

The IDF, adapting under pressure, instituted emission control protocols mid-campaign. Pager use was drastically curtailed. Certain secondary systems were abandoned outright, replaced by encrypted, hardened links whenever possible. Field commanders were briefed aggressively on communication discipline, with electronic warfare units tasked not only with offensive jamming but with monitoring and suppressing their own emissions. But these measures, though vital, could not fully erase the informational footprint already left across the battlefield. The early hemorrhage of metadata had shaped the operational landscape irreversibly.

Hezbollah, for its part, understood the clock was ticking. International mediation efforts, led by the United Nations and pressured by global powers, pushed toward a ceasefire. Resolution 1701, calling for a cessation of hostilities and the deployment of the Lebanese Army and UNIFIL forces into southern Lebanon, loomed on the horizon. The final weeks of fighting became a grim race—Israel seeking to achieve a decisive blow before diplomacy closed the window, Hezbollah seeking to survive and maintain its narrative of defiance.

When the ceasefire came into effect on August 14, it was less a resolution than a mutual exhaustion. Israel had inflicted enormous damage on Hezbollah's infrastructure but had not destroyed it. Hezbollah had survived the onslaught and, in doing so, had won a kind of asymmetric victory: survival as resistance, resilience as triumph. Both sides claimed strategic success. Both understood the war had exposed deep vulnerabilities.

For Israel, the Second Lebanon War forced a comprehensive reevaluation of military doctrine. The assumption that technological dominance in the air, on the ground, and in the digital domain would guarantee rapid victory was no longer sustainable. Operational security, once conceived primarily in terms of protecting classified information and high-value communications, expanded to encompass the entire electromagnetic spectrum—including administrative systems and legacy channels previously deemed insignificant.

Hezbollah emerged with new confidence, not merely in its ideological position, but in its tactical and operational methodologies. The war proved that asymmetric actors, armed not only with missiles and bunkers but with careful information harvesting and adaptive communications strategies, could impose real costs on a conventional military power. It validated the investment in electronic warfare, passive interception, and disciplined communications hygiene. It underscored the principle that in the modern battlefield, information was not just an advantage; it was survival.

The chaos of the war had been visible in the wreckage of towns and the loss of lives. But its deeper chaos, the one that would shape future conflicts, was invisible: the collapse of trust in wireless assumptions, the erosion of informational superiority by a patient and methodical adversary, the realization that control of the spectrum was not automatic but contested, vulnerable, and, if mishandled, fatal.

What had begun with an ambush and a captured soldier ended with a fundamental shift in how modern militaries understood the battlefield. It was not just the terrain that needed securing. It was the air itself—the signals, the emissions, the quiet, ambient infrastructure of communication that could no longer be trusted to remain unnoticed.

The Second Lebanon War was not the first modern conflict to feature electronic warfare. But it was among the first to show, on a broad operational scale, how even low-level, non-secure communications could shape the tempo and outcome of an entire campaign. It was a war fought with tanks and rockets and artillery—but also with antennas, pagers, and silent receivers hidden in the hills.

It was a war that signaled a new era, one in which the invisible spaces between transmissions were as dangerous, as decisive, and as thoroughly contested as any piece of ground.

And in that new era, there would be no such thing as an unimportant signal.

In the wake of the ceasefire, there was a moment of silence that carried a weight more profound than the noise of battle. It was the silence of reckoning. Both sides, battered but standing, turned inward to study what had happened—not only in terms of terrain lost or rockets fired, but in terms of the invisible war that had played out alongside the physical one. It was there, in the electromagnetic haze of unguarded signals and intercepted patterns, that the most enduring lessons would take root.

Inside Israeli defense circles, the realization that victory had been compromised by overlooked communications channels struck hard. Internal reviews launched within days of the ceasefire, even as units rotated home and commanders gave guarded press briefings. Communications security audits, previously routine exercises run against theoretical models, now focused on real events, real consequences, real bodies. The audits showed clearly that systems long considered safe by obscurity—paging systems, field maintenance relays, low-level coordination traffic—had been harvested, correlated, and turned into an intelligence engine by a non-state actor operating just across the hills.

The shock was not that vulnerabilities existed. All systems contain risk. The shock was that no one had expected those particular systems to matter. Encryption had been prioritized for high-level decision traffic. Digital hardening had focused on data centers, satcom terminals, command vehicles. But pagers? No one had budgeted time to review the configuration of 20-year-old paging infrastructure, still in use because it worked, because it was convenient, because it had never been a problem—until it was.

That was the deeper betrayal: not of a technical system, but of a mindset. The assumption that what is old is harmless. The belief that what is low-bandwidth cannot be high-risk. The quiet organizational faith that only the loud and the new need guarding. In 2006, those assumptions proved not only outdated, but dangerous.

Some of the reforms were immediate. Pagers were retired or replaced in every critical branch where exposure had been demonstrated. Where outright removal was impractical, usage policies were rewritten, emissions zones were created, encryption overlays were bolted onto surviving systems. But these were tactical patches. The strategic lesson, harder to absorb and much harder to teach, was that the threat surface was larger than any checklist could cover. Security could not be reserved for the glamorous systems. It had to be baked into the banal.

For Hezbollah, the war became a validation. Not merely because they had survived, or because they had withstood Israel's military might, but because their method had worked. Their doctrine—built on patient observation, on discipline in emission control, on passive listening rather than overt confrontation—had not just kept them alive, it had shaped the war's outcome. The war proved that asymmetric success was no longer the exclusive province of guerrilla ambushes and IEDs. It could now be achieved through informational maneuver—through out-seeing, not just out-fighting, the enemy.

Their electronic warfare cadre, once a secondary support element, gained prestige. Intercept operators who had spent long hours hunched over radios and decoders became heroes in Hezbollah's internal narrative—proof that intellect and perseverance could match Israel's global reputation for technological supremacy. It was a new mythology forming around a new kind of fighter: not the one with the RPG, but the one with the antenna.

And they would not stop there. In the months after the ceasefire, Hezbollah's EW infrastructure was not scaled back but expanded. Their intercept capabilities were reorganized and refined. Training programs were formalized, integrating lessons from the 2006 conflict into their standard operating procedures. Commercial receivers were upgraded. Antennas multiplied. Cross-training with external partners—particularly Iranian Quds Force units—accelerated. The next time Israel moved against them, they would be even more prepared. They had seen the advantage that informational discipline could deliver, and they intended to make it permanent.

For Israel, the transformation was slower, but ultimately deeper. The IDF launched a full post-war commission, one that examined not just tactical errors but structural assumptions. It exposed weak inter-branch coordination, over-reliance on airpower, poor readiness among reserve forces. But it also shined an uncomfortable light on the complacency surrounding secondary systems. The hard truth emerged: that a force with superior kinetic capabilities could still be paralyzed by its own communications if those systems bled information into contested airspace.

New initiatives followed. Spectrum hygiene became a standing operational discipline. EW units were empowered not only to disrupt enemy signals, but to police friendly emissions. Communications officers, once focused primarily on uptime and availability, were tasked with understanding adversarial interception models. The definition of operational security expanded to include every wireless device that touched the edge of the battlespace, no matter how mundane. Doctrine was rewritten. Exercises re-scoped. The electromagnetic environment was no longer a background condition. It was terrain.

This was the final lesson of the war, and the most difficult to institutionalize: that control of the spectrum was not an assumption—it was a fight. That even simple, low-power signals could be part of a high-stakes contest. That in modern warfare, no communication is neutral. Every emission is either a weapon, a vulnerability, or both.

By the time the smoke cleared and the headlines faded, both sides had drawn their conclusions. Hezbollah learned that information could amplify power. Israel learned that trust—particularly in legacy systems—was not a security model. The Second Lebanon War had not ended in decisive victory for either side, but it had redrawn the boundaries of where and how future wars would be fought.

The next conflicts would come. In Gaza. In Syria. Across a region increasingly saturated in signals. But after 2006, one thing had changed forever: everyone was listening now.

In the aftermath of conflict, lessons are often clear in retrospect but elusive in the moment. Commanders, politicians, and analysts scoured the ruins of the Second Lebanon War for meaning, for explanations, for the elusive threads that tied expectation to reality. Some clung to familiar narratives of political failure, operational miscalculation, or the unavoidable friction of war. Others, with more patience and less illusion, looked deeper into the invisible layers of the battlefield—the layers that had gone unnoticed until they turned against them.

It became increasingly clear that the war had not merely been a confrontation of military forces. It had been a confrontation of informational disciplines. One side had trusted its systems to remain obscure, sufficient in their traditional role. The other had assumed that every signal was a target, every emission an opportunity, and had acted accordingly. It was not the missiles alone that had carried the war beyond its expected scope. It was the quiet antennas, the captured pages, the reconstructed patterns.

Israel's technological edge had remained intact in the fields where it had invested heavily: precision airstrikes, cyber capabilities, command-level encryption. But war is rarely a contest of strongest points. It is a contest of vulnerabilities. Hezbollah had not needed to defeat Israel's best systems. It had only needed to exploit the systems left unguarded, the gaps left unexamined. The paging traffic, the unencrypted field reports, the routine logistics chatter—these had been the seams through which informational pressure flowed, destabilizing operations more effectively than direct strikes ever could.

What was most remarkable was how little technology

Hezbollah had needed to achieve this effect. No exotic encryption-breaking was required. No supercomputers, no massive cyber espionage campaigns. The war showed that simple tools, intelligently applied, could yield profound strategic dividends. A handheld receiver, a laptop, and disciplined analysis had outperformed assumptions that billions in defense spending had insulated against this kind of defeat.

It was a new model of conflict, or at least the public emergence of a model that had existed in theory but had rarely been demonstrated so clearly. In this model, the most powerful military in a theater could find its movements mapped not by satellite surveillance or deep-cover agents, but by its own communications' exhaust—the traces it left simply by operating in a contested spectrum without sufficient caution.

Hezbollah had turned Israel's strengths into liabilities not by confronting them head-on, but by finding the noise around them and listening with precision. And once they had learned the method, it became repeatable, scalable, and transmissible to others. Other non-state actors, nation-states, and insurgent groups studied the Second Lebanon War not simply for its kinetic tactics, but for its informational lessons. Quietly, the doctrine of passive interception, of spectrum exploitation, of wireless ambient intelligence became a new frontier in asymmetric warfare.

Inside Israel, the transformation was more painful but more thorough. Institutions rooted in traditional measures of security began to adapt to a world where the battlefield was ambient, where risk could emanate not just from a drone overhead or a sniper in a building, but from a signal emitted carelessly into the air. It forced a reckoning with legacy systems that had survived budget cycles, operational inertia, and bureaucratic neglect. It exposed how the trust baked into older technologies could outlive the conditions that had once made them safe.

The old truism that armies prepare to fight the last war had never felt more dangerous. The 2006 conflict had revealed that the last war was no longer a useful template. The enemy did not need to mass forces to be effective. The enemy did not need parity in tanks or planes or warships. The enemy needed access to the right information at the right time, and the discipline to act on it faster than the bureaucracy of a conventional army could respond.

And critically, the enemy did not need to break into the strongest vaults. He needed only to gather what was left lying outside them, unguarded, unexamined, waiting.

The collapse of wireless trust was not a single event. It was not a dramatic moment captured on film or described in after-action reports. It was an erosion, silent and patient, until the cliff gave way. It was a long series of small emissions, individually harmless, collectively devastating. It was the realization that security assumptions were only as strong as the most routine, least glamorous system still operating in the battlespace.

As both sides absorbed the lessons of 2006, the implications spread outward. Every new piece of equipment issued to soldiers, every revised field manual, every updated doctrine began to reflect a more adversarial understanding of the spectrum. Silence was no longer optional. Emissions were no longer invisible. Passive interception was no longer exotic. The air itself was contested, and it would remain so for every conflict to come.

The Second Lebanon War faded from headlines but deepened its imprint in professional militaries around the world. It served as a signal—a warning that the age of casual communication was over. That every transmission, from the most highly classified satellite link to the humblest pager chirping out a maintenance alert, was part of the battlefield.

And in the wars that followed, those who understood this

early would move faster, strike smarter, and survive longer. Those who did not would find themselves outmaneuvered not by superior firepower, but by superior patience and superior listening.

The chaos of the 2006 war was not merely the chaos of tanks and rockets and political missteps. It was the chaos born of a battlefield that had grown too complex, too saturated with signals, too trusting of its own noise. It was the first true glimpse of a future where dominance would be measured not just by who spoke the loudest, but by who listened the best.

And it was only the beginning.

In the years that followed the 2006 war, the lessons drawn from the invisible battlefield would begin to reshape the operational DNA of both Israel and Hezbollah. It would not happen overnight. Institutional change rarely does. But the war had broken something fundamental—the unspoken trust in ambient safety—and once broken, that trust could not be casually rebuilt.

For Israel, the transformation came in layers. At the tactical level, emissions discipline became embedded into training for every soldier, not just specialized communications units. Every piece of equipment capable of transmitting became subject to new scrutiny. Radios were reprogrammed with tighter frequency hopping. Field logistics systems were hardened with encryption overlays, even at the cost of convenience. Pagers and unsecured administrative messaging systems were systematically purged from critical command chains.

At the operational and strategic levels, the IDF integrated spectrum monitoring into every major exercise, treating the air as an actively contested domain rather than a neutral medium. Emissions security drills simulated interception not as a remote possibility but as a standing threat. Electronic warfare units were tasked with tracking their own side's signals as aggressively as they tracked the enemy's, understanding that every transmission was a potential leak if not tightly controlled. Commanders learned to treat the electromagnetic landscape the way they treated terrain—an environment that could be either occupied or denied, but never ignored.

Israel's intelligence agencies, too, recalibrated their focus. New programs emerged to detect, map, and characterize adversary emissions, including not only formal communications networks but ad-hoc, improvised systems that blurred the line between civilian and military traffic. The lessons of passive interception—of reading the metadata, of inferring intent from the rhythm and shape of transmissions rather than their decrypted content—became part of the professional bloodstream of Israeli SIGINT doctrine.

Yet the transformation was not purely technical. It was philosophical. The war had demonstrated that the difference between operational security and operational exposure was often a matter of organizational imagination—the ability to recognize what the adversary would value, even if it seemed trivial internally. It demanded a kind of cognitive adversarialism, a constant asking of the question: if I were them, what would I listen for? What would I watch?

For Hezbollah, the victory of survival—and the informational leverage that helped make it possible—became a foundation stone for future strategy. They did not rest on the methods that had worked in 2006. Instead, they adapted, refined, and expanded.

Hezbollah's electronic warfare capabilities, once cobbled together from commercial parts and battlefield improvisation, became more sophisticated. Passive intercept stations grew larger, more permanent, hidden inside the dense urban labyrinths of southern Beirut and the southern Lebanese hills. Training programs incorporated more advanced traffic analysis techniques, teaching operators not only to capture signals but to understand their operational context. Iranian support accelerated the process, providing technical expertise, equipment upgrades, and doctrinal experience drawn from Iran's own electronic warfare programs.

The philosophy that had served them so well—listen first, act second—deepened. Hezbollah increasingly viewed the electromagnetic spectrum as a primary battlefield, one that could be prepared, occupied, and exploited even before conventional fighting began. Their operational planning for future conflicts assumed that information, not just firepower, would determine survivability and success.

In parallel, Hezbollah invested heavily in emission control for their own forces. Radio discipline tightened. Hardwired communications replaced wireless links wherever feasible. Operational cells were trained to operate under conditions of complete radio silence, using dead drops, human couriers, and prearranged signals to coordinate attacks. The vulnerabilities they had once exploited in their adversary were now internalized as dangers to be mitigated within their own ranks.

Both sides, in their own ways, became mirrors of the invisible war they had fought. Israel, the nation of technological dominance, was forced to learn humility in the face of its own information noise. Hezbollah, the organization of asymmetric resilience, learned the power and necessity of operational discipline not just on the battlefield, but across the entire electromagnetic environment.

The Second Lebanon War did not end wireless exploitation. It initiated an arms race in the management and weaponization of ambient signals. It seeded new doctrines in militaries and insurgent groups around the world, all of whom studied the conflict's informational lessons as closely as its kinetic ones.

The world was becoming more connected, more wireless,

more saturated with emissions at every level of society. The tools needed to harvest those emissions were becoming cheaper, more accessible, more powerful. The advantage once held by nation-states in signals intelligence was eroding, bleeding outward into the hands of non-state actors, insurgents, terrorists, and private entities willing to listen carefully enough.

And so the battlefield expanded. Not just across hills and cities, but across the very air itself. Every unsecured signal became part of the contested space, each ambient transmission a quiet betrayal, each casual emission an unintentional invitation. The boundary between civilian and military collapsed, and with it the fragile line separating background noise from actionable threat.

The Second Lebanon War had been a war of rockets and tanks and ambushes. But at its core, it had been a war of awareness. A war between those who assumed they were unseen and those who made it their mission to see. A war between the comfort of legacy trust and the harsh reality of contested invisibility.

It was a war whose most enduring casualty was the simple, dangerous faith that what could not be seen could not be heard.

And it was only the first of many.

By the time official inquiries wrapped and after-action reports were shelved, the broader implications of the Second Lebanon War were becoming visible far beyond the borders of Israel and Lebanon. Militaries, intelligence agencies, and insurgent groups around the world absorbed the deeper lessons of the conflict. Some understood immediately. Others would learn more slowly, more painfully, in battles yet to come.

The idea that emissions alone could shape outcomes—without hacking into networks, without breaking encryption, without massive cyber operations—was no longer theoretical. It was no longer the subject of obscure academic papers or niche

SIGINT conferences. It had been demonstrated in the dirt and rubble of real battlefields, costing lives, influencing strategic decisions, dragging a technologically superior military into a fight it could not end on its own terms.

What the world saw in 2006 was the opening shot of a new paradigm: the battlefield was no longer limited to the visible or the obvious. It extended into the invisible architecture of modern life—the ambient emissions, the background signals, the casual communications we once trusted to remain private simply because no one had cared enough to intercept them.

And as technology advanced, the scale and scope of this invisible battlefield grew exponentially. New wireless standards emerged, connecting more devices, more vehicles, more sensors, more human beings than ever before. Smart cities bloomed, dripping with telemetry. Critical infrastructure modernized, wrapping itself in layers of wireless monitoring and remote management. Militaries digitized at every level, driving efficiency and capability but also vastly expanding their electromagnetic footprints.

The principles demonstrated by Hezbollah with scavenged gear and disciplined listening became global norms. State actors refined the art of passive interception into industrialized processes. Insurgent groups embedded spectrum harvesting into their guerrilla operations. Private companies built capabilities that once belonged solely to national intelligence services, turning ambient signal analysis into a commercial offering.

The result was a world where the margin for error shrank year by year. Where a forgotten signal, a default radio setting, an unsecured telemetry link could compromise entire operations without a single overt act of hacking. Where the most dangerous enemy might not be the one firing shots, but the one sitting silently with a receiver tuned to the right frequency, listening, recording, analyzing.

The old ideas of perimeter security, of clearly bounded operational theaters, became artifacts of an earlier age. The battlefield was everywhere signals flowed. The threats came not only from weapons systems but from metadata, from timing patterns, from the secondary and tertiary artifacts of communication. Silence became a weapon. Emissions became liabilities. The electromagnetic domain, once treated as support infrastructure, became a domain of warfare in its own right.

And yet, even as doctrine shifted and training adapted, the fundamental human tendency to trust what was convenient, what was habitual, persisted. The same forces that had allowed pager traffic to remain unsecured in 2006—cost, inertia, the prioritization of mission speed over mission security—continued to shape decisions in every domain. For every hardened network, a dozen unsecured peripherals. For every encrypted tactical radio, a maintenance system still broadcasting in the clear. For every secured headquarters, a contractor's laptop leaking telemetry into the open air.

The Second Lebanon War revealed the shape of this future, but it did not solve it. It forced awareness, but awareness alone is not resilience. Each new generation of wireless technology, each wave of innovation, brings fresh opportunities for exploitation alongside its promises of speed, efficiency, and ubiquity. The same structural vulnerabilities exposed by pager traffic persist today in Bluetooth beacons, Wi-Fi telemetry, satellite IoT links, civilian radio systems layered over critical operations.

Hezbollah's success in 2006 was not the triumph of exotic technology. It was the triumph of strategic patience and technical discipline over the assumptions of the modern battlefield. They did not need to defeat Israel's strongest systems. They needed only to recognize that every system, however humble, leaves a shadow—and that if you map enough shadows, you can see the object itself.

Israel's reckoning was painful but transformative. The conflict seeded a culture of adversarial thinking that would, over time, strengthen its defenses and reshape its approach to electromagnetic operations. But it also revealed that in the age of ubiquitous communications, no nation, no force, no system could consider itself immune from informational erosion.

The invisible battlefield is no anomaly. It is modernity itself — the new constant across every war, every conflict, every domain. Those who pretend otherwise, who allow convenience or inertia to reassert dominance over discipline, court the same vulnerabilities exposed in the hills of southern Lebanon.

In retrospect, the Second Lebanon War stands less as an isolated event than as an early case study—a preview of the informational fragility that would define the conflicts of the twenty-first century. A conflict where the lines between kinetic, informational, and psychological domains blurred beyond separation. A conflict where what was not said, what was merely emitted, became a source of strength or weakness.

It was not the last war to be shaped by invisible signals. It was merely the first to force the world to notice.

# CHAPTER 3 — HEZBOLLAH'S PLAYBOOK: LISTENING BEFORE SHOOTING

The art of interception was never accidental. It was a discipline born out of necessity, shaped by the conditions of asymmetric warfare, and refined by a culture that understood the value of patience over bravado. For Hezbollah, the road to mastering passive signal collection began long before the first shots of the 2006 war, in the shadow years following Israel's 2000 withdrawal from southern Lebanon.

During that interwar period, Hezbollah invested heavily in building an operational infrastructure that could not merely survive an Israeli return but actively bleed Israeli forces through attrition and disruption. Part of that investment was obvious: fortified bunkers, rocket stockpiles, hardened defensive positions buried under the villages of southern Lebanon. But another part remained invisible, woven into the hills and city rooftops — a network of listening posts, mobile intercept units, and small, disciplined signals intelligence teams tasked not with broadcasting but with harvesting the air.

The inspiration for this quiet campaign did not emerge solely from Hezbollah's internal ranks. External influences played a critical role. Iranian technical advisors, primarily from the Islamic Revolutionary Guard Corps' Quds Force, brought with them years of experience in electronic warfare doctrine, rooted both in Iran's internal security operations and in lessons absorbed from conflicts like the Iran-Iraq War. Russian equipment, much of it surplus from the decaying Soviet empire, found its way into Hezbollah's hands through Syrian channels. In particular, older Soviet-era spectrum monitoring systems, still capable of intercepting wideband communications, were adapted for field use.

Yet it would be a mistake to portray Hezbollah's interception capabilities as mere hand-me-downs from more sophisticated patrons. The true edge came from Hezbollah's own operational culture — a relentless drive to adapt commercial technologies for battlefield use, a willingness to tinker, to reconfigure, to fuse elements from disparate sources into functional, resilient systems. What Iran and Russia provided was raw material. What Hezbollah created was a uniquely agile, decentralized signals intelligence apparatus, suited not to massive headquarters or fixed listening stations, but to the rough, contested terrain of southern Lebanon.

In practice, Hezbollah's intercept teams operated with remarkable mobility. Some units worked out of innocuous-looking vans, modified with concealed antennas and packed with receivers and laptops running custom decoding software. Others occupied rooftop positions in towns and villages, blending among civilian infrastructure, their antennas hidden among satellite dishes or disguised as construction scaffolding. Still others worked in relay, moving from hilltop to hilltop with portable equipment, setting up temporary collection points to sweep the spectrum before packing up and relocating before detection.

The targets were predictable because the battlefield itself was saturated with emissions. Israeli military units, despite their high-end encrypted communications, still relied on unencrypted or weakly protected channels for administrative traffic, maintenance coordination, and medical logistics. Pager networks, operating on known frequencies, became a particular focus. Their signals, persistent and largely ignored by Israeli countermeasures, carried a steady pulse of operational metadata across the battlefield.

Intercepting pager traffic did not require breaking encryption, because in most cases, no encryption was used. It required only proximity, the right receiver, and enough technical sophistication to recognize, capture, and decode the relatively simple modulation schemes used by POCSAG and FLEX paging systems. These protocols, designed for efficiency and broad broadcast coverage, transmitted messages in cleartext bursts across open frequencies. In the Israeli battlespace, these bursts included everything from medical evacuation requests to logistical dispatches, each tagged with unit identifiers, times, and often rough locations.

Captured pager messages reconstructed fragments of the battlefield's invisible skeleton. In one series of reported intercepts, Hezbollah collected pages ordering medevac extractions from known staging areas, revealing where Israeli units had suffered casualties and allowing Hezbollah to infer which sectors were under strain. In another, maintenance alerts about fuel and water shortages gave clues about the operational tempo of armored formations, suggesting when tanks would be forced to halt or when supply lines would need reinforcement. Occasionally, personnel alerts surfaced, notifying field units of officer rotations or promotions, providing Hezbollah analysts with a living picture of Israeli leadership structures on the move.

The value of these interceptions was not in any single dramatic revelation. It was cumulative. Each message, each fragment, each administrative emission added a brushstroke to the operational portrait Hezbollah was building in real time. By correlating pages with observed battlefield events — rocket attacks, infantry movements, armor deployments — Hezbollah's analysts sharpened their predictive models, allowing commanders to anticipate Israeli reactions with increasing accuracy.

Listening was not a passive act. It was an act of engagement, of understanding, of building a parallel battlefield in the mind before committing forces to action. Shooting, in Hezbollah's doctrine, came after. Action without information was waste. Listening was the foundation upon which effective resistance was built.

The organization of Hezbollah's SIGINT efforts reflected this philosophy. Small teams operated semi-autonomously, each tasked with a specific slice of the spectrum or a defined geographical sector. Field interceptors collected raw signals, which were then relayed — often through hardwired fiber links rather than wireless — back to analysis centers hidden deep within civilian infrastructure. There, trained analysts, many with technical educations or operational experience from Iran's training programs, processed the captures, looking for patterns, anomalies, actionable intelligence.

The latency between collection and decision-making was astonishingly short for a non-state actor. In some cases, intercepted pager traffic led to Hezbollah repositioning rocket launchers or ambushing Israeli units within hours of the initial capture. The system was not perfect — not every intercept yielded usable intelligence, and not every inference was correct — but it operated with a flexibility and resilience that belied Hezbollah's public image as a purely guerrilla force. It was intelligence-driven warfare, conducted not from gleaming command centers but from cramped apartments, vans parked at the edges of towns, and disguised bunkers carved into hillsides.

What Hezbollah built was more than a signals collection network. It was an information architecture designed to exploit the fundamental structural weakness of modern militaries — the emissions they produce simply by functioning. It did not require superior technology. It required superior patience, discipline, and an operational culture willing to value information over immediacy.

This ethos, once proven on the battlefield of 2006, would become foundational to Hezbollah's broader strategic doctrine. The success of their passive interception campaign validated the idea that in modern conflict, the ear often precedes the fist, and that in the dense electromagnetic fog of war, those who listen first and listen longest win not through force, but through foresight.

The evolution of Hezbollah's interception capabilities was not a matter of isolated ingenuity alone. External support deepened over time, moving beyond the provision of surplus hardware into the realm of doctrinal training and operational methodology. Iranian advisors, already entrenched within Hezbollah's military and intelligence infrastructure, expanded their role in signals collection education. Where once the focus had been on basic technical proficiency—how to capture, how to demodulate, how to decode—new layers of training emphasized traffic analysis, pattern recognition, and the extraction of operational intelligence from unstructured signal environments.

This shift was transformative. Capturing a pager message was one thing; understanding its operational context was another. Iranian instructors, drawing from their own experience countering Iraqi forces and later Western intelligence efforts, taught Hezbollah operators how to think about signals not as isolated events but as elements of a living organism. Every emission, no matter how trivial it appeared, was a reflection of operational behavior—supply chain pressure, command post relocation, casualty rhythms, resupply urgency. The air was not filled with random noise; it was a chaotic symphony of logistics, fear, confidence, and vulnerability, waiting to be heard and interpreted.

Russian support, though less direct, contributed at the equipment level. As the Soviet Union collapsed and its military-industrial complex disintegrated, a flood of relatively sophisticated electronic warfare gear entered the global gray market. Through Syrian intermediaries, Hezbollah acquired portable direction-finding systems, spectrum analyzers, and wideband receivers capable of intercepting a broader range of frequencies than their earlier, more primitive setups. Although much of the equipment was dated by Western standards, it was perfectly suited for the interception of unencrypted or lightly protected Israeli communications.

Hezbollah's ingenuity remained the critical factor. Iranian and Russian tools were adapted, modified, repurposed. Civilian devices, originally designed for amateur radio enthusiasts or commercial telemetry work, were pressed into military service. Teams combined surplus hardware with local improvisation: directional antennas built from scavenged materials, power amplifiers modified for field use, signal processors augmented with custom scripts written by Hezbollah's small but capable cadre of technical specialists.

The architecture of their interception network expanded accordingly. Mobile units became more specialized. Some focused purely on capturing Israeli pager traffic, others monitored low-power tactical radios, while still others scanned civilian infrastructure for ancillary emissions that could reveal hidden military activity. Rooftop intercept stations dotted the landscape, blending invisibly into the urban sprawl. Fiber optic relays connected collection points to secure analysis centers, bypassing wireless vulnerabilities and allowing for rapid aggregation of captured data.

It was within this evolving ecosystem that Hezbollah achieved some of its most tactically significant successes. In several documented instances during the 2006 war, intercepted pager traffic allowed Hezbollah to predict Israeli maneuvers before they fully materialized.

One such case unfolded in the hills east of Tyre. Israeli armored columns preparing for an advance transmitted a series of logistical pager messages coordinating fuel resupply and maintenance checks. Although the content of the messages was administrative—requests for tank maintenance units, scheduling refueling stops—the timing and frequency of the pages, coupled with observed troop concentrations, signaled an impending armored thrust. Hezbollah analysts, synthesizing the intercepts with field observations, inferred the most probable axes of advance. Defensive positions were reinforced accordingly, anti-tank teams were pre-deployed, and ambush kill zones were prepared.

When the Israeli armor rolled forward, they encountered an unexpectedly dense network of anti-tank guided missile teams. Losses were inflicted at a rate far higher than Israeli planners had anticipated. What was intended as a swift, overwhelming penetration bogged down into a costly grind, eroding the momentum of operations and feeding into the broader perception of operational quagmire.

In another incident, medical pager traffic provided critical early warning. Following a series of rocket strikes against Israeli positions, Hezbollah intercept teams captured a sudden spike in medical evacuation pages. The pattern indicated mass casualty events in specific sectors. Interpreting the locations and frequency of these medevac requests allowed Hezbollah commanders to anticipate which areas of the Israeli front were under strain and thus more vulnerable to local counterattacks or increased rocket salvos.

These were not isolated strokes of luck. They were the fruits of a deliberate, systematic campaign of passive interception and analytical exploitation. Hezbollah's SIGINT efforts had matured from opportunistic eavesdropping into an operational art form—one that treated every emission as an artifact of intent and every decoded message as a tile in a mosaic of battlefield awareness.

What distinguished Hezbollah's intercept teams from mere technical hobbyists was their strategic patience. They understood that most emissions did not immediately translate into actionable intelligence. Instead, information had to be layered, corroborated, cross-referenced against observed enemy behavior. A single intercepted medevac page meant little in isolation. A pattern of medevac traffic correlated with satellite imagery, human observation, and prior resupply patterns painted a picture of systemic vulnerability.

This mindset—listening first, building context second, acting third—became part of Hezbollah's broader operational DNA. In an era where speed was often prized above comprehension, Hezbollah demonstrated that in the invisible war for information dominance, haste was the enemy of insight. The side that listened longer, with greater discipline, gained not just knowledge but the power to shape the battlefield before a shot was fired.

By the later stages of the 2006 conflict, Hezbollah's intercept network had evolved into a resilient, multi-layered intelligence apparatus. Hidden among water tanks and satellite dishes, these rooftop relays complicated Israeli targeting decisions, forcing ethical and legal dilemmas onto a battlefield already saturated with ambiguity. Mobile units, rooftop stations, field agents, and central analysis nodes worked in concert, sharing findings through secure links, adapting tactics in near real time. Even as Israeli forces adapted, curtailing some of their unsecured communications and enforcing stricter emissions discipline, Hezbollah's early gains in informational awareness continued to yield tactical advantages.

It was a stunning achievement for a non-state actor. It revealed a hard truth about modern warfare: that information dominance was not reserved for the richest, the best-equipped, or the most conventionally powerful. It was available to those who valued discipline over convenience, patience over immediacy, and listening over speaking.

And it established a model that Hezbollah would carry forward into every future conflict—a model where every battle would be fought twice: once in the electromagnetic spectrum, and only afterward in physical space.

Mobility had always been a core tenet of Hezbollah's operational philosophy, and nowhere was it more critical than in the realm of signals interception. Static stations, no matter how well concealed, were vulnerable to detection by Israeli electronic warfare units. Direction-finding teams operating from aircraft or ground platforms could, given enough time and emissions, triangulate the position of an active intercept site. Hezbollah understood that every transmission, every sustained capture operation, was a potential invitation to counterattack.

To survive, their interception teams became nomadic. Modified vans, outwardly indistinguishable from the battered civilian traffic of southern Lebanon, roamed the countryside with concealed receivers and processing equipment onboard. Antennas were hidden inside false roof compartments or disguised as luggage racks. The vehicles rarely stayed in one location for long. Once a target area was surveyed, data was either physically retrieved or, when risk allowed, exfiltrated over fiber-connected drops installed surreptitiously into urban telecommunications grids.

The van teams operated with a discipline that mirrored Hezbollah's broader tactical doctrine. Equipment setups were designed for rapid teardown. Personnel traveled light, carrying only the essentials to avoid detection during unexpected Israeli sweeps or airstrikes. When operational necessity forced longer dwell times, teams established redundant fallback positions—abandoned homes, empty storehouses, or makeshift camouflaged pits in wooded areas—ready to abandon a compromised site and reconstitute operations within hours.

Above them, on rooftops in the battered towns and cities

of southern Lebanon, a quieter but no less important component of the intercept network hummed. Small passive relay stations, often no larger than a shipping crate, blended into the clutter of water tanks, satellite dishes, and makeshift antennas. These rooftop sites extended Hezbollah's reach, allowing coverage of areas that mobile teams could not safely monitor. Some operated entirely passively, recording and storing emissions for later retrieval. Others, equipped with directional antennas, focused on high-value Israeli logistical corridors and staging grounds.

The rooftop sites were harder for Israel to detect and neutralize than mobile teams. Integrated into the civilian fabric of the urban environment, they presented a complex targeting problem. Striking every rooftop antenna would have risked massive collateral damage and international condemnation. Israel's policy of surgical airstrikes—necessary to manage global perceptions—made wholesale sweeps of suspected intercept locations infeasible. Hezbollah understood this dynamic well and leveraged it ruthlessly.

At the core of this decentralized architecture was an emphasis on emissions control. Hezbollah's own transmission discipline became an internal obsession. Mobile intercept vans did not broadcast unless absolutely necessary. Rooftop sites limited outgoing signals, favoring physical data retrieval or fiber-optic links. Field personnel used hardwired telephony where available, relying on encrypted short-burst transmissions only when other methods were impossible. Every effort was made to minimize the organization's electromagnetic footprint, to remain unseen even while seeing.

In this way, Hezbollah not only survived Israeli countermeasures but turned Israel's own operational hesitations against it. By embedding their intercept operations within the civilian landscape, by maintaining a constantly shifting network of collection points, and by minimizing their own emissions, they forced Israeli electronic warfare teams into a reactive, limited posture. Even when Israeli SIGINT units detected anomalous emissions, positive identification was often elusive, and opportunities for kinetic action were constrained by political and humanitarian considerations.

This operational resilience gave Hezbollah's intercept teams the time they needed to listen patiently and to build the layered informational pictures that allowed their forces to anticipate Israeli movements. It gave Hezbollah commanders a broader situational awareness than their technological inferiority would have otherwise allowed. And it reinforced a broader truth that modern militaries would struggle to internalize in the years ahead: that in the electromagnetic battlespace, survival and effectiveness are not dictated by who has the largest systems or the most advanced technology, but by who manages their emissions environment with greater discipline.

By late 2006, as the war ground into its attritional final phases, Hezbollah's mobile SIGINT teams were among the few components of the organization still operating at near full efficiency. Even as Israeli airstrikes leveled infrastructure and ground incursions battered fighting positions, the intercept vans and rooftop stations continued to operate, shifting constantly, adapting to the changing front lines. Their continuity of operations provided Hezbollah's leadership with a critical strategic asset: a persistent, adaptive view of the battlefield's informational currents even as the physical landscape around them shifted and burned.

The durability of Hezbollah's SIGINT architecture was not an accident of circumstance. It was the direct result of a doctrine that had been methodically built over years of preparation, informed by hard lessons from earlier conflicts, reinforced by external technical expertise, and hardened through internal cultural discipline. It reflected an understanding that in modern warfare, the electromagnetic spectrum was not simply an adjunct to combat power. It was a domain of warfare in its own right, demanding the same attention to mobility, concealment, and redundancy as any infantry company or rocket unit.

And it revealed something else, something more uncomfortable for traditional militaries built on assumptions of technological superiority: that the means of contesting the electromagnetic battlefield were no longer reserved for nation-states with billion-dollar budgets. With patience, discipline, and ingenuity, even small, irregular forces could harvest the ambient noise of the battlefield and turn it into actionable, asymmetric advantage.

This understanding would become a permanent feature of Hezbollah's operational mindset. It would inform how they built new communications networks, how they prepared for future conflicts, how they trained not just technical specialists but field commanders to think about the spectrum as part of the battlespace.

And it would serve as a blueprint for a new generation of asymmetric actors around the world, who studied Hezbollah's 2006 campaign not only for its kinetic lessons, but for the invisible war it fought—and won—across the air.

For Hezbollah, the real power of interception was never limited to avoidance. It wasn't just about knowing where Israeli forces were gathering so they could be avoided. It was about turning information into timing — learning when to strike, when to wait, and how to shape the rhythm of the conflict not through direct confrontation, but through insight. By the midpoint of the 2006 war, Hezbollah's use of captured pager traffic and related intercepts had matured from a defensive adaptation into an offensive enabler.

There were moments when Hezbollah seemed to strike just before Israeli units could solidify their positions — as though they were reacting not to observation, but to foreknowledge. In many cases, they were. One pattern emerged consistently in the war's central weeks: after Israeli logistics units transmitted pager alerts indicating resupply convoys or scheduled field maintenance, Hezbollah forces would maneuver into firing positions, pre-sight rocket launchers, and then delay their salvos until the exact window of vulnerability. Not random attacks, but sequenced pressure applied precisely when support columns were exposed and combat units temporarily focused inward.

The effect was unnerving to Israeli commanders. These attacks did not always cause large casualties, but they forced behavior changes. Units began holding back their own resupply movements until late night hours. Medical evacuations were delayed when possible, routed less efficiently, or called in under broader code systems. Commanders spent valuable time coordinating workaround procedures to mask emissions, slowing down tempo at a critical point in the campaign.

Hezbollah's response cycles, shortened by real-time signal ingestion and localized analysis, were never as fast as Israel's kinetic strike windows. But they didn't need to be. The advantage Hezbollah gained wasn't in pure speed. It was in anticipation. An Israeli tank battalion might be ready to push into a new sector with little resistance — but not if Hezbollah had spent the last four hours watching their pages calling in fuel resupply and shift rotations. In that time, maneuvering two or three small anti-tank teams into ambush positions required no miracle. Just the confidence that the enemy would arrive where and when predicted. Information replaced brute force.

Some of Hezbollah's most effective resistance cells worked backward from intercepted signals, building entire defensive plans around the predictable timing of Israeli emissions. Once a rhythm was understood — say, how long after a maintenance alert a convoy tended to move, or how often casualty reports were followed by air support — Hezbollah began staging decoy units. They created false concentrations in areas where Israeli medevac traffic had previously triggered strong responses. When Israel deployed in force expecting a firefight, they sometimes found abandoned buildings and carefully rigged explosives instead.

The same doctrine applied to rocket fire. With knowledge gleaned from intercepted communications, Hezbollah was able to time launches to coincide with known Israeli troop rotations. In at least one documented case, a barrage was launched just minutes before a known shift change at a regional command outpost. The strike caused minor physical damage but generated outsized disruption. Leadership handoff was delayed, radio procedures were temporarily jammed by overlapping communications, and response coordination stumbled. None of this happened by accident. It happened because someone had read the pager messages, counted the intervals, and chosen the moment when a single salvo could achieve more than a dozen would elsewhere.

This wasn't simply tactical awareness. It was the foundation of a different kind of warfare — one in which firepower was directed not by broad strategic objectives alone, but by the shape and tempo of the enemy's own behavior. Hezbollah began to develop a form of responsive warfare that didn't require command decisions to be made centrally. Small units could act with limited intelligence as long as they received cues from the broader intercept stream. They didn't have to know the entire operational plan. They only needed to understand what they were listening to and how to respond to what the air was already saying.

What emerged, by the war's final phase, was a decentralized resistance structure organized around a shared language of intercepted signal patterns. It resembled, in a crude but effective way, the kind of dynamic targeting feedback loop that Western militaries had spent decades refining in complex digital architectures. Except Hezbollah was doing it with analog hardware, scavenged parts, and an information discipline learned on the battlefield rather than in a classroom.

The impact was more psychological than technological. Israel had superior airpower, superior ISR assets, superior weapons. But superiority failed to guarantee predictability. And when a conventional military cannot control the rhythm of battle — when it cannot reliably predict the enemy's tempo or dictate the timing of events — frustration turns into hesitation. That hesitation creates delays. And delays, in asymmetric warfare, are often fatal.

By the time Israeli units adapted their emissions behavior, the damage had already been done. Pager systems were rapidly curtailed, some even disabled entirely in contested areas. Ad-hoc substitutes were patched in — hastily encrypted radios, field messengers, paper-based dispatch logs. These workarounds slowed Israeli logistics operations, strained unit coordination, and created friction between branches that had relied for years on the convenience of low-friction wireless messaging. But they were necessary. It had become clear that every unencrypted message sent into the air could, and often did, end up in the hands of the adversary before the intended recipient had time to act.

Hezbollah's strategic takeaway from this experience was clear: when your enemy leaks its behavior into the air, you don't need to overpower them — you need only to stay quiet long enough to listen. The first victory is in comprehension. Action comes second. It was this inversion of the traditional Western kill chain that gave Hezbollah its edge. Their chain began not with targeting, but with listening — and often ended without a shot fired, because action wasn't always necessary. Sometimes all it took was being seen where you weren't expected, or not being seen where a strike was presumed. Sometimes a signal denied was more powerful than one acted upon.

It was a doctrine Hezbollah would not abandon. The war was

proving not only that interception worked, but that it shaped the psychology of the enemy. It eroded their sense of control, it forced caution into places where boldness had once lived, and it bred an internal distrust of systems that had once been considered invisible, safe, and secondary.

The air was no longer neutral. It had become adversarial space. And Hezbollah had learned to occupy it — not with volume or brute strength, but with time, patience, and the discipline to hold fire until the signals said shoot.

By the time the guns fell silent and the ceasefire hardened into a tense, uneasy peace, Hezbollah's leadership understood they had done more than survive a war. They had validated a doctrine. They had proven that in a battlespace saturated with emissions, survival and advantage no longer belonged solely to those who fired first, but to those who listened longest and acted with the patience to turn information into opportunity.

In the months that followed, Hezbollah moved quickly to institutionalize the lessons of its interception campaign. What had started as a semi-ad hoc network of rooftop stations, mobile van units, and hardwired safehouses was reorganized into a more formal structure, blending technical specialists with tactical field units. Training that had once been informal — passed hand to hand among small cells — became codified into internal courses. Operators were taught not only how to capture signals, but how to interpret them, how to identify emission patterns, how to anticipate enemy intentions based solely on the rhythms and gaps of ambient communications.

The emphasis was no longer on collection alone. It was on interpretation. Hezbollah recognized that in a battlefield rich with noise, the key advantage would not go to the group with the most data, but to the group that could sift the signal from the static. Pattern recognition training became a priority. Operators learned to correlate the timing of medevac requests with troop movements, to match logistics pages to expected armor advances, to see the electromagnetic battlefield not as a blur of anonymous transmissions, but as a living, breathing organism that could be studied, mapped, and, if understood well enough, manipulated.

At the technical level, Hezbollah invested in upgrading its interception capabilities. Iranian advisors continued to provide access to more modern receivers and processing equipment. Russian-origin systems, particularly direction-finding arrays and wideband receivers, were refurbished and supplemented with civilian commercial gear that Hezbollah's technicians adapted for military use. Emphasis was placed on making systems modular, mobile, and difficult to detect — characteristics that had proven essential to survival during the 2006 conflict.

But Hezbollah's real innovation came in its philosophy of electromagnetic operations. They internalized the idea that the spectrum was not merely a place to gather information, but a place to wage war indirectly. They understood that the enemy's trust in their own communications systems could be weaponized against them. It was not enough to jam or intercept. The goal was to subtly pressure the enemy to mistrust their own signals, to force operational friction without ever firing a shot.

This approach extended beyond interception. Hezbollah began experimenting with limited forms of emissions denial. Not full jamming, which would have revealed their presence, but quiet, selective disruptions aimed at sowing doubt and delay. Faint interference patterns on known Israeli administrative frequencies. Timing their own low-power transmissions to create false impressions of troop concentrations. Using deception not through force, but through electromagnetic suggestion.

Their successes attracted attention far beyond Lebanon. Hezbollah's adaptation of commercial-off-the-shelf gear, combined with disciplined operational practices, became a case study for asymmetric forces around the world. Insurgent groups, militias, and even state actors facing technological overmatch studied the 2006 campaign, eager to understand how a small force had neutralized parts of a modern military's advantage simply by exploiting its informational exhaust.

Within Hezbollah itself, the interception model became a prototype for future conflicts. The organization invested not just in maintaining its passive SIGINT capabilities but in expanding them to cover the rapidly evolving communications landscape. As Israel moved to harden its communications, encrypt more of its logistics traffic, and enforce stricter emissions control, Hezbollah adapted in turn. They trained operators to detect metadata even from encrypted links — focusing on timing, frequency shifts, packet rates, and other side-channel indicators that could betray operational tempos even when content remained hidden.

They developed internal protocols for spectrum monitoring at every level of operation, from frontline fighters to central command nodes. Units in the field were taught to monitor the air continuously, not just for enemy transmissions but for subtle changes in pattern that could signal impending attacks, movements, or operational shifts. Every Hezbollah formation became, in effect, a passive signals collector, contributing small pieces to a distributed, constantly updating picture of the battlespace.

What emerged was not a top-down, centralized SIGINT system like those favored by traditional militaries, but a bottom-up, organic network of sensors, each contributing fragments of awareness. The model was messy, redundant, and sometimes inefficient — but it was resilient, hard to disrupt, and perfectly suited to the decentralized nature of guerrilla warfare.

The underlying philosophy remained consistent: in modern war, action should follow information, and information should follow listening. It was a philosophy that prioritized patience over impulse, understanding over reaction. It was a philosophy that fit Hezbollah's strategic culture of long-term resistance and tactical opportunism.

It also sowed the seeds for future capabilities that would extend far beyond pager traffic and field radios. As technology advanced, Hezbollah's intercept doctrine evolved to encompass cellular networks, satellite communications, and even low-power telemetry used in civilian infrastructure. The same principles applied. Listen first. Map the patterns. Exploit the assumptions. Act only when the signal landscape offered a decisive, asymmetric opportunity.

The war had ended, but the playbook Hezbollah had written — with scavenged receivers, rooftop antennas, and battered intercept vans — was only beginning its long, quiet journey across the emerging battlefields of the twenty-first century. It would shape not only how Hezbollah fought its next wars, but how others, watching closely, learned to wage their own invisible battles across the air.

The quiet war Hezbollah waged in the electromagnetic spectrum did not end with the last page captured or the last transmission intercepted. The deeper impact was cultural. Within Hezbollah's hierarchy, the lessons of the 2006 campaign became part of the organization's self-image, woven into the mythology of resistance alongside the rockets, bunkers, and ambushes. It was not enough to be brave. It was not enough to fight with skill. To truly resist, one had to master the air.

The success of their interception strategy seeded a new doctrine inside the organization, one that viewed information as a fluid, contested resource rather than a static asset to be guarded or stolen. Information was alive. It was mobile. It could be harvested not only from the enemy's mistakes but from the normal operational rhythms that modern militaries had come to take for granted. Every emission was an opportunity. Every overlooked signal was a potential lever of advantage.

Hezbollah's internal training materials began to reflect this shift. New cadres of operators were instructed from the start to see the electromagnetic spectrum as terrain — not abstractly, but as concretely as hills, rivers, and roads. Recruits were taught that the air had channels, bottlenecks, blind spots, and dead zones, just like physical terrain. Mastery of the air was no longer seen as the exclusive domain of specialized technical units. It was the responsibility of every fighter, every commander, every planner.

The structure of their operations changed accordingly. No major deployment moved without a corresponding plan for electromagnetic masking. No ambush was staged without considering how the surrounding signals environment might reveal or conceal movements. No unit was left without basic training in signals detection, discipline, and avoidance. And at the core of every operational briefing was a renewed assumption that the enemy was listening — just as Hezbollah was.

The enduring genius of Hezbollah's 2006 playbook was not simply that it used interception to gain tactical advantages. It was that it reframed the entire concept of what could and should be considered a battlefield. Where traditional doctrine divided warfare into physical domains — land, air, sea — and later added cyber as a distinct realm, Hezbollah collapsed the distinctions. In their model, the electromagnetic spectrum was not a separate domain layered atop physical reality. It was an integral part of it, fused to every movement, every decision, every action.

This collapse of boundaries allowed Hezbollah to fight with an agility that defied conventional expectations. In places where Israeli commanders saw only open terrain or hardened bunkers, Hezbollah's intercept operators saw patterns of signals — dense here, thin there, moving in rhythms that revealed concentration, fatigue, rotation, and vulnerability. The battlefield was layered, dynamic, and alive. And they could listen to it unfold.

Over time, Hezbollah's lessons seeped outward. Other groups paid attention. Insurgencies and non-state actors operating in Africa, the Middle East, and parts of Southeast Asia began adopting elements of passive interception into their own operations. Military academies, especially those focused on counterinsurgency and asymmetric warfare, quietly studied Hezbollah's 2006 signals campaign as a case study in low-cost, high-impact operational adaptation.

The phenomenon was subtle at first. Increased incidents of counter-timing, where insurgent attacks coincided suspiciously with shifts in coalition force rotations. Patterns of roadside bombs placed at predictable chokepoints revealed not by human surveillance but inferred from captured communications traffic. A global echo of the same operational DNA first hardened in the hills of southern Lebanon.

And yet even among traditional nation-states, the lesson was often slow to take root. The bias toward securing classified communications while neglecting lower-tier emissions remained a persistent weakness. Logistics, maintenance, medical coordination — all the small, vital arteries of modern operations — continued to rely, in many cases, on less protected systems. The cost of upgrading, the inertia of established practices, the political optics of investing heavily in unseen security over visible firepower — all conspired to delay adaptation.

Hezbollah's 2006 playbook served as a quiet warning. It showed that supremacy in firepower, technology, and intelligence gathering could be neutralized, at least partially, by adversaries who were willing to invest first and most heavily in the art of patient listening. It proved that asymmetric advantage did not require the invention of new weapons or the discovery of new doctrines. It required only the disciplined exploitation of what already existed — what had been trusted, overlooked, and allowed to speak freely into the contested air.

In the years that followed, this approach would be refined even further. The tools would become smaller, cheaper, more powerful. Software-defined radios that once cost thousands could now be assembled from hobbyist components for a fraction of the price. Open-source decryption and signal analysis software proliferated. Civilian technology blurred ever closer into the operational spaces once reserved for militaries.

The democratization of interception was underway. And Hezbollah had been among the first to show what was possible when an irregular force treated the electromagnetic terrain with the same seriousness, the same strategic weight, as conventional forces treated the ground under their feet. Around the world, irregular forces learned to harvest the air as Hezbollah had — turning emissions into opportunity, noise into foresight.

The playbook they wrote — with antennas hidden among satellite dishes, with receivers wired into vans parked on city streets, with operators who understood that waiting could be deadlier than shooting — became a foundation for a new era of warfare. An era where dominance is measured not only by the speed of one's trigger finger, but by the quiet, disciplined patience to let the enemy's own voice betray them.

It was a victory that made little noise at the time. No parades. No declarations. Just the silent accumulation of awareness, turned against an enemy who had assumed that if they could not be seen, they could not be heard.

The world was louder now. More connected. More saturated

with emissions at every frequency, from every device, from every human action. And in that world, those who learned to listen first would not merely survive.

They would shape the battles yet to come.

For all the operational discipline and quiet efficiency Hezbollah demonstrated, some glimpses of their interception successes eventually slipped into the public record. After the war, a handful of after-action reports, military leaks, and journalistic investigations illuminated the hidden architecture of the electromagnetic battle that had unfolded in parallel to the kinetic one.

One category of interception that emerged repeatedly in reporting was Hezbollah's use of Israeli medical evacuation pages. These messages, often dispatched over aging pager systems still used by Israel's northern command and associated medical logistics units, were transmitted in the clear and contained details about casualty pickups, staging areas, and emergency resupply needs. Analysts working for Hezbollah intercepted these pages in real time, tagging locations and times to build a dynamic vulnerability map. In several cases, the sheer frequency of medical dispatch traffic alerted Hezbollah units to stress points in the Israeli operational tempo — areas where battalions were suffering higher than expected losses, opening temporary gaps in the front.

Specific examples surfaced. In one, a series of pager transmissions referenced repeated medical evacuations in the vicinity of Maroun al-Ras, a small village near the Israeli border. Hezbollah's intercept teams, correlating the timing and clustering of the messages with visual observations of Israeli helicopter movements, concluded that a local unit had been hit harder than Israeli public statements suggested. Within hours, Hezbollah launched a concentrated series of rocket and mortar attacks against nearby Israeli staging areas, forcing a redeployment of forces already strained by casualties. The attacks were not random. They were informed by the invisible map drawn through intercepted signals.

In another instance, maintenance alerts sent over unencrypted channels inadvertently revealed an armored brigade's need to pause movements for urgent repair work. Pager messages detailed the dispatch of recovery vehicles, the scheduling of fuel resupply, and the anticipated downtime for several combat vehicles. Hezbollah analysts, reading the cadence of these administrative pages, correctly inferred that the armored column would be stationary and vulnerable for a critical window of several hours. Rocket fire was timed accordingly. Even though physical damage to Israeli armor was limited, the disruption to movement plans and the forced reallocation of support assets delayed operations across an entire sector.

Captured or leaked after-action reports from the Israeli side, although careful in language, occasionally hinted at the consequences. References to "unexpected anticipatory fires," to "operational tempo disruption from unknown sources," and to "enemy tactical adjustment correlating with friendly logistical movements" peppered internal assessments. Israeli commanders understood that their unguarded administrative communications had been harvested and exploited. In some units, restrictions on pager usage and administrative radio traffic were instituted mid-campaign — too late to undo the informational advantage Hezbollah had already accrued.

What these fragments reveal is not merely the technical capacity of Hezbollah's intercept teams. They reveal the larger operational philosophy at work — the idea that even the smallest emissions, the most seemingly trivial signals, could have outsized effects when harvested with discipline and applied with tactical patience. Hezbollah did not need to capture battlefield orders or encrypted strike plans to shape Israeli behavior. They needed only to understand the heartbeat of operations as reflected in logistics, maintenance, medical, and administrative chatter.

Each intercepted page, each decoded logistical alert, was a piece of a puzzle that, once assembled, allowed Hezbollah to fight smarter, faster, and at lower cost than would otherwise have been possible. It allowed them to bleed an adversary far superior in firepower without engaging directly on equal terms. It allowed them to stretch the war into weeks, to survive where annihilation had been expected, to shift the political calculus from decisive victory to uneasy stalemate.

The success of this model emboldened Hezbollah to invest further in spectrum dominance in the years that followed. During later conflicts, reports surfaced of Hezbollah extending its interception efforts beyond pager and radio traffic to include low-power cellular infrastructure, Wi-Fi telemetry, and even attempts to harvest satellite uplinks. The basic doctrine remained unchanged — listen first, map second, act third — but the tools and targets expanded alongside the evolving technologies of modern battlefields.

The war for the air — for the invisible signals that stitched together the movements, logistics, and decisions of conventional militaries — was no longer the exclusive domain of large state actors. Hezbollah had shown that a disciplined non-state force could enter that domain and thrive, exploiting the very informational currents that larger powers had assumed were safe simply because they were unacknowledged, unmonitored, or deemed unworthy of protection.

The echoes of this victory reverberated outward. Around the world, irregular forces studied the 2006 campaign. Lessons filtered into insurgent groups operating against Western forces in Iraq and Afghanistan, where intercepted radio chatter, open-broadcast blue force trackers, and unsecured administrative networks offered the same kinds of informational leverage Hezbollah had pioneered. State actors watched carefully too, recognizing that the democratization of interception posed threats and opportunities alike in the coming age of hybrid warfare.

In southern Lebanon, among Hezbollah's leadership, the war was remembered less for its physical battles and more for its informational triumphs. It became a proof point that in a world drowning in emissions, survival and influence belonged not necessarily to those who shouted loudest or struck first, but to those who listened longest and understood most deeply.

And it was understood that the battlefield of the future would not just be one of tanks, rockets, and rifles. It would be one of antennas, signals, and the relentless, patient, invisible accumulation of awareness.

The lessons drawn from Hezbollah's signals exploitation campaign did not remain frozen in the tactics of 2006. In the years that followed, as technology advanced and new wars erupted, the underlying principle evolved: where there is wireless communication, there is exposure. Where there is exposure, there is advantage for those who learn to harvest it first.

In the decade after the Second Lebanon War, the global battlespace became even more saturated with wireless emissions. Unmanned aerial vehicles flooded the skies, each dripping telemetry, video feeds, and command links. Armored vehicles were outfitted with battlefield management systems, communicating over ad-hoc networks. Troops carried personal radios, GPS trackers, biometric sensors, and networked tablets. Entire supply chains and medical infrastructures went wireless, transmitting data assumed to be too trivial for anyone to intercept — precisely the kind of data Hezbollah had shown could be weaponized.

Hezbollah adapted accordingly. Their operators expanded from passively listening to pagers and radios to harvesting side-channel data from battlefield electronics. Signals intelligence was no longer merely about capturing voice traffic or paging alerts; it became about pattern analysis across a kaleidoscope of low-power emissions. Wi-Fi beacons leaked positional data. Cellular handshakes mapped movements. Drone telemetry betrayed surveillance priorities. Even the heartbeat of a network, the regular pings and acknowledgments between devices, became a form of intelligence that could be gathered, processed, and exploited.

The underlying philosophy remained untouched: patient listening was a weapon more powerful than any rocket or rifle. Action could wait. Understanding could not.

This evolution mirrored the broader changes sweeping across hybrid warfare. Nation-states and non-state actors alike began blending cyber operations, electronic warfare, and traditional kinetic action into seamless campaigns. Hezbollah's intercept playbook, first proven with scavenged receivers and discipline in 2006, foreshadowed this integration. Where others saw discrete domains — cyber here, SIGINT there, kinetic warfare elsewhere — Hezbollah increasingly treated them as facets of a single continuous battlespace.

The shift was subtle but profound. In this model, a captured pager message, a cloned Wi-Fi access point, a hijacked video feed, and a targeted rocket barrage were not separate actions requiring separate chains of command. They were linked expressions of the same operational goal: to understand the adversary faster, to disrupt him more efficiently, to shape his decision-making from the shadows.

As the years passed, Hezbollah's information warfare capabilities grew more sophisticated, not always through indigenous development, but through the careful adoption of proven tactics. Open-source intelligence gathering, network mapping, passive surveillance of civilian communication infrastructure — all were folded into their operational planning. The same patience that once characterized their rooftop listening posts now extended to their cyber and electronic warfare strategies.

Yet even as their technical methods evolved, the cultural discipline remained the same. They continued to teach their operators that silence was survival, that emissions were vulnerability, that the air itself was an open battlefield to be contested with the same seriousness as any hilltop or village. It was this fusion of old-world patience with new-world technology that gave Hezbollah an enduring edge.

The implications of Hezbollah's evolution extend far beyond Lebanon. They offer a clear warning to any modern military, any intelligence agency, any security planner who believes that dominance in the electromagnetic spectrum is a given. The Second Lebanon War showed that informational superiority is not a permanent condition bestowed by technology alone. It is a fragile, perishable advantage — one that must be earned and re-earned continuously against adversaries willing to listen, to wait, and to act without revealing themselves.

Trust in the invisibility of communications was shattered in 2006. The wireless world, once treated as an ambient convenience, was exposed as an adversarial medium. What Hezbollah demonstrated was not that secure communications were impossible, but that organizational culture determines vulnerability far more than technology does. It is not enough to encrypt battle orders while leaving logistics and maintenance to leak unguarded. It is not enough to secure the headquarters while emissions from the field radiate unnoticed. It is not enough to armor the visible while neglecting the invisible.

Hezbollah's playbook was simple to describe but difficult to execute. It demanded discipline across weeks and months of boredom, listening to streams of seemingly meaningless data. It demanded restraint in the face of tempting half-information, patience to wait for patterns to emerge rather than rushing toward action. It demanded a kind of humility often absent in insurgent movements — the humility to admit that the enemy would betray himself without being provoked, if only one listened closely enough.

In the global wars that followed, these lessons manifested again and again. In Afghanistan, in Iraq, in Syria, in Ukraine. Whenever wireless infrastructure expanded faster than security measures, whenever emissions were treated as invisible or irrelevant, adversaries harvested them. Whenever armies trusted the air without securing it, they left a trail that careful enemies could follow.

The tools have changed. Encryption is stronger. Wireless standards have evolved. Electronic countermeasures are more aggressive. But the human behaviors that create informational vulnerability remain stubbornly consistent. Convenience, trust in legacy systems, the prioritization of speed over security — these factors continue to erode even the most sophisticated defenses.

Hezbollah's contribution to this global shift was not technological innovation. It was operational innovation. They proved that information dominance is not the exclusive domain of those who can afford it. It belongs to those who prioritize it — those who are willing to adapt their entire concept of warfare to include the invisible, to embrace the spectrum as a terrain to be fought over, shaped, and exploited.

The war for the air, for the signals that carry life, movement, and command across the battlefield, continues. And it is not always the side with the most satellites, the largest jamming arrays, or the newest encryption protocols that wins it. Victory often belongs to those who listen longest, wait most patiently, and act when the enemy forgets that invisibility is never free.

Hezbollah remembered.

They listened before they shot.
And in doing so, they rewrote the rules of a battlefield that still surrounds us today — unseen, but never silent.

# CHAPTER 4 — A TACTICAL SHIFT: INTERCEPTION MEETS ACTION

When Hezbollah first began systematically intercepting Israeli pager traffic, the advantage it sought was informational. Awareness, foresight, and battlefield mapping were the initial goals. But as the war unfolded and the intercept data accumulated, a transformation occurred. Awareness shifted into precision. Intelligence became action. And in the chaotic, crowded battlespace of southern Lebanon, Hezbollah learned to turn quiet listening into deadly timing.

Their operators did not treat every intercepted message as a call for immediate response. That would have flooded the battlefield with noise and undermined their discipline. Instead, they treated each pager intercept like a thread, gathering it, weighing its context, matching it against the growing internal map they were building of Israeli operational rhythms. Most messages were triaged, cataloged, and added to pattern libraries maintained by Hezbollah's tactical analysts, working from hidden rooms deep inside civilian areas or from mobile analysis hubs moved frequently to avoid Israeli detection.

Over time, the sheer volume of captured pager data revealed the predictability buried within the apparent chaos of war. Logistics pages consistently preceded major unit movements. Medical evacuations clustered around vulnerable sectors. Maintenance alerts forecasted armor immobilization. Even administrative messages about shifts and rotations, mundane on their surface, betrayed the human operational tempo underneath Israeli military planning. Hezbollah's intercept teams learned not to chase every signal, but to look for convergences, to watch for the buildup of chatter that preceded action.

When the convergences appeared, so did the strikes.

Rocket teams, operating from hidden launch positions buried beneath civilian structures or camouflaged into the natural folds of the terrain, received coded alerts from Hezbollah field commanders who had synthesized the intelligence. Sometimes the timing was tight — less than an hour between a spike in pager chatter around a maintenance depot and a rocket barrage landing on the same coordinates. Other times, the attacks were held in reserve, launched hours later to coincide with anticipated troop arrivals or logistical bottlenecks.

The strikes were not indiscriminate. In areas where intercepted pager traffic indicated concentrated resupply or high-value personnel movement, Hezbollah's rocket fire became uncharacteristically precise for a guerrilla force. Salvos were timed not to the hour but to the phase of an enemy operation, with barrages adjusted based on fresh interception data flowing back from Hezbollah's decentralized listening teams.

The most devastating effects were not always physical. While rockets destroyed vehicles, supply dumps, and occasionally killed soldiers, the greater impact was psychological. Israeli units began to suspect — correctly — that their movements were being anticipated. Confidence in rear-area security, once taken for granted, eroded. Soldiers moving through what should have been protected corridors found themselves under sudden, targeted fire. Convoys delayed by maintenance issues became targets precisely during their immobilization windows. Medical evacuations, once routine, became fraught with anxiety, knowing that the very act of calling for help could attract fire.

In one documented case, an Israeli medical evacuation

helicopter was forced to abort a landing after incoming rocket fire saturated its intended pickup zone. The decision to wave off, made in the critical seconds before touchdown, was not based on visual identification of Hezbollah forces but on the unexpected precision of the incoming barrage — a barrage that had been timed almost perfectly to the window between the transmission of the medevac request and the helicopter's scheduled arrival.

Incidents like this accumulated over weeks of conflict, creating a steady, corrosive pressure on Israeli operations. The belief that Hezbollah somehow "knew" when and where they were most vulnerable took hold in the ranks. It was not a mystical fear; it was a rational response to consistent, observable patterns of exposure and exploitation. Israeli soldiers did not need to know the technical details of Hezbollah's interception campaign to feel its effects. They lived them every time a movement order was followed by a shelling. Every time a resupply convoy moved under the cover of darkness only to find itself bracketed by artillery moments after a logistics page was transmitted. Every time a planned rotation of tired troops was delayed because the enemy seemed to anticipate the schedule.

The psychological toll was enormous. Soldiers operating under constant uncertainty began to distrust their own systems. Confidence in radios, pagers, and even internal dispatches weakened. Field commanders, under pressure to maintain operational tempo, grew more cautious, spending precious minutes devising ad hoc communications workarounds rather than moving swiftly along pre-planned routes. Each hesitation compounded the tactical friction already imposed by Hezbollah's fortified defenses and guerrilla ambushes.

This erosion of confidence extended up the chain of command. Israeli operational planners, facing mounting evidence that logistical and administrative emissions were being harvested, were forced to reevaluate standard operational practices in the middle of an active conflict. Restrictions on pager use were tightened. Certain administrative communications were ordered transferred to encrypted networks, even if doing so introduced delays. Troop movement orders were sometimes hand-carried rather than transmitted. But these adaptations, however necessary, slowed Israel's operational tempo precisely when speed was needed to overwhelm Hezbollah's defensive networks.

Hezbollah, for its part, understood exactly what they had achieved. Internal communications captured after the war reveal a clear self-awareness among Hezbollah commanders of the psychological impact their interception-driven operations were having. They discussed the enemy's growing fear of exposure. They documented the slowdown in Israeli tempo. They celebrated not just the casualties inflicted but the perception of inevitability they had created — the feeling among Israeli soldiers that no matter how careful they were, they were being watched, anticipated, and targeted before they could act.

This psychological warfare was a byproduct of tactical discipline. It was not achieved through massed forces or spectacular technological breakthroughs, but through the patient, methodical exploitation of signals that had always been there, floating invisibly across the battlefield. It was victory achieved not in the traditional decisive battle sense, but in the slow, grinding corrosion of enemy confidence, tempo, and cohesion.

By the time the ceasefire came, the informational victory was nearly complete. Israeli forces remained potent, capable of striking with overwhelming force at points of their choosing. But they moved more hesitantly, communicated more cautiously, improvised more frequently. Every delay, every diversion from planned operations, every added layer of security protocol imposed because of the fear of exposure was a silent victory for Hezbollah's passive, patient, invisible campaign.

And those victories were cumulative. They did not disappear when the rockets fell silent. They lived on in the doctrinal reforms, in the after-action reports, in the quiet acknowledgments among Israeli commanders that in 2006, their dominance had been contested not only on the ground and in the air but across the very architecture of information itself.

Hezbollah had learned to listen first, but now they had proven they could act based on that listening with devastating effect. It was not simply an enhancement to their defensive posture. It was the emergence of a new offensive doctrine, one that blurred the lines between intelligence collection, psychological operations, and kinetic action. A doctrine that would not be abandoned in the wars to come.

It would not always be rockets or mortars that struck first. Sometimes, the first blow would be a signal heard, a pattern recognized, a movement anticipated — and only afterward, at the moment of maximum effect, would the strike follow.

The transformation was complete. Hezbollah had shifted from harvesting the battlefield's invisible chatter to shaping the battlefield itself based on what they heard.
They had entered the heads of their adversaries — and once inside, they were very hard to remove.

On the ground, the impact of Hezbollah's information-driven tactics rippled through Israeli forces in ways that after-action reports only partially captured. In unit debriefings after firefights, soldiers spoke not only about enemy firepower or fortifications but about a creeping sense that Hezbollah was predicting their movements before they made them. It was not merely that ambushes happened. It was that they happened with eerie timing, hitting units during moments of fatigue, after key resupply convoys, during known shift rotations — the precise windows when operational vulnerability was highest.

Frontline commanders began to observe a behavioral shift among their troops. Soldiers moved more cautiously between positions, sometimes hesitating at natural chokepoints even without direct orders, as if expecting contact. Communications discipline tightened, but the underlying fear remained. Every call for a resupply, every request for a medical extraction carried an unspoken question: who else might be listening?

Field adaptations followed. Platoon leaders, no longer trusting the security of their own emissions, began adopting informal countermeasures. Supplies were staggered in smaller convoys rather than concentrated in predictable windows. Troop movements were delayed or rerouted based on perceived signal security rather than tactical necessity. Units increased their use of pre-arranged hand signals, runners, and line-of-sight confirmations to replace reliance on radio communications wherever possible.

These improvisations, born of necessity, degraded efficiency. Where orders might once have moved across the battlefield in seconds, they now took minutes or longer. Where units might have coordinated tightly around pre-planned synchronization points, they now operated under a fog of delayed or fragmented orders. Each disruption was small in isolation, but cumulatively, they sapped momentum and strained unit cohesion at the exact moment Israeli planners sought rapid, overwhelming pressure against Hezbollah's defensive belts.

Hezbollah exploited these disruptions ruthlessly. Their small-unit tactics, already well-suited to decentralized fighting, were enhanced by the fluid flow of intercept intelligence. When an Israeli company delayed a scheduled push, Hezbollah fighters were often ready to reposition to fresher ambush sites, realigning anti-tank teams or laying new mines along anticipated paths of movement. Even when Israeli units did not delay, Hezbollah's tactical cells were quick to infer from intercepted logistical signals when resupply gaps or unit exhaustion might create exploitable vulnerabilities.

One documented example came from operations near the Wadi Saluki, where an Israeli armored column planned a coordinated crossing under the cover of darkness. Original timing, captured in part by logistical pager traffic regarding bridge-layer deployments and maintenance status updates, provided Hezbollah with enough warning to preposition anti-tank teams equipped with AT-14 Kornet missiles. When the Israeli crossing was delayed several hours due to internal coordination difficulties — themselves exacerbated by stricter radio discipline reducing real-time synchronization — Hezbollah's teams were able to rest, resupply, and re-aim before the armored vehicles finally began their push. The result was devastating: several tanks were hit in quick succession, forcing a tactical withdrawal and handing Hezbollah a localized but symbolically powerful victory.

It was not simply tactical prowess that delivered these results. It was the marriage of interception discipline with action timing. Hezbollah's fighters were trained to absorb the lessons of the intercepted air, to act not merely when given direct orders, but when patterns told them where Israeli forces would be, when they would be vulnerable, and how long they would likely remain exposed.

This semi-autonomous decision-making, grounded in real-time signal harvesting and pattern recognition, gave Hezbollah an elasticity that traditional hierarchical armies often struggle to achieve in combat. Small cells operated with partial information, but enough to take effective action within narrow windows of opportunity. They didn't need complete battlefield awareness. They needed localized superiority — superiority gained by listening and moving faster than larger, slower command structures could react.

The Israeli response evolved mid-war, but at a cost. Units began adopting low-emission posture drills, limiting radio usage even during active engagements. Emissions discipline drills, previously reserved for high-intensity training scenarios, were improvised in real time under battlefield pressure. Field commanders increasingly moved toward "dead signal" operational cycles, where units transmitted only at randomized intervals in brief, encrypted bursts, avoiding continuous radio chatter and reducing signal footprint.

These adaptations were partially effective. As Hezbollah's interception picture grew less clear, the precision of their ambushes and strikes decreased. But the damage had already been done. The initial advantage Hezbollah had built by exploiting the early war's communication habits allowed them to shape key phases of the conflict, buying time, bleeding momentum, and imposing operational hesitation on an adversary whose doctrine depended on speed and aggressiveness to win decisively.

Beyond the tactical sphere, the psychological impact compounded. Israeli troops, who had trained for superiority in maneuver, firepower, and coordination, found themselves fighting an enemy who did not seem to fear detection, who struck precisely when Israeli formations were at their most disorganized, and who always seemed one step ahead in the fluid chessboard of local engagements. It became harder to maintain the narrative of dominance when every logistical move felt like it was broadcast to an unseen, omnipresent observer.

Field reports captured this frustration in subtle ways. References to "uncanny timing" of Hezbollah counterattacks. Complaints about supply convoys drawing rocket fire shortly after dispatch. Mentions of "operational exposure without clear cause" in officer debriefings. Even in a military as experienced and hardened as the IDF, the psychological weight of fighting a war where the enemy seemed to see your moves before you made them took its toll.

At the command level, Israeli intelligence analysts began piecing together the extent of Hezbollah's passive interception efforts. Signals surveys detected patterns suggesting widespread spectrum monitoring. Emissions pattern analysis confirmed that areas with high volumes of unencrypted logistical traffic correlated with higher rates of Hezbollah counteraction. Tactical intelligence bulletins circulated among field units warning against casual radio and pager usage, but by then the informational terrain had already been tilted in Hezbollah's favor.

The war continued, but with each passing week, Hezbollah's informational pressure distorted the battlespace further. Israeli units adapted defensively, limiting the damage. But the strategic tempo — the ability to move, to mass, to strike on initiative — was never fully recovered. Every step forward required more planning, more counter-countermeasures, more caution.

Hezbollah had proven that by mastering the invisible domain of intercepted signals, even a force outmatched in firepower could shape the flow of battle. Not by meeting strength head-on, but by reading its intentions before they solidified into action, and by striking at the connective tissue of military operations rather than the armored fist alone.

This shift — from interception for awareness to interception for shaping the battlefield itself — marked a turning point in asymmetric warfare. No longer was passive listening merely a defensive measure. It had become the first movement in a broader offensive dance, one where timing, patience, and insight replaced the blunt instruments of mass and velocity.

And for Israeli soldiers moving cautiously through the hills and ruins of southern Lebanon, the change was felt not as an abstraction, but as a constant, gnawing awareness that someone was listening. Someone was waiting. Someone was already adjusting the battlefield, even before the next order was given.

As the war stretched on, the subtle corrosion of Israeli operational tempo became increasingly difficult to contain. Every adaptation meant to counter Hezbollah's interception campaign came at a price. Encrypting more communications reduced speed. Curtailing emissions complicated coordination. Delaying medical evacuations out of caution risked morale and increased battlefield fatalities. The invisible pressure Hezbollah exerted through their signals exploitation did not need to break the Israeli war machine directly. It only needed to slow it, to complicate it, to bleed its momentum until strategic objectives slipped out of reach.

Inside Israeli command posts, debates intensified. Intelligence officers warned of systemic vulnerabilities in legacy communication systems. Signal Corps advisors advocated for radical shifts toward more hardened, low-emission operational models. Field commanders, faced with the daily tactical realities of coordinating battalion-sized maneuvers under threat of immediate retaliation, pushed back against measures that added friction to already strained operations. Speed was life in ground warfare. Yet the very tools that enabled speed — radios, pagers, logistical broadcasts — had become liabilities.

The resulting tension shaped operational decisions in ways that often favored Hezbollah. Israeli units that might once have launched rapid exploitation attacks after battlefield successes instead paused to confirm that emission discipline was in place. Supply routes that would once have operated in steady, predictable cycles grew erratic, delaying resupply of forward positions. Coordination between infantry and armored elements, always a delicate dance under fire, was further strained by new protocols forbidding real-time radio chatter except under extreme necessity.

Hezbollah's fighters, meanwhile, adapted alongside their shifting adversary. As Israeli emissions discipline improved, Hezbollah's intercept teams became more sensitive to secondary signals — the faint administrative beacons still leaking from support units, the barely noticeable bursts of encrypted traffic that, while opaque in content, betrayed timing and movement patterns. A short encrypted burst at a consistent time each day from a frontline logistics officer could, if watched carefully enough, reveal when resupply was occurring. A spike in tightly scheduled, short-range communications among command posts could suggest impending maneuver.

The transition from cleartext interception to side-channel analysis marked a maturation of Hezbollah's informational doctrine. Even when deprived of direct content, they could infer operational rhythms from the metadata of communications alone. The battlefield had grown quieter in electromagnetic terms, but it had not grown opaque. To those willing to listen patiently enough, the patterns still spoke.

At the same time, Hezbollah's exploitation of their informational advantage became increasingly psychological. It was no longer enough to strike tactically at vulnerabilities revealed by intercepted signals. They began to shape the perception of omnipresence deliberately.

Selective rocket attacks, timed precisely to anticipated movements but occasionally withheld even when opportunities were clear, created a climate of unpredictability. By choosing when not to strike as carefully as when to strike, Hezbollah kept Israeli forces guessing. Convoys that braced for attack sometimes passed unharmed, only to be targeted later when their guard lowered. This selective application of firepower, based on intercepted operational signals, fed into the broader perception that Hezbollah was always watching, always waiting, always choosing.

The psychological weight grew heavier. Israeli soldiers described feeling hunted, exposed not just during assaults but during the banal moments of military life — resupply, medical care, administrative reorganization. The rituals that kept armies functioning began to feel like vulnerabilities rather than strengths. Fear shifted from the front lines into the rear areas. The battlefield's geography of danger expanded, blurring the distinction between safe zones and active combat zones.

Unit after-action reports reflected the strain. Comments about "constant electromagnetic pressure," about "feeling seen even without contact," about "an enemy that anticipated our needs" appeared with greater frequency. Casualties inflicted directly through Hezbollah's intercept-driven strikes were significant but secondary to the broader operational erosion taking place.

At the strategic level, the Israeli high command recognized the implications. Victory in southern Lebanon had always depended on the ability to move fast enough to shatter Hezbollah's defensive belts before international pressure forced a ceasefire. Every day lost to hesitation, every hour spent recalibrating to avoid emissions exposure, tipped the clock further in Hezbollah's favor. Tactical victories, achieved at high cost, were undermined by a tempo Hezbollah's informational dominance had slowed to a crawl.

Hezbollah's leadership, too, understood the broader battlefield they had shaped. Internal communications captured postwar reveal a high level of self-awareness. Their commanders discussed not only the tactical successes enabled by interception, but the strategic delay it imposed on Israeli operations. Time, always the hidden currency of asymmetric warfare, had been bought in weeks and days measured not by battlefield conquests but by informational attrition.

The tactical shift — interception meeting action — had created strategic dividends.

It proved that a disciplined, patient, listening enemy could turn modern militaries' reliance on wireless coordination into a lever of control. It proved that psychological dominance could be achieved without air supremacy, without numerical superiority, without massive technological overmatch. It proved that in the age of ambient wireless communications, battlefield initiative could be contested by those who chose to fight not just with weapons, but with understanding.

Israeli commanders facing the final weeks of the war carried the burden of this realization. It was not merely that Hezbollah had survived. It was that Hezbollah had shaped the conditions of survival through informational mastery. Every battle fought in southern Lebanon after that realization became, in part, a battle against the invisible weight of being heard.

And for Hezbollah, the lessons were clear. In the wars to come, they would not need to outgun their adversaries. They needed only to out-listen them, outwait them, and act precisely at the cracks created by an enemy's unguarded emissions.

It was a doctrine that had begun with rooftop antennas, scavenged receivers, and patient ears. Now it had become a core pillar of Hezbollah's evolving military strategy — an enduring advantage crafted not with overwhelming firepower, but with invisible pressure applied relentlessly until operational structures cracked under their own weight.

And in the minds of the soldiers and officers who lived through it, the memory of that invisible battlefield — of an enemy not seen but always felt — would linger far longer than the ruins of the visible one.

When the ceasefire finally took hold, the physical lines of battle in southern Lebanon were etched in rubble and blood, but the more enduring scars were invisible. They lived in the lessons both sides carried away from the electromagnetic battlespace, in the quiet recalibrations of doctrine, and in the changed mental landscape of soldiers who had fought under the steady, unseen gaze of an adversary who listened before he struck.

Inside Israel's postwar commissions, a difficult reckoning began. No after-action report could easily measure the compounded cost of informational exposure. It was not just a matter of how many rockets landed or how many tanks were lost. It was the cumulative price of lost tempo, of decisions delayed, of movements second-guessed, of confidence eroded in the invisible air that once seemed harmless. Commanders tasked with explaining the war's sluggish progress and uneven tactical returns found themselves citing factors rarely named in traditional operational summaries: degraded communications trust, electromagnetic vulnerabilities, adversary pattern analysis.

For years, the Israeli military had invested heavily in technological superiority — encrypted command nets, secure satellite links, hardened air-ground coordination channels. These systems had performed their roles under enormous strain. Yet around and beneath them, the less glamorous arteries of operational life — maintenance schedules, medevac coordination, fuel requests, resupply updates — had continued to bleed information into the air, vulnerable, visible, and ultimately fatal.

The reality was stark. The enemy had not needed to defeat Israel's strongest systems. Hezbollah had targeted the connective tissue, the background noise, the spaces where complacency thrived because risk was assumed to be low. They had weaponized metadata long before that term became common in global security discourse. And they had done it with patience, with discipline, and with an understanding of the enemy's human rhythms, not just his technological signatures.

The psychological wounds inflicted were slower to heal. Soldiers returned from the war with an acute awareness that invisibility was an illusion. The feeling that every movement, every request, every emission could invite retribution gnawed at operational culture in ways no immediate policy reform could fully address. Communications protocols were tightened. Signal Corps training was overhauled. New systems were fielded with improved emissions security. But beneath the technical adaptations lay a deeper anxiety: the knowledge that even in the best-guarded networks, the simple fact of operational necessity — the need to move, to supply, to evacuate, to survive — would always generate signals. And signals could always be heard.

For Hezbollah, the war became a validation. Their postwar assessments brimmed with confidence not simply because they had survived Israeli assault, but because they had shaped Israeli behavior. They had demonstrated that informational dominance was achievable not through massive technological investment, but through the strategic application of discipline and patience. They had proven that an attentive ear could be more dangerous than a raised weapon, that shaping the enemy's perception could matter as much as inflicting physical losses.

The tactical shift Hezbollah pioneered — interception feeding into action — would not be abandoned. It would be refined, expanded, iterated upon. In the years following the Second Lebanon War, Hezbollah's forces continued to invest in spectrum dominance, building more sophisticated interception arrays, integrating cyber reconnaissance, experimenting with low-profile active collection systems designed to harvest metadata from increasingly encrypted environments.

But the foundational lesson remained unchanged: listen first, understand patiently, act precisely. The doctrine that had once grown out of necessity — from scavenged Soviet receivers and commercial pagers — had become a deliberate strategic choice. Hezbollah no longer viewed interception as an adjunct to warfare. It was warfare. The air itself was a battlespace, and in that battlespace, even the most powerful adversaries could be made hesitant, reactive, and ultimately vulnerable.

The Israeli experience in 2006 offered a brutal case study in this shift. The technical details of interception could be debated. The ethics of embedding listening posts in civilian areas could be challenged. But the operational consequences could not be denied. When the enemy knows your rhythms better than you do, when he listens longer than you are willing to stay silent, when he acts based not on your visible formations but on the invisible pulse of your logistics and support systems, the terms of engagement are no longer yours to dictate.

This was the new reality that emerged from the hills and shattered towns of southern Lebanon. A battlefield shaped as much by what was heard as by what was seen. A war fought not just with rockets and tanks, but with antennas, receivers, and a discipline of patience that could erode superiority one intercepted signal at a time.

The soldiers who fought in that war carried these lessons forward, sometimes consciously, sometimes unconsciously. In future conflicts, greater care would be taken to harden communications, to minimize emissions, to treat the air itself as a hostile environment rather than a neutral medium. But the deeper lesson — the cultural vulnerability that had allowed casual emissions to persist — would remain a shadow on the doctrine of even the most advanced militaries.

For Hezbollah, the success of their tactics meant that future wars could be approached with confidence in a principle often forgotten by conventional forces: that in modern warfare, information is not a byproduct. It is a primary weapon. Harvested, refined, and applied correctly, it can shape battlefields before the first round is ever fired.

And for anyone willing to listen, the war of 2006 still speaks. Not in the headlines or the photographs of ruined villages, but in the quiet, invisible layers of conflict where emissions bleed intent and patience turns knowledge into power.

It is there, in the unseen air, that the next battles will be shaped — and perhaps, before they are even fought, decided.

In the years after the ceasefire, the effects of Hezbollah's tactical shift reverberated outward in ways neither side could have fully anticipated during the heat of the war. The invisible battlefields of electromagnetic space, once treated as ancillary to the terrain of hills, towns, and highways, began to emerge at the center of how asymmetric actors understood modern warfare. It was not a matter of Hezbollah inventing a new way to fight. It was a matter of proving that a listening force, if disciplined enough and patient enough, could fundamentally alter the initiative without ever matching firepower for firepower.

Around the world, others were paying attention. Militias, insurgent groups, and even some nation-state militaries quietly studied the details that filtered out of the 2006 conflict. What Hezbollah had shown was that the dominance of technologically superior militaries could be eroded not through direct confrontation, but through the exploitation of their dependencies — their need for coordination, for logistics, for medical evacuation, for the complex, constant flow of internal communications that kept modern military machines functioning.

It was not necessary to defeat these forces head-on. It was enough to corrupt their rhythms, to make them hesitate, to force them into procedural caution at moments when momentum mattered most. It was enough to create uncertainty, to inject friction into processes once treated as secure and invisible simply because no one had looked closely before. Hezbollah had rewritten part of the operational manual of modern conflict, and others would adopt variations of their model in battles yet to come.

In Iraq, in Afghanistan, in Syria, in Yemen, echoes of this approach could be heard in the invisible background noise of those wars. Insurgent groups began harvesting not just direct battlefield chatter but logistical coordination signals, helicopter dispatch frequencies, supply convoy scheduling information. The tools varied — from simple civilian scanners to more advanced, often externally supplied collection gear — but the principle remained constant: listen first, map second, act third.

Hezbollah's success with interception-fed targeting also inspired a deeper understanding among irregular forces that information, once captured, could be shaped and weaponized in more subtle ways than direct attacks. Disinformation seeded into intercepted channels, false movement patterns generated to lure enemy forces into ambushes, even the selective leaking of true information to create operational overreactions — these tactics evolved from the foundations laid in southern Lebanon, where passive listening had first been married to active shaping.

For the Israelis, and later for Western militaries facing complex hybrid threats, the lesson proved hard but ultimately transformative. Emissions control, once the domain of specialized signal units and cyber commands, became a general operational concern. Spectrum monitoring was embedded deeper into tactical planning. Communications discipline, encryption by default, rapid shift protocols for compromised networks — all of these adaptations grew in direct response to the kind of informational exploitation Hezbollah had demonstrated could be decisive.

Yet adaptation came at a cost. The very act of defending the electromagnetic perimeter — the need for increased caution, emissions reduction, signal masking — introduced friction into operations that traditionally relied on speed, autonomy, and rapid concentration of force. In this way, Hezbollah's 2006 playbook continued to exact a price long after the last rocket was fired. Every operation slowed for emissions review, every convoy delayed for communications security, every hesitation forced by the fear of being heard was a lingering echo of the war fought, in part, across the invisible battlefield.

In Hezbollah's own doctrine, the lessons were institutionalized. Future operations — from intelligence activities abroad to internal defensive preparations at home — incorporated the assumption that any opponent, no matter how powerful, could be rendered hesitant through careful informational pressure. Listening, in Hezbollah's post-2006 evolution, was no longer a preparatory phase. It was a form of attack. Every intercepted signal was a blow. Every hesitation forced was a victory.

This strategic patience, bred in the mountains and villages of southern Lebanon, became a cultural asset as much as a tactical one. Fighters trained not only in the use of weapons but in the use of awareness. Commanders briefed on battlefield conditions that included electromagnetic maps of signal flows and vulnerabilities. Analysts taught to correlate the faintest hints of logistical movements into actionable intelligence. What began with scavenged commercial gear had evolved into an operational philosophy as deeply ingrained as traditional concepts of maneuver and fire.

In many ways, Hezbollah's approach reflected a broader shift in the character of modern conflict — away from the raw application of firepower alone and toward the shaping of adversary behavior through informational dominance. It was a war fought before the visible war, a conflict of patience and perception that decided many battles before the first physical contact was made. And it was a war that Hezbollah had helped pioneer, not because they had the most sophisticated technology, but because they had the cultural discipline to understand what listening could achieve.

By the end of 2006, Hezbollah was no longer simply a

resistance movement in the traditional sense. They had become a proving ground for a new kind of hybrid warfare doctrine, one that blurred the lines between intelligence gathering, psychological operations, and direct kinetic action. Their successful fusion of interception and targeted strikes showed that in the modern era, informational mastery could erode the advantages of even the most formidable opponents, one intercepted signal at a time.

And for those Israeli units who had fought through the thick air of southern Lebanon, carrying with them the heavy knowledge that their movements and intentions had been mapped by an enemy they could not see, the lesson was personal and lasting. The fear of being heard did not dissipate with the ceasefire. It remained, embedded in every cautious transmission, every double-checked coordinate, every encrypted order shouted across a battlefield that, once, they had assumed was theirs alone.

In the wars to come, that assumption would never again be taken for granted.

Even as the visible combat operations ended and political negotiations filled the void left by the fighting, the invisible war Hezbollah had waged continued to evolve beneath the surface. The world Hezbollah revealed — a world where passive interception could shape outcomes as surely as artillery and rockets — did not close with the ceasefire. It expanded, creeping into the doctrine of both state and non-state actors, into the architecture of modern conflict, into the very psychology of how war would be fought.

Hezbollah's experience in 2006 institutionalized a foundational truth that would persist across decades: interception is not an accessory to war. It is war.

No longer would listening be treated as a preparatory phase for action. It would become action itself, blurring the distinction between reconnaissance and engagement, between gathering and shaping, between perception and pressure. In a world saturated with emissions, the act of listening became the first strike, and the patient accumulation of signals, patterns, and behavioral rhythms became the slow application of strategic force.

The discipline Hezbollah demonstrated — to harvest before acting, to resist the impulse to strike prematurely, to understand the battlefield not only geographically but informationally — gave them a reach far beyond their physical size. It allowed them to touch the tempo, the decisions, the very thinking of a superior adversary without direct engagement. That ability, once proven, was not something easily countered by traditional means.

To harden a network, to encrypt a radio signal, to change frequencies — these were tactical responses. But to change a military culture that had grown reliant on convenience, that assumed the background noise of operations was beneath the interest of an adversary, was a far more difficult challenge. It required a fundamental shift in how militaries thought about their own emissions, about their own logistical heartbeat, about the very fact that the act of existing in a battlespace was itself an act of vulnerability.

Hezbollah's triumph was to make this vulnerability felt. Tangibly. Psychologically. In the bodies of soldiers who hesitated at crossroads, in the minds of commanders who second-guessed routine movements, in the protocols rewritten after the war to account for the silent enemy in the air.

And it was not a transient victory. As other conflicts erupted — in Gaza, in Iraq, in Afghanistan, in Ukraine — the patterns reemerged. Forces over-reliant on unsecured emissions found themselves exposed. Insurgent groups, militias, hybrid forces increasingly integrated passive interception into their operational cycles. Whether through scavenged commercial gear, captured military radios, or increasingly sophisticated side-channel analysis, the principle remained unchanged. Those who listen long enough gain a foothold in the enemy's decision loop, and once inside, they shift the balance of initiative.

Hezbollah had shown that it did not require technical parity to contest the electromagnetic battlespace. It required patience, discipline, and a deep understanding that information — real, partial, or even misinterpreted — could be weaponized if applied with precision.

The broader strategic implications were profound. It meant that no military force, however dominant in conventional terms, could afford to ignore the invisible battlefield. It meant that superiority was not a permanent state but a condition contingent on maintaining not just firepower, but emissions hygiene, informational discretion, and operational humility.

For Hezbollah, the Second Lebanon War was not merely survival. It was validation. A proof that a listening enemy could bleed a superior force dry not by defeating it in pitched battles, but by forcing it to bleed time, tempo, and trust. It was the beginning of an era where every movement, every request, every maintenance call and medical dispatch had to be considered not merely operationally necessary but operationally hazardous.

The tactical shift Hezbollah achieved — from passive interception to active operational shaping — was not a footnote to the war. It was one of its defining outcomes. It marked a turning point in the character of conflict itself, where the lines between intelligence, operations, and psychological warfare blurred into a seamless continuum of pressure and adaptation.

And it left behind a battlefield where silence was no longer neutral. It was contested ground. Where noise was no longer harmless. It was a signal. Where every unguarded whisper carried the potential weight of tactical exploitation.

The lessons of 2006 are not relics. They live on in every battlefield where emissions are harvested, where rhythms are mapped, where understanding precedes action. They live in the way modern forces now treat their own signals with suspicion, in the way soldiers are trained to recognize that being heard can be as dangerous as being seen.

They live in the enduring fact that the first battle is for awareness. And in that battle, the one who listens longer, more patiently, and more precisely, often wins before a single shot is fired.

Hezbollah's playbook was simple.
It was not easy.
And it changed the future of war.

The aftermath of the war left traces not just in doctrine, but deep in the habits and instincts of those who had lived through it. Israeli field commanders returning from southern Lebanon carried with them an unease that no after-action report could entirely sanitize. It was not merely a technical realization about emissions security or a procedural update to communications protocols. It was a visceral awareness that their enemy had been inside their decision cycles, predicting movements, shaping outcomes, not through superior force but through superior patience.

For many, the battlefield had changed forever. No longer was security measured only in the thickness of armor or the strength of fortifications. Security had become something more ephemeral, something harder to trust: the belief that one's own communications, one's own rhythms, could be relied upon without fear of betrayal. That belief had been quietly shattered. In its place came a new caution — not fear in the traditional sense, but a wariness that slowed decisions, that demanded second and third confirmations, that introduced a latency into action where once there had been speed.

At the institutional level, reforms followed quickly. Entire branches of the Israeli Defense Forces were tasked with emissions hygiene, electromagnetic discipline, and spectrum awareness in ways that had once been the exclusive domain of specialized signal units. Training cycles were rewritten. New generations of soldiers were taught not just how to fight, but how to avoid being heard — a skill once treated as peripheral, now recognized as fundamental to survival.

Yet even these adaptations bore the mark of Hezbollah's influence. Every additional layer of security, every communication blackout imposed for operational safety, every hour spent rehearsing low-emission tactics was time and energy spent reacting to a doctrine first proven not by a global superpower, but by a guerrilla force operating out of battered towns and rural strongholds.

The broader strategic community absorbed the lessons as well. Analysts across NATO, in Washington, in European capitals, in defense ministries from Asia to Latin America, quietly studied the 2006 conflict and drew conclusions that rippled into the structure of modern hybrid warfare. Electromagnetic spectrum operations became an integrated pillar of military planning. Cyber and signals intelligence fused operationally, no longer treated as separate realms but as complementary aspects of the same battlespace. The air — the invisible architecture of communication, coordination, and control — was now a battlefield as surely as any hilltop or river crossing.

And at the center of this transformation lay a simple, enduring reality: the side that listens longer and more precisely gains an advantage before a single traditional battle begins.

Hezbollah had not merely resisted. They had shaped the future of conflict. They had demonstrated that interception, once the silent handmaiden of traditional operations, could itself become the primary theater of contest. They had shown that informational shaping was not ancillary to war; it was war. That the erosion of confidence, the disruption of rhythms, the sowing of hesitation could break momentum as surely as artillery or airstrikes.

For Hezbollah, the lessons of 2006 were not just lessons learned. They were lessons codified, internalized, and passed forward into the organization's bloodstream. Every subsequent conflict, every strategic plan, every future engagement was shaped by the knowledge that careful listening could create time, space, and survival where brute force alone could not.

In the hills and villages of southern Lebanon, they listened first — and only later, precisely, they struck. The lessons written in intercepted air would outlast the battles that carved the earth.

And for the militaries that studied them, the price of adaptation would be perpetual vigilance. A new battlefield had been opened — one with no front lines, no clear edges, no permanent defenses. Only discipline, humility, and the willingness to see every emission as a potential exposure could offer any hope of resilience.

The war of antennas and silence had begun in earnest — not with rockets or declarations, but with the patience to listen longer than the enemy could act.
It began in the hills and villages of southern Lebanon.
And it had not ended. It had only expanded.

# CHAPTER 5 — THE ISRAELI BLIND SPOT

The seeds of Israel's exposure in the electromagnetic domain were not sown in the chaos of the 2006 war. They were planted years earlier, during a long period of dominance that allowed certain habits, certain assumptions, to take root and harden into doctrine. In a military machine built on speed, confidence, and decisive action, small vulnerabilities could persist unnoticed for years until a patient, listening enemy turned them into liabilities.

Paging systems had become woven into the fabric of Israeli military logistics during the 1980s and 1990s. Initially introduced to speed medical coordination, administrative alerts, and maintenance requests, pagers were seen as a simple, low-cost solution to streamline rear-area operations without burdening frontline tactical communications. In peacetime exercises and localized security operations, they worked well. Messages moved quickly. Casualty reports flowed without choking command nets. Supply dispatches and movement confirmations could be issued without dragging precious tactical bandwidth away from maneuver elements.

But the very success of pagers in these administrative roles sowed complacency. As the broader communications architecture of the Israel Defense Forces modernized — with encrypted radios, satellite links, and hardened battlefield management systems — pagers remained in their original form, largely unsecured, largely unchanged, drifting into a gray zone of operational thinking. They were neither considered critical enough to secure with the full rigor applied to combat networks, nor insignificant enough to abandon. They occupied a convenient, habitual middle space, tolerated because they made the military function more smoothly.

Culturally, the IDF prized agility. Doctrine emphasized speed of maneuver, rapid concentration of force, the ability to shift operational weight faster than any opponent could adapt. Against conventional Arab armies in previous decades, this approach had yielded stunning successes. Agility was not an abstract principle; it was a visceral reality experienced by generations of Israeli officers who had grown up believing that speed, flexibility, and superior coordination would always offset material inferiority.

In that environment, friction was the enemy. Systems that introduced delays — encryption requirements, emissions control protocols, communications blackouts — were seen not as necessary defenses, but as potential barriers to the tempo of warfighting. Pager systems, which allowed logistical and medical coordination to operate on parallel, frictionless tracks without interfering with tactical command nets, fit perfectly into this ethos.

No one set out to build an insecure system. No deliberate choice was made to expose critical operational rhythms to interception. The risk simply never rose high enough in the institutional mind to force a change. Other threats loomed larger. Conventional armored attacks. Ballistic missile barrages. State-sponsored cyber intrusions against high-value command centers. In that hierarchy of concern, pager transmissions moving back and forth between field hospitals, maintenance crews, and supply depots seemed almost quaint.

The vulnerabilities were technical, but the blind spot was cultural. It rested on an implicit trust that the electromagnetic environment — especially in rear areas — was permissive, that background communications could be allowed a degree of sloppiness without serious risk. It was a trust born of decades of fighting adversaries who lacked the technical sophistication or the operational discipline to harvest low-level emissions at scale.

In Lebanon, Hezbollah shattered that trust.

When the war broke out, the IDF found itself operating across a complex, fractured battlespace where the distinctions between front lines and rear areas blurred rapidly. Towns became battlefields. Convoys became combat elements. Medical stations found themselves within rocket range. In this environment, the administrative functions supported by pagers were no longer confined to the safety of rear bases. They moved into the tactical sphere, their emissions bleeding directly into areas contested by Hezbollah's patient, listening forces.

The fast-moving nature of Israeli operations compounded the exposure. Brigades surged forward, rotated units, called for supplies, organized evacuations, improvised new positions — all while relying on the same pager systems that had served them so well in structured peacetime drills and linear border conflicts. The acceleration of operations demanded rapid coordination. Rapid coordination demanded simple, accessible communication channels. And the simple channels, trusted out of habit, broadcast operational rhythms into the open air where Hezbollah's intercept teams waited.

Signals discipline, even in elite units, began to fray under the combined pressure of tempo and habit. Orders to limit radio chatter were issued. Reminders about emissions security circulated. But pagers, tucked into operational routines so deeply that few questioned them, continued to pulse administrative lifeblood through exposed, unsecured frequencies.

This was not a failure of individual discipline. It was a systemic blind spot. The soldiers and officers using pager systems did not see themselves committing a security violation. They were doing what the institution had trained them to do: move fast, coordinate flexibly, prioritize speed over friction. The cultural inertia around pagers was so strong that it survived even the first evidence of exploitation — rocket strikes timed suspiciously close to medevac dispatches, ambushes aligned with supply movements, enemy repositioning that mirrored Israeli logistical concentrations.

As Israeli commanders realized that informational leakage was enabling Hezbollah's tactical timing, the slow process of countermeasure implementation began. Orders restricting pager use filtered down. Units improvised encryption overlays. Some brigades instituted messenger relays or fallback to hardened radio circuits for sensitive movements. But these were late-stage adaptations, deployed into a battlefield already seeded with Hezbollah's informational advantage.

Pagers, once the quiet servants of efficiency, had become the unintentional narrators of Israeli operational rhythms. They spoke clearly to those patient enough to listen — and Hezbollah had listened longer than anyone expected.

The breakdown was not technical first. It was conceptual. It was the result of treating some signals as unimportant because their immediate content seemed administrative, detached from the lethality of maneuver and fire. It was the result of assuming that the communications battlefield was a segmented space, where tactical nets needed rigorous security but logistical arteries could remain largely open.

In the modern electromagnetic environment, that assumption proved fatal.

Hezbollah's genius was not in out-inventing Israeli communications technology. It was in recognizing that no modern army, however advanced, could function without emitting — and that the emissions least guarded often revealed the most exploitable truths. Where Israeli planners focused on protecting command nodes and encrypted warfighting orders, Hezbollah's intercept teams mapped the quieter, steadier pulse of maintenance, medicine, and movement. And from that pulse, they built a picture of Israeli operations accurate enough to time attacks, anticipate maneuvers, and erode tempo.

The exposure of pager communications was a symptom. The deeper issue was a mindset that assumed operational privilege over the airwaves. A mindset that failed to recognize the battlefield had already expanded into spaces once considered benign, harmless, too minor to matter.

In Lebanon's hills and cities, Hezbollah demonstrated that no emission was minor. Every burst of data, every logistical call, every administrative message was a brushstroke in the painting of an army's intent. And when an enemy could see the painting before the final strokes were even laid, the outcome could be shaped long before the first direct clash of forces.

Israel's blind spot was not that it failed to encrypt every message. It was that it failed to recognize how little needed to be heard to shift the balance of initiative. It was a blind spot born of success, hardened by habit, and exposed by an adversary willing to wait longer, listen deeper, and act with precision when the hidden rhythms of war revealed themselves.

By the midpoint of the war, Israeli commanders recognized that the electromagnetic environment was not neutral. The cumulative weight of precision-timed Hezbollah attacks, ambushes that seemed to mirror logistical movements, and the unnerving sense of anticipation in enemy actions forced a reckoning inside the IDF's operational core. Pagers, once ignored in security briefings, became a point of acute concern.

Emergency directives issued from higher command instructed units to curtail pager transmissions where possible. Field commanders, facing the reality of interception-driven attrition, were told to shift critical coordination to encrypted radio nets. In some areas, standing orders demanded a complete cessation of unsecured transmissions within operational corridors, pushing logistical coordination into face-to-face relays, courier systems, or pre-arranged communications windows tied to hardened channels.

But cultural change, especially under the duress of active combat, moves slower than the issuance of new orders. Soldiers and junior officers, already saturated with the tempo and exhaustion of complex operations, struggled to internalize a new doctrine of communications discipline overnight. Habits built over years do not dissolve in days. Even as units adapted outwardly, building new processes for movement coordination and medical dispatches, the echoes of old patterns lingered.

In moments of crisis — under fire, during urgent casualty evacuations, amid the chaos of urban clearing operations — the need for speed overwhelmed the freshly imposed communications discipline. Pagers were used out of instinct, out of immediacy, out of the simple human need to act fast when lives hung in the balance. These lapses were not failures of will or understanding. They were the predictable outcomes of trying to reengineer operational culture mid-battle, against an enemy already tuned to listen for any signal of opportunity.

Hezbollah did not need perfect coverage. They did not need every page, every logistical message, every dispatch. A fragment was often enough. A cluster of medevac pages from a certain sector. A spike in maintenance alerts along a known approach route. A burst of activity in an otherwise quiet administrative channel. Hezbollah's intercept teams were trained not just to collect, but to interpret partial pictures, to synthesize fragments into actionable insights with a speed and confidence that belied their comparatively primitive collection tools.

As a result, Israeli adaptations, though necessary and partially effective, came too late to unseat Hezbollah's informational advantage. Damage was already embedded in the operational tempo. Units moved with a new caution born not of battlefield obstacles, but of electromagnetic fear. Every resupply mission demanded a calculus of exposure. Every movement coordination carried the unspoken question of what else might be listening.

The IDF's efforts to secure communications were genuine. In many areas, encryption was tightened. Emergency spectrum management protocols were invoked. Emission control drills, long treated as afterthoughts in pre-war training, became frontline imperatives. Commanders began shifting from open-band coordination to hardened, frequency-hopping systems where available. But these corrections operated within a battlespace Hezbollah had already shaped.

The fragility of the Israeli communications architecture under sustained electromagnetic contest was a hard lesson. It revealed that technological superiority at the system level — encrypted radios, hardened command nodes, redundant satellite links — could be undermined if low-level, habitual systems were left exposed. It showed that the spectrum was not segmented neatly between critical and trivial traffic. To a patient, disciplined enemy, all traffic had value. All noise could be signal.

The failure was not simply one of technical security, but of operational imagination. Israeli planners had long prepared for the interception of command orders, for jamming of tactical nets, for attacks on strategic communications hubs. What they had not fully prepared for was the quiet harvesting of background emissions — the ambient administrative signals that, when mapped and interpreted, gave away the skeleton of the operational plan without ever touching the core warfighting channels.

This was the real nature of the blind spot. It was not just overconfidence in pager security. It was a systemic underestimation of how small, persistent emissions could become strategic vulnerabilities when collected with patience and analyzed with rigor.

Even as the IDF adjusted, Hezbollah adapted as well. When direct pager intercepts became rarer, Hezbollah shifted attention to metadata flows, the timing of bursts, the correlation of minor radio traffic to logistical actions. In some cases, the very act of Israeli units clamping down on pager usage revealed priorities. Sectors that suddenly went dark in the electromagnetic spectrum became obvious candidates for Israeli offensives. Silence, like noise, spoke volumes.

The war became, in many ways, a contest of who could read the gaps more effectively — who could see in the noise and in the absence of noise the true intentions of the other. In this contest, Hezbollah's earlier patience had given them a running start.

For Israeli commanders on the ground, the operational friction introduced by the communications crisis was cumulative. Each new procedural step designed to secure transmissions added seconds, minutes, sometimes critical hours to movement and coordination. Each additional layer of confirmation slowed the tempo of exploitation after successful engagements. Each unit forced into tighter emissions control lost a fraction of the fluidity that had long been the IDF's tactical signature.

In a conventional fight, these might have been manageable costs. Against an adaptive, deeply embedded, information-driven adversary like Hezbollah, they were decisive.

In the final analysis, Israeli forces adapted admirably to the conditions imposed upon them. They survived, maneuvered, inflicted heavy damage. But they did so under conditions of constant informational pressure, with the knowledge that their every movement risked echoing into the enemy's ear. That pressure distorted not just tactics, but strategy. It bought

Hezbollah the most precious resource an asymmetric force can possess: time.

Time to reinforce. Time to reposition. Time to survive.

The pager systems were only one symptom of a broader cultural exposure. An exposure born of a world where battlefield communications had been treated as a spectrum of importance, where some signals were secured and others ignored. Hezbollah showed that in a saturated battlespace, no emission is unimportant. No frequency is safe by habit alone.

The lesson for Israel, and for every modern military that followed, was stark: communications security is not merely about protecting secrets. It is about protecting behavior. It is about denying the enemy the ability to infer, to predict, to shape your operations from the footprints you leave in the air.

And once that footprint is mapped, recovering initiative is no longer a matter of firepower. It is a matter of time. Time that, once lost, may never be regained in the life of a war.

Inside Israeli command circles, the realization of what had occurred triggered a deeper, more uncomfortable reflection. It was not enough to blame the exposure on a single system like pagers. It was not enough to patch the immediate technical vulnerabilities. The exposure had revealed a deeper truth — that even a military as sophisticated and operationally aggressive as the IDF could fall victim to cultural inertia. And that in the face of an adaptive, patient adversary, every unexamined assumption was a crack waiting to be widened.

The psychological impact of Hezbollah's interception campaign was not limited to the battlefield. It radiated backward into the IDF's institutional self-image. Israel's armed forces had built a reputation for innovation, for tactical adaptability, for aggressive exploitation of enemy weaknesses. The very idea that they had operated for so long with an invisible vulnerability — and that an adversary had systematically harvested that vulnerability to shape operational tempo — struck at the heart of Israeli military pride.

This was not simply a technical embarrassment. It was a doctrinal shock. It forced a confrontation with the reality that superior firepower, superior intelligence platforms, and superior tactical execution could all be undermined by gaps left open through habit, through convenience, through misplaced trust in legacy systems.

In the postwar period, internal reviews and reform commissions tasked with studying the failures of the Second Lebanon War placed significant emphasis on communications discipline. New regulations mandated tighter control of emissions even at the lowest tactical levels. Training cycles incorporated electromagnetic spectrum awareness as a core competency, not a niche specialty. Units were restructured to include embedded communications security specialists capable of monitoring emissions exposure in real time during operations.

But behind these structural reforms lay a harder task: the cultural recalibration of a force accustomed to operational flexibility at all costs. The IDF had long prioritized tempo over rigidity, believing that speed covered weaknesses and that initiative solved problems faster than defensive caution. Now, a balance had to be struck between speed and invisibility, between initiative and exposure.

This recalibration did not happen easily. It required reeducating generations of officers who had risen through a system that viewed communications as a solved problem, one whose challenges had been addressed by encryption protocols, secure radios, and hierarchical command discipline. The notion that emissions themselves — not merely the content of transmissions, but their timing, their patterns, their metadata — could reveal operational intent was a harder concept to internalize.

Younger soldiers adapted more readily. Trained in a world where digital footprints were second nature, they understood instinctively that visibility in the electronic domain carried consequences. Older generations, steeped in an era where radio chatter was synonymous with battlefield control, needed time to absorb the new reality.

Meanwhile, Hezbollah, having reaped the benefits of their informational campaign, wasted no time institutionalizing their successes. Signals intelligence was no longer treated as a supporting activity but as a core pillar of operational design. Interception training was expanded. Pattern analysis became a formalized discipline. Even as Israel worked to close its vulnerabilities, Hezbollah invested in sharpening its ability to exploit any that remained — not necessarily through better technology, but through better understanding of the human behaviors that shaped emissions.

The battlefield had expanded permanently. It was no longer bounded by terrain features or frontline engagements. It stretched invisibly across every node of communication, every burst of coordination, every logistical heartbeat. And in this new battlefield, victory would belong not only to those who moved fastest or struck hardest, but to those who listened longest, waited most patiently, and understood most deeply the human rhythms leaking into the air.

The Israeli blind spot had been exploited not through hacking into secret plans or jamming critical nodes, but by simply observing the unguarded flows of daily operational life. In an era saturated with wireless communication, that observation was enough to shape outcomes — to steal initiative, to deny tempo, to introduce friction where fluidity once reigned.

The lesson was enduring. It meant that no piece of information, however trivial it appeared, could be safely ignored. It meant that no transmission could be treated as benign simply because it lacked strategic content. It meant that in a saturated, contested electromagnetic environment, the very act of communicating became an act of vulnerability.

For the IDF, this was a bitter but necessary evolution. It would shape future conflicts, drive the development of more agile, more secure communications architectures, and instill in new generations of commanders a wary respect for the invisible war always unfolding beyond the reach of their immediate senses.

It would also serve as a cautionary tale for militaries around the world — a reminder that informational exposure is not always the result of enemy penetration or sophisticated cyberattack. Sometimes, it is the natural consequence of assuming that the air itself is neutral, that emissions belong solely to the sender, that movement through the electromagnetic terrain can be casual, habitual, unseen.

Hezbollah shattered that illusion. They taught that silence could be a weapon, and that noise, if gathered patiently enough, could be turned into an instrument of disruption.

And in doing so, they left behind not only the ruins of a war fought across hills and villages, but a permanent change in the nature of how modern militaries think about the air around them.

A change that no encryption protocol alone can ever fully undo.

The vulnerabilities exposed during the Second Lebanon War were not unique to Israel. They were endemic to every military culture that had grown accustomed to treating certain layers of communication as safe by tradition rather than by continuous validation. Across the globe, modern armed forces had layered sophisticated security around their most prized assets — encrypted command systems, satellite links, drone control channels — while leaving the mundane arteries of war largely exposed.

It was easy to understand why. The human mind gravitates toward dramatic risks. High-level breaches, catastrophic system failures, public cyber attacks — these were tangible, alarming events that demanded action. A slow bleed of background emissions, a trickle of logistical chatter, the steady pulse of administrative coordination seemed too small to warrant urgent attention. And yet, when those small leaks accumulated in the hands of a patient adversary, they could erode the foundations of operational security more effectively than any direct assault.

Israel's experience in 2006 served as a harsh reminder that battlefield dominance cannot be preserved by focusing only on the visible centers of gravity. It must extend to the periphery, to the margins, to the quiet spaces where daily functions occur and where habitual patterns emerge. In modern warfare, those margins are no longer secondary. They are primary fields of contest.

The IDF's historical emphasis on speed, flexibility, and initiative had created one of the most tactically dynamic militaries in the world. But it also nurtured an implicit assumption that the electromagnetic terrain would remain permissive as long as core communications were secured. Hezbollah dismantled that assumption with methodical patience, using outdated interception equipment and disciplined operational interpretation rather than technological superiority.

The IDF's late-stage adaptations during the war proved that the institution could evolve under pressure. But it also demonstrated the latency between cultural realization and effective behavioral change. Even with direct evidence of exploitation, shifting the embedded practices of emissions carelessness proved to be a monumental task. Orders could be issued in a day. Mindsets, forged over decades of operational success, changed only through the slow, grinding accumulation of battlefield consequences.

This asymmetry — between the speed at which vulnerabilities are exploited and the slowness of systemic adaptation — is the central danger in the modern electromagnetic battlespace. It favors the listener, the observer, the enemy who requires no decisive breakthrough, only a steady harvest of overlooked exposures.

Hezbollah understood this before many conventional militaries did. They demonstrated that when speed and efficiency are purchased by relaxing discipline over informational emissions, the adversary does not need to break your strongest walls. He only needs to listen long enough to predict when and where you will lower your guard.

The problem was not simply technical. It was philosophical. It was a failure to continuously validate assumptions about the environment — to question whether the systems and processes that had served well in previous conflicts were still fit for a world where invisible interception had become not a specialist's task, but a standard operational threat.

In this sense, the Israeli blind spot was not isolated to Lebanon. It became a global cautionary tale. It showed that militaries built for fast maneuver could be slowed not by kinetic resistance, but by informational shaping. It showed that sophisticated forces could be made hesitant, reactive, cautious not through force of arms, but through the silent shaping of perceptions and decision loops.

The events of 2006 initiated a quiet but profound shift across global security communities. Electromagnetic spectrum operations, once niche specialties, were elevated to core mission areas. Forces began developing doctrines for emissions control, not just encryption. Communications discipline drills became standard even for frontline combat units. Operational security measures expanded to include not just content protection, but pattern protection — the deliberate management of signal timing, density, and flow to mask behavioral rhythms.

But even as these adaptations took hold, the fragility remained. The fundamental vulnerability was not technological but behavioral: the tendency of human organizations to assume that what has worked will continue to work, that habits formed in relative security will endure in contested spaces. The real battlefield, as Hezbollah revealed, was not the radios or the pagers themselves. It was the invisible lattice of trust and habit that surrounded their use.

Hezbollah's success in exploiting Israel's blind spot was not simply tactical. It was conceptual. They forced a rethink of the electromagnetic domain from the ground up, showing that interception was not merely a prelude to action, but a form of action in itself — capable of shaping decisions, slowing operations, and altering the psychological balance of a conflict before the first shots were fired.

And they did it without needing technological parity. Without massive investments in cyberwarfare platforms or satellite constellations. They did it with patience, with understanding, with a relentless focus on the human dimensions of communication — the patterns, the cadences, the overlooked messages that told the story of an army's intent more clearly than its encrypted orders ever could.

Israel, for all its military innovation, had simply not yet learned to see itself as an emitter in an adversarial environment where every signal, every emission, every logistical ripple could be weaponized against it. Hezbollah taught them. And through that brutal education, the entire structure of how future wars would be fought began to change.

The blind spot was not technical. It was not operational. It was cultural.
And like all cultural vulnerabilities, it could only be corrected through painful experience.

Experience that cost time, initiative, and — as it always does in war — lives.

By the end of the war, it was clear that the electromagnetic spectrum was no longer simply a medium through which battles were coordinated. It had become a terrain in its own right — dynamic, contested, unforgiving. And the institutions that adapted first would have the advantage not because they built stronger walls around their secrets, but because they recognized that survival depended on minimizing the signals that could be gathered, interpreted, and turned against them.

For Israel, the painful lessons of the Second Lebanon War became part of a broader, ongoing transformation. Operational plans that once prioritized speed and mass began to fold in new layers of emissions control. Movement orders were rewritten with an eye toward minimizing signal leaks. Logistical operations, once treated as background noise to the real business of combat, were recast as potential critical vulnerabilities requiring just as much care as frontline engagements.

The IDF was not alone in this evolution. Militaries around the world, studying the reports that trickled out of the conflict, began to understand that the future would not belong to the side that simply encrypted their critical orders most effectively. It would belong to the side that understood the broader electromagnetic signature of their operations — the cumulative, composite footprint of every transmission, every burst, every acknowledgment, every request for fuel or medical aid.

In this new reality, cultural arrogance — the belief that certain systems were secure enough, that emissions were harmless unless content was compromised — became as dangerous as technological obsolescence. It was a reminder that the soft edges of conflict, the quiet spaces filled with routine communication, were often the points where hardened military machines could be bent and slowed by an adversary willing to harvest what they left exposed.

Israel moved swiftly to close these gaps. New training regimens embedded emissions awareness into the earliest phases of soldier education. Units deployed spectrum monitors as part of standard reconnaissance. Commanders were drilled not only in how to maneuver their forces but in how to maneuver their electromagnetic footprint, masking movements through emissions discipline as carefully as through physical camouflage. Signals intelligence, once seen primarily as a strategic asset for large-scale operations, was integrated into the tactical bloodstream of unit-level planning.

But change came at a cost. Operational tempo, once the IDF's signature advantage, slowed as coordination had to account for emissions security. Units accustomed to rapid, decentralized movement found themselves bound by new constraints, new checks on their freedom of action. And while these measures were necessary to deny enemies like Hezbollah the informational advantage they had once enjoyed, they also introduced friction into a system that had long thrived on fluidity.

Hezbollah, for their part, had already begun moving on to the next phase. Their doctrine, sharpened by success, continued to evolve. Passive interception remained a cornerstone, but it was now supplemented by active deception, spectrum shaping, and, in some areas, offensive cyber operations aimed at manipulating not just what Israeli forces communicated, but how and when they communicated it. The war for the air had expanded — and Hezbollah, having learned the value of patience and pattern exploitation, adapted faster than many had anticipated.

The blind spot that Israel revealed in 2006 was not an isolated phenomenon. It was a reflection of a broader truth about modern war: that convenience, habit, and cultural assumptions about security are themselves vulnerabilities.

That the pace of technical advancement often outstrips the pace of cultural adaptation. And that in the electromagnetic domain, visibility is not a momentary condition — it is a persistent risk that demands constant, ruthless discipline to manage.

Israel's reforms were real, and their lessons internalized. But the deeper change was cultural — a caution not born of fear, but of respect: a hard understanding that the adversary could hear even what was not intended for him — would mark every subsequent Israeli military operation. From Gaza to Syria to operations beyond the region, the invisible battlefield was no longer ignored. It was mapped, monitored, contested at every step.

And yet the war between the need for speed and the need for silence continues to shape operational choices. Every commander must now weigh the risk of exposure against the imperative for momentum. Every staff planner must think not only about the movement of tanks and infantry but about the movement of emissions, the flow of invisible signatures across the battlespace. Every soldier is a potential broadcaster of critical information, whether he carries a sophisticated encrypted radio or a simple logistical pager.

The electromagnetic battlespace is now fully fused with the physical one. There are no longer two wars — one seen and one unseen. There is only one, and it unfolds simultaneously in both domains. Hezbollah understood this before many others did. They built their victories not just on firing rockets or launching ambushes, but on listening longer, waiting deeper, and acting with the precision that comes from knowing an enemy better than he knows himself.

The Israeli blind spot — that cultural, operational, and psychological vulnerability — was not unique. It was simply the first and most visible example of a broader phenomenon that would repeat itself in conflicts to come. Wherever militaries moved faster than they could protect their own emissions, wherever operational necessity outpaced security discipline, adversaries stood ready to listen, to map, to shape.

And wherever that happened, it would no longer matter how powerful the forces were, how advanced their weapons, or how brilliant their strategies. If they could be heard — truly heard, patiently and systematically — then they could be slowed, disrupted, and eventually neutralized.

This was Hezbollah's ultimate lesson. It was not a lesson about pagers, or radios, or encryption keys. It was a lesson about human behavior, organizational culture, and the slow erosion of advantage by those willing to wait just long enough for the next unguarded signal to tell them what they needed to know.

And it was a lesson that no military — not then, not now — can afford to forget.

The larger implications of the Israeli blind spot stretched far beyond the hills and valleys of southern Lebanon. They reached into the foundational assumptions of modern militaries everywhere. It was no longer sufficient to encrypt communications and harden command centers. It was no longer acceptable to assume that operational life could be divided into critical and non-critical emissions. In a battlespace saturated with passive collectors, active listeners, and patient interpreters, everything emitted became potential information.

The transformation that began inside the IDF after 2006 was painful, but it was necessary. It marked a shift from viewing electromagnetic protection as a specialty concern to treating it as an operational baseline. It changed the definition of success from seizing ground quickly to moving without broadcasting intent. It reframed the concept of battlefield presence from a matter of physical mass to one of informational opacity.

But while Israel moved forward, the lesson it had learned — or more accurately, been taught by Hezbollah — remained relevant for others who had not yet faced the same trial. In militaries accustomed to clear battlefield boundaries, to secured rear areas, to clean divisions between combat and support, the notion that a supply dispatch could be as critical a vulnerability as a frontline tactical plan remained difficult to fully internalize. The trust in infrastructure, in convenience, in the routine flows of military life persisted.

And therein lay the enduring relevance of Hezbollah's achievement. They proved that in modern warfare, the low-level emissions of daily operations — the heartbeat of an army — were no less revealing than its formal orders. That vulnerabilities did not announce themselves with alarms and sirens but crept in through the unexamined habits of organizations.

The evolution of warfare after 2006 bore out this realization. Conflicts from Ukraine to Syria to the Sahel showed that passive interception, pattern analysis, and side-channel exploitation had become baseline tactics for irregular forces and state actors alike. Sophistication was no longer a prerequisite. Patience, discipline, and a basic understanding of emissions rhythms were enough to contest the advantage of even the most technologically advanced opponents.

For Israel, the experience left an indelible mark. It embedded a skepticism toward emissions that could not be encrypted or masked. It hardened a culture of operational discretion that extended beyond radios to include every device, every system, every digital breath exhaled onto the electromagnetic spectrum. It was a transformation not only of tactics, but of mindset.

It also raised broader philosophical questions that have yet to be fully answered. In a world where emissions are unavoidable, where even the act of moving generates a signature, what does operational security truly mean? Is it a matter of perfect concealment, or of managing visibility strategically, presenting signals designed to confuse as much as to conceal? Is silence achievable, or must it be replaced with managed noise, deliberate misdirection, controlled exposures?

The IDF's journey after 2006 suggested that the answer lay not in seeking total invisibility — an impossible goal in an interconnected, high-emission world — but in cultivating a new kind of operational literacy. A literacy that treated the electromagnetic environment as fluid, contested, and dynamic. A literacy that assumed exposure unless proven otherwise. A literacy that taught soldiers, commanders, and planners alike that every emission was a choice, and that every choice carried consequences.

It was a harsh education, bought at the price of operational friction, lost tempo, and strategic opportunity. But it was an education that would, in time, better prepare Israel for the wars that followed — wars where the air was never silent, where the battle for information unfolded alongside and within the battle for terrain.

Hezbollah, through their exploitation of the Israeli blind spot, had proven that the patient listener could not only survive against a stronger enemy but could shape the conditions of survival before a single shot was fired. They showed that informational asymmetry, leveraged with discipline and insight, could level the field in ways that armor and aircraft could not.

In doing so, they shifted the trajectory of modern conflict. They demonstrated that dominance in the electromagnetic domain was not a luxury or a specialist's concern. It was a survival imperative.

And they reminded the world that in war, the greatest vulnerabilities are often those hidden in plain sight — habits too small to notice, too familiar to question, too deeply embedded to discard until the damage is already done.

Israel's blind spot was not unique. It was merely the first to be illuminated, harshly and undeniably, by an enemy who understood that in the battles of the twenty-first century, information is not a support function. It is the battlefield itself.

And that battlefield, once opened, can never again be closed.

In the years that followed, the Israeli blind spot became less a story of failure and more a story of transformation. The vulnerabilities exposed by Hezbollah's interception campaign forced not just technical adaptations but a cultural realignment inside the IDF. It was not enough to close specific gaps, to encrypt specific systems, to monitor specific emissions. The deeper requirement was to change the way operations were conceived — to view communication itself not as a neutral process, but as a continuous negotiation with exposure, risk, and adversarial awareness.

This shift did not make Israeli operations slower in the long term. It made them sharper. It bred a generation of officers who understood that movement without emissions discipline was not movement at all, but an invitation. It cultivated a force more attuned to the invisible terrain over which every war now passed — a force that understood that initiative was no longer seized only through physical speed, but through the careful management of what could be seen, heard, inferred.

It was a hard-earned lesson. And it came with the understanding that the next adversary, whoever they might be, would likely have learned the same lessons as Hezbollah — or would invent new ways to harvest the signals that armies leave behind.

The electromagnetic spectrum had changed from a support medium into a full-spectrum battlespace. And in that battlespace, victory would belong not to the side with the loudest weapons, but to the side that could see without being seen, hear without being heard, and move without leaving footprints for others to follow.

Israel's blind spot had been temporary. Its consequences had been lasting.

Victory would no longer belong to those who merely moved fast. It would belong to those who remembered that every heartbeat, every breath of signal, once thought benign, could narrate their defeat to an enemy who never stopped listening.

The war of 2006 did more than reveal a vulnerability. It helped define a new era —
An era where survival, success, and dominance would belong to those who fought not just for the ground they stood on, but for the very air they breathed.

# CHAPTER 6 — LEGACY SYSTEMS IN A MODERN BATTLEFIELD

The persistence of legacy systems in modern battlefields was never a simple matter of oversight or negligence. It was, more often, a byproduct of realities far deeper than technological preference: realities shaped by cost, logistics, institutional inertia, and the ever-widening gap between innovation at the strategic level and practicality at the operational edge.

Pagers, analog radios, unencrypted maintenance dispatch systems — all were relics from earlier eras of military communication. They were systems built for speed and simplicity at a time when the risks of interception were manageable, when adversaries lacked the technical sophistication or the operational patience to exploit low-level emissions. Their design reflected the assumptions of an earlier information environment, one where mobility, accessibility, and redundancy outweighed the still-theoretical risks of mass interception or real-time metadata analysis.

And yet these systems endured long after their vulnerabilities became obvious to those who studied the electromagnetic battlefield closely. They endured not because militaries failed to see their risks, but because the institutional machinery of warfare is slow to adapt, and because replacing entire layers of operational infrastructure is far more complex than issuing a new directive or purchasing newer equipment.

In most armed forces, modernizing core communications meant focusing first on the systems deemed critical: secure command links, encrypted tactical radios, hardened datalinks for air-ground coordination, battlefield management systems with layered authentication and encryption. These investments were expensive, but justifiable. They defended the obvious centers of gravity where strategic risk was highest.

Below those high towers of attention, however, stretched a dense web of older systems that made daily military life possible. Medical evacuation alerts, maintenance dispatches, convoy scheduling, administrative coordination — all ran through technologies that had once been cutting-edge and were now functionally invisible. Their emissions filled the background noise of every operation, trusted not because they were inherently secure, but because they had always been there, woven into the fabric of organizational life.

Replacing these systems was expensive in ways that went beyond procurement costs. It demanded retraining thousands of personnel, rewriting operational procedures, reconfiguring networks and maintenance schedules, re-certifying supply chains built around decades-old standards. It demanded a disruption to the quiet flow of logistics that no commander wanted to interrupt unless absolutely necessary. And in a world where military budgets were increasingly strained by rising costs of advanced platforms — aircraft, satellites, precision munitions — there was always a temptation to push the modernization of rear-echelon communications another year down the priority list.

Institutional inertia did the rest. In every bureaucracy, technological transitions are fought not only on technical grounds but on cultural ones. Systems that work — or that appear to work — resist replacement. The costs of change are immediate and visible: retraining headaches, temporary loss of efficiency, procurement fights, political battles over funding priorities. The costs of staying the course, by contrast, are hidden until they are exposed in the pressure cooker of actual combat.

This dynamic explains why, decades into the twenty-first century, so many militaries entered conflicts still reliant on communications technologies that were vulnerable by design.

Analog radios, sending unencrypted bursts across predictable frequencies. Pagers broadcasting plaintext logistics and medical alerts into the open air. Maintenance coordination channels secured by little more than obscurity and the assumption that no one would bother to listen.

It was not laziness. It was a rational, if short-sighted, calculation. The need to preserve operational fluidity, to prioritize the most visible threats, to defer disruptions that could cascade into logistical chaos. It was a calculation that worked — until it didn't.

Modern conflicts, from Lebanon to Ukraine to various proxy wars across Africa and the Middle East, exposed the hidden liabilities embedded in this layered technological debt. Forces that prided themselves on hardened command centers found their logistical movements mapped by adversaries harvesting unencrypted maintenance requests. Units operating with sophisticated encrypted radios still lost surprise when their supply routes were inferred from pager traffic or analog convoy coordination.

The battlefield had shifted beneath their feet. The invisible air around every operation was no longer passive. It was contested space. Every emission, no matter how trivial it seemed, could be collected, correlated, and weaponized against the force that had allowed it to persist unchecked.

Legacy systems, once relegated to administrative backwaters, had become unexpected cyber front lines. Not because they were connected to the internet in the traditional sense, but because they emitted data — radio waves, pager broadcasts, analog signals — that could be captured, analyzed, and turned into operational intelligence.

In this new environment, the term "cyber" no longer referred only to network intrusions and malware attacks. It encompassed any exploitation of information flows, any interception of emissions, any mapping of behavior through ambient data. Legacy systems, many of which had no conception of cybersecurity at the time of their design, were now part of this battlespace by default.

The cost of ignoring them was measured not only in compromised movements and delayed operations but in lost initiative, eroded morale, and strategic setbacks. Forces that failed to account for their full emissions footprint — including the emissions of their oldest, least glamorous systems — found themselves fighting not only against enemy weapons but against the ghosts of their own technological past.

The challenge was compounded by the nature of asymmetric warfare. Non-state actors, militias, and hybrid forces often lacked the resources to contest hardened command networks directly. But they could field cheap scanners, modified commercial receivers, and improvised signal analysis teams to harvest the low-hanging fruit of exposed legacy communications. They could listen where militaries assumed no one was listening. They could map logistics patterns, anticipate medical evacuations, detect concentrations of forces not by hacking encrypted systems, but by harvesting the soft signals that leaked from unguarded, outdated infrastructures.

The war for information had democratized. It no longer required supercomputers or access to elite cyber capabilities. It required only the willingness to listen patiently, to correlate fragments, to treat every emission as a potential breadcrumb leading to operational insight.

Legacy systems, in this environment, became more than outdated tools. They became vulnerabilities that shaped the tempo and structure of modern battle. They created avenues of exposure that no amount of kinetic superiority could fully offset. They imposed friction on forces that needed speed and secrecy. They handed initiative to enemies who, by simply refusing to move faster than their comprehension allowed, could use the technological complacency of their adversaries against them.

And still, legacy systems persisted. Not everywhere. Not always. But in enough places, in enough ways, to shape the outcomes of battles and campaigns across the early twenty-first century. The simple, inescapable fact was that militaries are organisms as much as machines. They carry their histories within them. Their strengths, their blind spots, their habits, their compromises — all written not only in the weapons they buy but in the systems they carry forward long after their design assumptions have become obsolete.

The story of legacy systems in modern battlefields was not a story of accidental oversight. It was a story of how war evolves faster than institutions. A story of how enemies adapt faster than budgets can. A story of how the air, once taken for granted, became the battlefield over which every action, every decision, every movement would now be contested.

And it was a story that had only just begun.

The vulnerability of legacy systems was no longer theoretical. It had manifested again and again, in conflicts where the sophistication of the frontline technology was betrayed by the emissions of the systems that trailed behind it. In Ukraine, during the early stages of the Donbas conflict, separatist forces and their backers demonstrated a clear understanding of how to exploit unencrypted analog radio communications. Ukrainian units, equipped with a mix of modern digital systems and Soviet-era analog gear, often found their positions triangulated not through hacking, but through the simple harvesting of open-band radio transmissions. Artillery strikes, informed by passive listening rather than active surveillance, fell with unnerving precision on units that believed themselves unseen.

The problem was not unique to Ukraine. In Syria, both regime forces and various opposition groups relied heavily on legacy radios, old commercial satellite phones, and ad hoc communications rigs built from scavenged parts. In the crowded electromagnetic spectrum over Syria's shattered landscape, emissions became a currency of survival. Those who managed their noise survived longer. Those who failed became visible, and visibility often meant death delivered by drones, airstrikes, or precision artillery. In such environments, legacy systems were not merely inefficient. They were liabilities that marked their users for targeting.

Even Western militaries, with their vast technological advantages, were not immune. In Afghanistan, despite years of modernization, coalition forces often relied on a patchwork of systems to connect with local allies, logistics convoys, and support elements operating at the periphery of the main battlespace. Field expedience sometimes dictated the use of unencrypted or minimally protected communications to maintain tempo in areas where terrain, distance, and equipment shortages made the ideal solutions impractical. The Taliban, with its focus on patience and adaptation rather than direct technological competition, made effective use of passive interception to anticipate convoy movements, mass forces, and evade drone patrols.

The theme repeated itself across battlefields large and small: the edge of technology, the tip of the spear, was often well protected. The body that supported it was less so. And adversaries, especially those fighting from positions of material disadvantage, targeted the body rather than the spearpoint. They harvested signals, mapped rhythms, inferred operations, and turned the presence of legacy systems into a tactical advantage.

Hybrid vulnerabilities emerged as militaries tried to bridge the gap. Instead of replacing entire communications architectures, many forces layered encryption wrappers, VPN tunnels, or frequency hopping overlays atop older infrastructure. These measures improved security in theory but often created brittle systems that failed under battlefield pressure. When the new layers collapsed — due to misconfiguration, equipment failure, or operator error — units defaulted back to legacy modes of communication. In moments of crisis, the path of least resistance led straight back into exposure.

Attackers knew this. They understood that war was messy, that friction stripped away ideal protocols, that chaos favored the patient collector over the hurried operator. They listened for fallback channels. They mapped emergency relays. They profiled which units reverted to old habits when under duress. And they positioned themselves not just to exploit failures when they occurred, but to create the conditions that would make those failures inevitable.

The persistence of legacy systems also revealed a critical truth about cyber warfare in the real world. The glamorous image of cyber conflict — of elite hackers penetrating hardened networks from darkened rooms — was far less relevant in many cases than the slow, patient accumulation of environmental exposure. Cyber did not always begin with a keystroke. It often began with a poorly secured radio, a reused maintenance frequency, a pager system that no one thought to encrypt. The boundary between cyber and signals intelligence, between electronic warfare and cyber exploitation, blurred until the distinctions became operationally meaningless.

This convergence meant that the simplest signals, the oldest emissions, were often the most profitable targets. It meant that a force's digital hygiene could be undone not by a zero-day exploit against a hardened network, but by the ambient leakage of systems that had long been forgotten by procurement officers and cybersecurity planners alike.

Legacy systems, in this sense, became not just tactical vulnerabilities, but strategic liabilities. They shaped how forces moved, how they communicated, how they projected power across contested spaces. They forced commanders to trade speed for security, to choose between frictionless coordination and operational invisibility. They introduced hesitation where once there had been tempo. They bled time — and in modern war, time was often the decisive currency.

For the forces that adapted, the path forward was painful but clear. It required ruthless audits of emissions across the entire operational stack, from front-line radios to rear-echelon administrative traffic. It required retraining at scale, embedding emissions discipline into every echelon of command. It demanded a shift in procurement priorities, recognizing that low-level systems — the ones that seemed least glamorous, least critical — could become the single point of operational failure if left exposed.

For those who failed to adapt, legacy systems became the silent agents of their undoing. No matter how sophisticated their front-line technology, no matter how lethal their strike capabilities, they found themselves bleeding information into the hands of adversaries who needed only to listen, to map, to wait.

The modern battlefield had no sympathy for historical attachment. It cared nothing for the reasons why a system remained in place. It measured exposure in outcomes, not excuses. And it rewarded those who treated every emission, every broadcast, every unsecured signal, not as a benign convenience but as a potential vector of defeat.

Legacy systems, once trusted allies of operational efficiency, had become a new front line — silent, invisible, and as contested as any trench or fortified village. They bore the weight of decades of organizational assumptions. And in the crucible of modern war, those assumptions cracked open under the steady, patient pressure of an enemy who needed only to listen long enough to hear what was never meant to be said.

As militaries struggled to harden legacy systems against growing threats, many turned to patchwork solutions designed to buy time rather than address root vulnerabilities. Encryption overlays were added onto analog radio systems. Pager messages were routed through ad hoc gateways that applied basic obfuscation before rebroadcast. Maintenance dispatch protocols were modified to include codewords and circumlocutions meant to mask the true nature of requests.

At first glance, these adaptations appeared effective. Emissions still flowed, but they carried fewer obvious signals for adversaries to intercept and interpret. Commanders could claim that efforts were being made, that exposures were being managed, that the vulnerabilities of older systems were being closed without the disruption of full replacement.

But in practice, these patches often created new attack surfaces. Encryption wrappers around fundamentally insecure analog transmissions introduced latency, synchronization problems, and a false sense of security. When the encryption layers failed under battlefield conditions — due to equipment incompatibility, environmental interference, or human error — operators reverted to their original, unsecured practices out of necessity.

The same pattern appeared with improvised obfuscation protocols. Codewords that were meant to obscure intent became, over time, predictable. Patterns emerged as units reused phrases, forgot variations, or relied on context clues that were obvious to attentive listeners. It did not take sophisticated decryption techniques to map these adaptations. It took patience, the ability to gather samples over time, and the discipline to correlate weak signals into stronger patterns.

Adversaries, especially those familiar with the friction and disorder of war, learned to exploit these hybrid vulnerabilities ruthlessly. They harvested partially encrypted or partially obfuscated emissions not for immediate tactical use, but for building operational models — models that revealed rhythms, priorities, and vulnerabilities even when the raw content of the communications remained hidden.

Some groups went further. They moved from passive collection to active manipulation of legacy systems. Spoofing attacks against analog radios became increasingly common. In several conflicts, false convoy orders were broadcast on unencrypted frequencies during moments of operational stress, sowing confusion and redirecting forces into ambush zones. Fake maintenance requests were transmitted into administrative bands, luring support elements into artillery kill boxes. False medevac calls were injected into unsecured pager networks, disrupting casualty evacuation chains and degrading morale.

The exploitation of legacy systems thus evolved from passive listening to active shaping. It was no longer enough to protect critical orders or encrypt the movement of front-line combat units. Entire support ecosystems — the mundane, unseen arteries of war — had to be hardened or risk becoming vectors for disruption far beyond their perceived importance.

And yet the task was immense. Legacy systems were not neatly isolated. They were embedded in the daily functioning of militaries, integrated into supply chains, maintenance workflows, medical services, and administrative operations. They formed a living, breathing organism whose emissions mapped not only the movements of armies but the structure of the institutions that sustained them.

Every patch applied to a legacy system bought only limited time. Every improvised security measure masked only some fraction of the risk. True resilience required a complete reimagining of the communications landscape — a willingness to tear out and rebuild from the ground up, to treat emissions management as a fundamental operational function rather than a technical afterthought.

Few militaries had the resources, the political will, or the operational patience to undertake such transformations at scale. The pressures of immediate readiness, of visible battlefield performance, of bureaucratic inertia, all worked against the kind of deep, disruptive change needed to truly close the vulnerabilities exposed by legacy systems.

And so, in conflict after conflict, the same patterns repeated. Sophisticated front-line capabilities coexisted uneasily with aging, exposed support infrastructures. Battles were shaped not only by who fired first or maneuvered fastest, but by who managed their emissions most intelligently — or who failed to, and suffered the consequences.

Legacy systems became not just passive vulnerabilities but active battlegrounds. Their continued existence forced commanders to make hard choices about operational tempo, emissions discipline, and the acceptable trade-offs between speed and exposure. They became pressure points that patient adversaries could exploit to erode morale, disrupt logistics, and bleed time — the most precious resource in modern war.

The battle for the electromagnetic spectrum was no longer fought only between sophisticated jammers and cutting-edge electronic warfare suites. It was fought in the spaces where assumptions lingered, where old systems persisted, where habits outpaced doctrine. It was fought in the invisible leakage of unguarded communications and the slow, steady mapping of behaviors that had once gone unnoticed.

The survival of legacy systems on modern battlefields was not simply a story of technological lag. It was a story of institutional inertia, of human factors, of the slow erosion of operational security through habits too small to notice and assumptions too convenient to challenge.

It was a reminder that the greatest vulnerabilities are often those that seem too mundane to warrant attention — until they are harvested, analyzed, and turned into weapons by an enemy willing to wait.

And in the wars to come, that patience would prove to be one of the deadliest weapons of all.

The persistence of legacy systems did not affect all forces equally. In militaries with layered structures — regular armies, reserve components, paramilitary auxiliaries — the modernization gap often became a chasm. Frontline units received newer equipment first, hardened communication systems, advanced encryption. Support units, reserve forces, logistics commands, and civil-military coordination elements were often left operating with older platforms, their upgrades deferred or deprioritized in favor of more immediate combat needs.

This uneven modernization created fractures within the electromagnetic footprint of operations. To an adversary skilled in passive collection and pattern analysis, those fractures became maps of vulnerability. They revealed where hardened communications ended and where exposure began. They indicated which units were likely to revert to analog or legacy protocols under stress. They painted a picture not only of battlefield deployments but of the internal hierarchies, priorities, and assumptions of the forces they faced.

In conflicts where asymmetric adversaries had the time and patience to gather such data, these patterns became operational tools. Entire offensive campaigns were shaped not by penetrating hardened networks, but by exploiting the seams between modern and legacy systems. Attacks were timed against resupply convoys coordinated by unsecured radio. Ambushes were laid for reserve units relying on analog push-to-talk systems. Drone strikes were called against medical stations whose pager traffic betrayed casualty movements before they could be concealed.

The enemy did not need to defeat the best-protected elements of the force. It was enough to target the connective tissue — the logistics, the support, the secondary echelons — and bleed the operational capacity of their opponents through a thousand small cuts, each enabled by emissions that had never been fully brought under control.

Even where technological upgrades were uniform, behavioral inertia often recreated old vulnerabilities. Troops trained on legacy systems often fell back into familiar habits under pressure. Encryption modules were bypassed for the sake of speed. Emissions protocols were relaxed in the name of urgency. Complex multi-layered communications plans collapsed into simple, exposed radio nets when operations bogged down, when movement was delayed, when friction rose to unbearable levels.

Adversaries learned to provoke these collapses deliberately. Spoofed signals injected into legacy channels disrupted command and control just enough to create localized confusion. Deception campaigns, built on partial knowledge gleaned from emissions monitoring, forced units into emergency maneuvers that exposed fallback communications paths. By attacking the stress points of human behavior, they brought legacy vulnerabilities back to the surface, even in forces that believed they had hardened themselves against them.

The exploitation of legacy systems thus became a form of psychological warfare as much as a technical one. It created uncertainty, hesitation, mistrust of one's own communications environment. It eroded the confidence that modern forces depended upon to maneuver quickly and decisively. It made commanders question the integrity of their own operational picture, not because it was penetrated directly, but because it was infected by the slow seepage of invisible compromises.

In this environment, the notion of emissions discipline

evolved from a narrow technical requirement into a comprehensive operational mindset. It was no longer sufficient to trust that high-value systems were protected. Commanders had to assume that every device, every radio, every pager, every maintenance terminal could become a node of exposure. They had to lead operations with an eye not just toward movement and fire, but toward minimizing the invisible signatures their forces left behind.

Training pipelines shifted slowly to reflect this reality. New soldiers were taught not merely how to operate their communications equipment, but how to think about emissions in the abstract — to understand that every transmission, however routine, created an opportunity for adversaries. Exercises incorporated emissions control drills alongside traditional maneuver and fire missions. Unit-level leadership courses emphasized the management of electromagnetic profiles as a critical battlefield function, no less vital than cover and concealment.

Yet the transformation was uneven, and the threat remained dynamic. Adversaries adapted alongside the forces they targeted. As newer systems replaced older ones, the methods of exploitation shifted. Instead of listening for plaintext pager messages, they mapped the metadata patterns of encrypted logistical networks. Instead of spoofing analog radios, they injected false signals into the decision-making cycles by exploiting timing anomalies and signature analysis.

The battle against legacy vulnerabilities thus became part of a larger, ongoing contest between adaptation and inertia, between modernization and habit, between the visible battles of fire and maneuver and the invisible battles fought across the electromagnetic terrain. And like all contests in war, it was one where patience, discipline, and deep understanding of the adversary mattered as much as — and sometimes more than — raw technological superiority.

For militaries that failed to internalize this reality, the consequences would be cumulative and devastating. Small exposures, overlooked emissions, trivial-seeming compromises would add up over time until operational momentum was lost, until initiative shifted, until decisions had to be made reactively rather than proactively.

Legacy systems, once taken for granted as harmless background functions, had become the persistent ghosts of every operation. They haunted not only the forces that still used them directly, but the entire architecture of modern warfare, from the highest levels of strategic planning down to the smallest tactical engagement.

And defeating them — truly defeating them — required more than new equipment or updated protocols. It required a change in thinking as profound as the changes that once reshaped warfare with the advent of gunpowder, the radio, or the airplane. It required seeing every movement, every transmission, every logistical pulse as part of a contested battlespace.

A battlespace where the enemy was always listening.
Where silence was never perfect.
And where history, embedded in the systems and habits of armies, could become the deadliest vulnerability of all.

The realization that legacy systems constituted a persistent operational threat led some militaries to attempt deeper reforms. The approach was not simply to encrypt better or to monitor more aggressively, but to confront the uncomfortable truth that no patch, no wrapper, no bolt-on solution could fully remove the vulnerabilities embedded in the architecture of obsolete systems. The only true solution was lifecycle management — the deliberate, methodical retirement of systems once they outlived their ability to survive in a contested information environment.

But even that strategy was fraught with challenges.

Legacy systems were not isolated. They were entangled with procedures, training cycles, logistical networks, and procurement schedules that had grown around them over decades. Removing them meant more than unplugging devices. It meant reengineering how entire portions of a military force functioned. It meant admitting that the invisible threads that made an army flexible, efficient, and fast could themselves become liabilities if not constantly revalidated against the evolving threatscape.

Managed obsolescence — the planned, phased elimination of legacy systems — offered a theoretical path forward. It required militaries to think beyond short-term operational needs and invest in systemic transformation, replacing not just hardware but the institutional habits that made insecure communications acceptable in the first place. It demanded a shift in risk calculus: to weigh not only the costs of modernization but the far greater strategic costs of cumulative exposure over time.

In the few cases where such efforts were pursued seriously, they paid dividends. Forces that aggressively retired outdated communications architectures found that their operational tempo improved not simply because their systems were newer or faster, but because commanders regained trust in their ability to maneuver without broadcasting their every movement to attentive adversaries. Forces that systematically audited emissions, enforced disciplined lifecycle retirements, and trained every echelon to view communications as contested terrain found themselves operating inside a cleaner, quieter battlespace.

But for most militaries, the path was neither quick nor smooth. Budgetary pressures pushed modernization timelines into the indefinite future. Political realities made the retirement of legacy systems — often domestically produced or tied to influential industrial bases — a contentious issue. Logistical inertia meant that even when new systems were fielded, old ones remained in service far longer than intended, kept alive by expedience, habit, or simple bureaucratic momentum.

Meanwhile, adversaries continued to evolve. As new generations of encrypted systems came online, hostile signals intelligence teams adapted by focusing on the emissions patterns that surrounded them: the maintenance schedules, the status reports, the logistical chatter that still leaked from auxiliary systems. They understood that even in a hardened network, the points of integration between old and new offered seams through which insight could be extracted.

In this way, the battlefield of emissions became a mirror of the battlefield of terrain. There were no perfect fortresses, only defenses layered carefully enough to slow an enemy's advance. No communications system was truly unexploitable; there were only operational practices disciplined enough to minimize exposure, confuse pattern analysis, and deny adversaries the easy harvest of actionable data.

The forces that succeeded were those that treated emissions as a living ecosystem rather than a static asset. They invested not only in technology but in doctrine, in training, in the daily discipline of emissions awareness. They embedded signals security into the heartbeat of their operations, treating every movement, every dispatch, every administrative cycle as a potential battleground.

Those that failed fell into predictable cycles. Exposure led to interception. Interception led to shaping. Shaping led to operational erosion — slower movements, missed opportunities, reduced initiative. Victory slipped not because of catastrophic defeats in battle, but because of cumulative informational losses that reshaped the conflict at every level.

Legacy systems were never simply about the hardware. They were about the habits that surrounded them, the assumptions that permitted them to persist, the blind spots that allowed vulnerabilities to be normalized. Defeating their corrosive influence required a cultural shift — a constant, ruthless reevaluation of every system, every emission, every assumption about who might be listening.

It demanded humility: the willingness to admit that convenience today could become exposure tomorrow. It demanded vigilance: the continuous pressure to map not just the enemy's capabilities but one's own vulnerabilities. And it demanded patience: the understanding that resilience was not built in bursts of procurement but in the slow, disciplined reshaping of how entire institutions thought about information, security, and survival.

In the wars to come, the armies that endured would be those that internalized these lessons most deeply. Not those with the flashiest new radios, or the most hardened cyber defenses, but those who understood that in a saturated, contested electromagnetic environment, the true contest was not for information alone, but for the silence between emissions — the space where operational freedom could be preserved or lost.

The armies that adapted would treat every system, new or old, as a living part of a larger electromagnetic organism — one that had to be shaped, shielded, and disciplined constantly.

The ones that failed would find themselves fighting not only their enemies, but their own past, their own habits, their own inertia.

And on a battlefield where the patient listener could defeat the hurried transmitter, that failure would not take the form of dramatic collapse. It would come slowly, invisibly, one leaked rhythm at a time, until initiative drained away and survival became a race against exposures no encryption could undo.

The pressure to eliminate legacy vulnerabilities will only grow sharper as the nature of war itself continues to evolve. Autonomous systems, artificial intelligence-driven operations, and network-centric warfare models are already transforming how militaries move, fight, and coordinate. Yet beneath these advances, the same ancient risks persist: emissions exposure, pattern leakage, systemic inertia.

Modernization introduces its own forms of legacy. Each wave of new technology leaves behind remnants, integrations, and fallback modes that carry forward the vulnerabilities of the past. The unmanned aerial system controlled by encrypted links may still broadcast status updates over maintenance frequencies designed decades earlier. The advanced battlefield management suite may still rely on backend logistics databases that were hardened only by obscurity, not by design. The faster and more interconnected militaries become, the more seams emerge — and the more those seams can be mapped by adversaries who understand that complexity itself can be an attack surface.

Future wars will not be defined solely by who fields the best platforms or the most advanced networks. They will be defined by who manages the invisible infrastructure of information most ruthlessly. By who audits their emissions not once, but continuously. By who recognizes that the battlefield is not just the terrain underfoot, but the electromagnetic skin that wraps around every movement, every intention, every decision.

Legacy systems will persist, not only because they are hard to eliminate, but because in every system, even the newest, yesterday's choices shape today's exposures. What is cutting-edge today becomes background noise tomorrow. What is secure now may bleed under tomorrow's listening disciplines. The very architecture of speed and efficiency that modern forces prize carries within it the seeds of future vulnerabilities unless disciplined from the outset.

The adversaries that succeed in future conflicts will be those who practice this discipline religiously. They will see emissions not as an unavoidable byproduct of operations, but as a primary operational factor. They will weave emissions management into the DNA of planning, training, and execution. They will hunt for the remnants — the fallback systems, the administrative relays, the recovery channels — knowing that war stress will push even hardened forces back toward their oldest, least-secure habits.

They will listen not only to the obvious, but to the forgotten. They will map the legacy hidden within the new. And when the moment comes, they will act with the confidence of those who know their enemy better than the enemy knows himself.

For the modern military planner, the message is stark: the war for the electromagnetic terrain is no longer optional. It is existential. It touches every echelon, from the strategic to the tactical, from headquarters to supply depot, from encrypted datalink to analog maintenance relay. The ability to survive and prevail in future conflicts will rest not on what forces believe about their technological sophistication, but on what they refuse to assume about their own exposures.

The blind spots that once allowed pagers and analog radios to leak operational intent are the same blind spots that, if left unaddressed, will compromise AI coordination systems, autonomous logistics networks, and integrated fires platforms. The tools have changed. The vulnerability — the persistence of legacy within operational culture — remains.

To defeat it requires not merely better encryption, faster innovation, or more rigorous procurement. It requires cultural discipline — the ability to question convenience, to suspect habit, to understand that in a battlefield soaked with emissions, operational survival demands not just the ability to strike, but the ability to be silent when it matters most.

The future will not reward those who move first without emissions control. It will reward those who move wisely, whose presence is felt only when they choose, whose rhythms remain hidden even under the most intense pressure.

Legacy systems taught this lesson.
The next generation of war will demand that it finally be learned.

In the end, legacy systems were never just about technology. They were about time. About the residue left by decisions made under different pressures, for different wars, with different expectations about who would be listening and how closely. They were about human comfort with the familiar, institutional resistance to disruption, and the slow erosion of operational purity in the face of everyday necessity.

Every battlefield carries its own ghosts. In the modern electromagnetic battlespace, those ghosts are the lingering signals of past architectures, past habits, past assumptions. They flicker across the airwaves long after the technologies themselves have been declared obsolete. They live on in fallback procedures, in emergency communications drills, in the quiet corner systems no one thought to audit because they had always been there.

The adversaries who shape the wars of the future will not need to build the most powerful jammers or the most complex cyberweapons. They will need only the discipline to listen for the past embedded within the present. They will map the pathways where modernization faltered. They will harvest the emissions of systems designed before the current threatscape was even imagined. And they will act at the seams — at the junctions where pride in technological superiority blinds forces to the vulnerabilities still carried invisibly within them.

No army is free of history. No network is free of legacy. Every institution carries forward fragments of its previous wars, previous communications, previous compromises. The battle is not to eliminate that history, but to control it — to audit it relentlessly, to shape it consciously, to deny it as a weapon to those willing to dig patiently enough into the noise.

Future wars will be shaped not only by the capabilities each side builds, but by the legacy each side fails to abandon. The emissions forgotten, the fallback channels left unsecured, the procedural shortcuts tolerated too long — all of them will become part of the contested battlespace, silent actors in the struggle for initiative and survival.

The armies that recognize this reality will shape their forces with a different kind of ambition. Not only to move faster, strike harder, or see farther, but to operate cleaner — with fewer trails, fewer leaks, fewer echoes of the past left for an enemy to trace.

The ones that fail will find that their history fights against them, that the battlefield is filled not only with adversaries they can see, but with the ghosts of their own neglected vulnerabilities.

The war for emissions control, for the silent shaping of the battlespace, has already begun.

And in that war, the past is never truly past.
It is alive in every signal, every transmission, every habit that lingers just a moment too long.

# CHAPTER 7 — LEARNING THE HARD WAY: ISRAEL'S ELECTRONIC AWAKENING

The failure of 2006 was not forgotten inside Israel's military and intelligence circles. It left marks too deep, wounds too visible, to be dismissed as an anomaly or blamed solely on the fog of war. The exposure of communications rhythms, the bleeding of logistical patterns, the slow erosion of operational initiative — these were not peripheral failures. They cut to the heart of how Israel's armed forces thought about the battlefield itself. And once seen, they could not be unseen.

The realization that the electromagnetic spectrum had been ceded, passively and invisibly, to an adversary like Hezbollah, provoked an internal reckoning. In war rooms and commission hearings, in quiet after-action reviews and bitter interagency meetings, the conclusion was inescapable. The assumption of environmental permissiveness, the reliance on old systems and habitual practices, had allowed a smaller, less equipped enemy to erode the core Israeli advantage: the ability to move faster, coordinate more precisely, and strike with confidence.

Nowhere was the sting sharper than within Israel's premier signals intelligence and cyber units, especially the vaunted Unit 8200. Known for its technical sophistication, for its deep infiltration of regional communications, for its ability to harvest intelligence across borders, Unit 8200 found itself forced to confront an uncomfortable truth: that superior strategic capabilities had masked operational fragilities. That mastery of enemy communications at the highest levels had not translated into mastery of the electromagnetic battlespace at the tactical edge.

The failure was not technological ignorance. It was a failure of cultural vigilance — the slow creep of convenience, the acceptance of legacy exposures because they seemed manageable, the misplaced trust that certain channels and emissions were beneath the threshold of enemy exploitation.

In the immediate aftermath of the war, a quiet but profound reorganization began. New mandates were issued. New operational priorities were defined. Unit 8200, along with other branches of Israel's intelligence and cybersecurity community, pivoted sharply toward securing not only the visible arteries of command, but the background noise of daily operations. Encryption, once treated as essential for command orders but secondary for logistical chatter, became universal. Every message, every dispatch, every transmission was reassessed through the lens of potential enemy exploitation.

Encryption was not enough. Lessons absorbed from the battlefield emphasized that even encrypted emissions revealed patterns: timing, volume, distribution, and rhythm. Operational security measures evolved from simple content protection to behavioral camouflage. Denial and deception strategies, long employed at the strategic level to mask Israeli intentions from foreign intelligence services, were now brought down into tactical and operational planning cycles.

New doctrines emerged around emissions discipline. Units were trained not just to minimize what they transmitted, but to manipulate what they emitted. False traffic was generated to flood known collection channels. Timing windows were randomized. Supply requests were layered with noise traffic to obscure real movements. Deception cells, once focused primarily on misleading human intelligence collectors or radar operators, expanded into electromagnetic deception, crafting signature profiles designed to create ambiguity, to frustrate enemy mapping efforts, to blur the outlines of real operations.

Unit 8200's role shifted subtly but decisively. No longer just a collector and analyzer of enemy signals, it became an active architect of Israel's electromagnetic presence on the battlefield. Signals intelligence became signals shaping. Cybersecurity efforts, once largely defensive and system-focused, began to integrate with operational planning. Every major Israeli operation in the years that followed bore the fingerprints of this transformation: tight emissions control, aggressive deception, and an understanding that the air itself was a contested domain requiring continuous maneuver.

The cultural shift was not limited to elite units. It filtered outward through the IDF's broader force structure. Basic training was revised to introduce emissions awareness earlier. Officer courses emphasized the management of electromagnetic exposure alongside traditional maneuver and fire disciplines. Reserve forces, long reliant on older systems and practices, were re-equipped and retrained with a focus on emissions hygiene. Communications protocols were rewritten with an assumption of hostile collection even in rear areas.

The transformation was uneven at first, resisted in some quarters by those who saw it as a burden on tempo, on initiative, on the aggressive, rapid style of warfare that had long defined Israeli military success. But the hard lessons of 2006 had left deep scars, and those scars gave reformers the leverage they needed to push through change. No one could credibly argue that the old assumptions were safe anymore. Not after Hezbollah had listened, mapped, and acted faster than their technological means should have allowed.

Over time, the changes hardened into institutional reflexes. Israel's forces began to operate with an invisible shield of emissions discipline wrapped around them, an operational armor built not of steel or ceramic, but of carefully shaped signals and controlled silences. Movement orders were designed to minimize signature bursts. Maintenance schedules were randomized to break predictive patterns.

Medical evacuation channels, once plaintext and easily mapped, became ghost corridors of encrypted, irregular traffic.

The psychological shift was profound. Soldiers and commanders alike began to view the electromagnetic spectrum as a live battlefield, not a neutral backdrop. Every transmission was seen as a potential exposure. Every emission carried the implicit question: who else might be listening? Where once speed alone was prized, now speed without stealth was seen as reckless, dangerous, a gift to the enemy's patient ears.

This new mindset laid the foundation for a broader transformation that would ripple outward beyond traditional signals discipline. It fed into Israel's growing investment in cyber warfare, in offensive electronic operations, in the active shaping of adversary information environments. The same cultural shift that demanded control over one's own emissions also drove a hunger to manipulate the emissions of others. If the electromagnetic battlespace could be shaped defensively, it could also be shaped offensively — to confuse, deceive, disrupt, and paralyze adversaries before a single shot was fired.

Israel's electronic awakening after 2006 did not happen overnight. It was not a revolution in a single year or even in a single war. It was a grinding, relentless transformation driven by necessity, fueled by the humiliation of exposure, shaped by the realization that even the most sophisticated technological advantage could be undone by cultural complacency.

And once that lesson was learned, it was internalized with the same relentless intensity that had characterized Israeli adaptations in past wars. The air itself became a contested space. Silence became a weapon. Noise became a tool. Deception became as important as maneuver. And the electromagnetic terrain, once assumed to be permissive, became a dynamic battlespace to be shaped, dominated, and if necessary, weaponized.

Israel's modern hyper-aggressive cyber posture — its willingness to strike first in cyberspace, to manipulate information environments, to conduct operations that blurred the lines between espionage and battlefield shaping — can trace much of its DNA to the hard lessons of 2006. The failure that exposed the IDF's vulnerabilities became the catalyst for a transformation that would make Israel one of the world's most formidable players in the invisible wars of signals, cyber, and information.

It was not born of academic foresight or theoretical planning. It was born of pain, of exposure, of the bitter taste of initiative lost because the enemy had listened better, longer, and more patiently.

And it ensured that in the wars that followed, Israel would never again assume that the air was empty.

They would shape it. They would weaponize it.
And when necessary, they would make sure that it betrayed only those who failed to learn the same hard lessons.

The practical results of Israel's electronic awakening became visible in the years following the Second Lebanon War. The change was not theoretical. It manifested in the field, in the quiet evolutions of how Israeli forces moved, how they communicated, and how they fought invisible battles that shaped the outcomes of visible ones.

One of the earliest signs of this transformation was the aggressive deployment of emissions control protocols across all echelons of operations. Where once movement orders were transmitted with minimal concern for interception, now every dispatch, every coordination request, every logistical update was filtered through a lens of exposure risk. Silence became operational doctrine. Units operated in communications blackouts as a matter of standard practice. Rapid, encrypted burst transmissions replaced continuous chatter. Tactical commanders were drilled to operate with incomplete information rather than risk revealing their intentions through unnecessary communications.

At the same time, Israel began to institutionalize emissions deception as a proactive tactic. Operations were preceded by carefully crafted electromagnetic feints — bursts of traffic designed to suggest false assembly areas, staged medical alerts implying casualty flows where none existed, maintenance orders hinting at armor concentrations that would never arrive. It was not enough to deny information to the enemy. The goal was to pollute their collection efforts, to drown them in plausible falsehoods, to make listening itself a dangerous exercise in misinterpretation.

This blending of denial and deception matured into a form of operational shaping that extended beyond traditional signals intelligence. Israel's cybersecurity and electronic warfare units began working hand in hand with kinetic planners. Every major operation included a cyber-electronic shaping phase designed to destabilize the adversary's decision-making loop before the first physical engagement took place.

In Gaza, this manifested in the conduct of operations where Hamas command elements found themselves blinded by sudden disruptions of internal communications, misdirected by spoofed messages, paralyzed by the sudden collapse of their assumptions about Israeli force movements. Israeli units maneuvered through environments where the electromagnetic map seen by the adversary was not merely incomplete, but actively manipulated — a hall of mirrors crafted through emissions control, deception, and precision cyber operations.

The same approach extended into strategic realms. Cyber operations attributed to Israel — though rarely officially acknowledged — showed the fingerprints of this post-2006 mindset. Operations like the Stuxnet campaign against

Iranian nuclear facilities bore the hallmarks of a doctrine that viewed the manipulation of information flows, system behaviors, and operational perceptions as integral to warfare. Stuxnet was not merely a cyber weapon; it was a carefully crafted attack that blended physical sabotage with the shaping of the target's operational environment, creating confusion and delay without immediate visible confrontation.

The line between traditional electronic warfare, cyber operations, and strategic deception blurred. Israeli doctrine no longer treated these as separate disciplines. Instead, they were fused into a single operational philosophy: control the flow of information — both your own and the enemy's — and you control the shape of the battle long before weapons are fired.

This fusion required changes not just in technology but in human factors. Training pipelines for Unit 8200 and other cyber-electronic elements shifted to emphasize not only technical skills but operational intuition. Analysts were trained to think like commanders. Operators were taught to see the battlespace not as isolated signals or networks, but as dynamic, contested ecosystems where every transmission, every disruption, every deception could ripple outward into strategic effects.

Operational planners, too, absorbed this change. Where once cyber or electronic warfare support was appended to major operations, it now became foundational. Plans began with an assumption of electromagnetic contest. Kinetic movements were designed not only for physical advantage but for emissions advantage — to operate inside adversary detection loops, to mask real actions behind layers of feints and misdirection, to create a battlespace where the enemy could never be sure what was real and what was shaped.

This new posture was aggressive, patient, and unapologetic. It reflected a cultural shift inside the Israeli defense establishment, a recognition that the price of electromagnetic and informational complacency was far too high to pay again. It also reflected a deeper understanding that in modern conflict, direct confrontation was only one method of victory. Shaping perception, distorting understanding, manipulating enemy decision cycles — these were paths to victory that could yield strategic gains before a single physical target was engaged.

Israel's electronic awakening was not perfect. Mistakes were made. Adversaries adapted. The dynamic nature of cyber-electromagnetic warfare meant that every advantage was temporary, every deception technique had a shelf life, every emissions control measure had to evolve continuously under operational pressure. Yet the underlying cultural transformation endured. It created a defensive mindset that assumed the enemy was always listening, always mapping, always looking for the seam between discipline and habit. It created an offensive mindset that treated information itself as terrain to be seized, contested, and denied.

By the late 2010s, Israel was recognized not just as a regional military power, but as a world leader in cyber operations, electronic warfare integration, and information dominance. This reputation was not built on a singular technological leap or a dramatic battlefield victory. It was built on the accumulation of hard lessons learned in the fields of southern Lebanon — lessons about the cost of being heard, the fragility of habitual exposure, and the unforgiving nature of an invisible battlespace.

It was built on the understanding that modern war would be decided not only by who could strike hardest, but by who could see first, deceive best, move fastest without being seen, and strike into an adversary's confusion before clarity could return.

The scars of 2006 had reshaped Israel's defense philosophy at every level, from tactical emissions control to strategic information shaping. They had embedded a cultural humility that recognized how easily technological advantage could be squandered through operational arrogance. And they had created a relentless drive to ensure that in every future conflict, Israel would shape the electromagnetic and informational terrain — or at the very least, deny it to the enemy.

This transformation was not born of fear. It was born of survival.
The survival of initiative.
The survival of tempo.
The survival of operational freedom in a battlespace where noise, silence, and deception were now as decisive as fire and steel.

The transformation that reshaped Israel's military posture after 2006 did not remain confined within barracks and bases. It spilled outward into the civilian sector, into industry, into national policy. The same cultural shift that demanded emissions discipline and information shaping on the battlefield fostered an entire ecosystem built around cybersecurity, electronic warfare innovation, and digital operational dominance.

At the center of this transformation was the steady migration of talent and doctrine from Israel's military cyber and signals intelligence units into the private sector. Veterans of Unit 8200 and related organizations, steeped in the new realities of contested information environments, carried with them not only technical expertise but a deeply operational mindset. They understood that cybersecurity was not merely about building walls higher, but about shaping perceptions, about disrupting decision cycles, about operating inside an adversary's assumptions.

This mindset fueled a wave of innovation that reshaped Israel's economy. Cybersecurity startups, often founded by former intelligence officers, proliferated rapidly. Many of these companies were not focused solely on defense — on building better firewalls or intrusion detection systems — but on proactive, intelligence-driven cybersecurity. On active threat hunting, deception architectures, and pre-emptive disruption of adversary campaigns before they could fully mature.

The operational aggressiveness forged after 2006 flowed naturally into civilian cybersecurity. Israeli firms marketed themselves not as passive defenders, but as active hunters — operating inside adversaries' decision cycles, predicting movements, cutting campaigns off at the root. This approach mirrored the doctrine that had emerged inside the IDF and Unit 8200: dominate the information environment early, or risk being shaped by it later.

At the national level, Israel's government embraced this shift fully. Cybersecurity was elevated to a national strategic priority, placed alongside air, sea, and land defense. The National Cyber Directorate was established not as a reactive body, but as a proactive one — tasked with not only defending critical infrastructure but shaping the entire cyber ecosystem to favor Israeli interests. Policies were crafted to encourage rapid innovation, fast integration of new technologies, and close cooperation between government agencies, private sector firms, and military units.

This fusion of military doctrine, civilian innovation, and national strategy produced an environment where cybersecurity was not a siloed specialty but an integrated component of national defense planning. Israel moved aggressively to secure its critical systems, yes, but also to project power in cyberspace — to develop offensive capabilities that could be deployed preemptively or in retaliation as needed.

The world took notice. Israel's emergence as a cyber power was not gradual. It was rapid, visible, and unapologetic. It was a posture born from the recognition that informational dominance was no longer optional, and that operational freedom in the twenty-first century depended on shaping the digital battlespace as surely as it depended on maneuvering tanks or aircraft.

Yet beneath this visible success, the core cultural lesson of 2006 remained. Israeli cyber doctrine did not rest on the belief that technology alone would secure victory. It was built around the understanding that human behavior — habits, assumptions, operational patterns — was the true battlefield. It was built on the recognition that the enemy would always adapt, that advantage was temporary, that information environments were living organisms to be shaped daily through discipline, vigilance, and creativity.

This philosophical foundation distinguished Israel's approach from many of its peers. Where some nations treated cyber operations as extensions of technical superiority, Israel treated them as extensions of operational cunning — as campaigns of shaping, deception, and maneuver within contested informational terrain.

It was an approach that valued patience as much as speed, shaping as much as striking, denial as much as dominance. It reflected the painful understanding, earned through the failures of 2006, that in a world saturated with emissions, with signals, with leaks of intention and position and plan, survival demanded not only the ability to shield oneself but the ability to create illusions for the enemy.

The soldiers and engineers who had lived through the bitter experience of being heard — of having their movements mapped, their rhythms predicted, their initiatives stripped away by patient enemy ears — carried that awareness into every system they built, every operation they planned, every cyber campaign they launched.

They understood that the contest was never static. That every advantage eroded over time. That operational discipline had to be renewed constantly. That every new system introduced new signals, new patterns, new habits — and therefore new vulnerabilities to be ruthlessly mapped, understood, and masked.

In this way, Israel's modern cyber posture was not an accident of talent or technology alone. It was the operational maturity born of humiliation, recovery, and relentless cultural adaptation. It was the institutionalization of hard lessons learned not in the glow of theoretical war games, but in the cold realities of a battlefield where failure to control emissions had meant failure to control the tempo of war itself.

And it was a reminder that in the invisible wars of the present and future, technology would be necessary, but it would never be sufficient. Discipline, humility, and the ruthless shaping of the information environment would remain the decisive factors — the difference between moving freely through the battlespace or moving under enemy observation, hesitation, and fire.

Israel learned this the hard way.
And once learned, it became an unshakable part of how it fights — not just with weapons, but with silence, with noise, with shape, and with shadow.

The evolution of Israel's electronic posture did not end with the absorption of the lessons from 2006. It continued to mature through every subsequent conflict, every skirmish, every shadow engagement that unfolded in the years that followed. Each new operation became a laboratory for testing the principles of emissions discipline, information shaping, and electromagnetic deception.

In Gaza, during operations such as Pillar of Defense and Protective Edge, Israel's forces demonstrated how deeply the new doctrines had permeated tactical and operational planning. Before ground operations commenced, cyber units moved to disrupt Hamas' internal command structures, injecting false communications, seeding confusion among leadership nodes, and fragmenting the adversary's situational awareness. Drone flights were choreographed not simply for reconnaissance or targeting, but for electromagnetic shaping — broadcasting controlled emissions, misleading enemy intercept teams about force concentrations and attack vectors.

Units on the ground moved with a level of emissions discipline that would have been unimaginable a decade earlier. Communications blackouts were enforced at critical moments. Deception traffic was layered over real movement orders. Combat teams drilled contingency operations designed to function with minimal radio communication, relying on pre-coordinated timing, signals, and rehearsed flexibility rather than real-time updates that could betray their intentions.

At the strategic level, Israel's growing comfort with shaping operations manifested in its willingness to strike deep into Syria, targeting weapons convoys, Iranian-backed militias, and critical infrastructure. These strikes often came without warning, preceded by minimal emissions exposure, coordinated across multiple service branches without the kind of signal leakage that once would have betrayed preparations. Even when the strikes were detected after the fact, their planning and execution unfolded inside an informational blackout engineered by meticulous emissions control, cyber-enabled disinformation, and the aggressive disruption of enemy surveillance networks.

Meanwhile, Israeli cyber operations — those publicly disclosed and those inferred through forensic investigation — reflected the same operational DNA. Where early cyber efforts had been tightly targeted, focusing on specific system disruptions or espionage objectives, later operations grew more ambitious. They sought to shape entire operational environments, to create persistent uncertainty inside adversary command structures, to destabilize decision-making at both the tactical and strategic levels.

The campaign against Iranian infrastructure, both physical and digital, bore the hallmarks of this mature posture. Attacks were not isolated incidents but sustained efforts to degrade, delay, and disorient. Information was not merely stolen or destroyed; it was manipulated, altered, weaponized to create secondary effects far beyond the immediate targets. The line between cyber, electronic warfare, and psychological operations blurred into a seamless continuum of pressure, disruption, and control.

Israel's emergence as a full-spectrum electronic warfare and cyber power was not the product of one great innovation or one decisive conflict. It was the accumulation of refinements made under pressure, the hardening of doctrine around the lived experience that in modern war, the electromagnetic and informational battlespaces were not ancillary to combat — they were its foundations.

The emphasis on emissions discipline spread beyond the military. It became part of national security culture, influencing how intelligence agencies operated, how critical infrastructure was defended, how diplomatic and commercial operations were secured against surveillance and cyber exploitation. The understanding that every transmission, every data flow, every administrative process could be contested and weaponized led to a national security posture that treated silence, deception, and informational ambiguity as essential elements of statecraft.

This culture also recognized that victory in the informational domain was never permanent. Every advantage decayed. Every innovation triggered countermeasures. Every operational rhythm, no matter how carefully masked, risked becoming a pattern over time if not deliberately varied and refreshed.

Israeli doctrine embraced this instability. Rather than seeking static defenses, it pursued dynamic dominance — the continuous shaping of the environment, the constant renewal of emissions profiles, the aggressive hunting of adversary collection efforts, the rapid adaptation of deception strategies to prevent enemy acclimatization.

In this way, Israel accepted the uncomfortable but inescapable truth of modern war: that informational supremacy was not something to be achieved and held, but something to be fought for every day, with every transmission, every silence, every calculated misdirection.

The ghosts of 2006 were never fully exorcised. They lingered, not as operational weaknesses, but as permanent reminders of what was at stake. They informed every operational plan, every training cycle, every new system architecture. They whispered caution into the ears of commanders who might otherwise have trusted too much in the convenience of easy communications, the speed of unsecured coordination, the comfort of assumed electromagnetic superiority.

And so, Israel continued to operate not as a nation assuming dominance, but as a nation remembering vulnerability — and through that memory, crafting a posture that treated every emission as a choice, every silence as an asset, every false trail laid for the enemy as a form of maneuver no less decisive than the thrust of a tank column or the firing of a missile.

This was not the Israel that went to war in 2006. It was something leaner, sharper, quieter. A force that moved in both the physical and electromagnetic domains with a calculated, predatory patience.

And in the long, invisible battles that increasingly defined modern conflict, that patience — the patience to shape, to deceive, to dominate without being seen — became one of Israel's most formidable weapons.

The journey from exposure to dominance was not linear. It

was shaped by cycles of adaptation, counter-adaptation, and the relentless realization that the battles of the future would be fought first, and often decisively, in the domains that could not be seen. In electromagnetic fields, in digital corridors, in the subtle patterns of traffic flow and silence that revealed intentions long before forces met in physical space.

Israel's electronic awakening was never about achieving invulnerability. That lesson had been burned away by the failures of 2006. No force, no matter how disciplined, could eliminate every leak, every signal, every whisper of operational activity into the contested air. The real victory was understanding this truth, and building a way of war that accounted for it — that treated emissions not as background noise to be ignored, but as a living, dynamic battlespace to be shaped, contested, and used.

The posture that emerged was defined by a kind of disciplined aggression. Israel no longer moved through the electromagnetic spectrum carelessly, but neither did it move fearfully. Silence, when needed, was maintained with rigor. Noise, when useful, was crafted with precision. Deception was woven into operational planning as naturally as logistics or fire support. Information shaping was no longer the preserve of intelligence agencies or psychological operations units alone; it was an organic function of maneuver, embedded in the bloodstream of every serious engagement.

This approach demanded constant vigilance. Every new technology introduced new risks. Every new system brought new emissions to be mapped, understood, and managed. It was not enough to secure networks. The very act of existing in a networked battlespace carried risks that had to be continuously anticipated, masked, redirected.

Commanders learned to live inside this tension. Every operational choice — when to transmit, when to receive, when to move silently, when to create controlled noise — became a conscious act of battlefield shaping. Every layer of the force, from the highest headquarters to the lowest tactical element, operated under the assumption that the enemy was listening, mapping, and preparing to act upon what could be heard.

This cultural shift was profound, but it was not static. It continued to evolve with every conflict, every confrontation, every technological leap. Israel's ability to maintain its edge rested not on the achievements of a single war or generation, but on the willingness to accept that the contest was permanent, that adaptation was continuous, that informational dominance was never fully achieved, only rented for as long as discipline could be maintained.

The transformation that began in the aftermath of the Second Lebanon War was not a shift in equipment or even doctrine alone. It was a shift in identity. Israel had come to see itself not merely as a nation fighting battles on land, air, and sea, but as a nation permanently engaged in the shaping of unseen spaces — in the contest over information, over perception, over decision-making loops that unfolded before conventional warfare even began.

This identity shaped not just how Israel fought, but how it saw its adversaries. No enemy was underestimated again simply because they lacked high-end technology. Every force, no matter how primitive in appearance, was assumed capable of listening, mapping, interpreting. Every operation began with an assumption of contested space, and with plans not only to maneuver forces, but to maneuver perceptions, to outpace the adversary's ability to make sense of what he was seeing and hearing.

Israel's modern cyber-electromagnetic posture grew directly from this foundation. It was a posture built not only to defend and attack in the digital realm, but to control the tempo of information itself — to deny the enemy clear understanding, to delay his reactions, to paralyze his operations under the weight of uncertainty, deception, and misinformation.

And at its core remained the hard memory of 2006 — the memory of what happens when an army forgets that the air itself can be turned against it. The memory of what happens when operational convenience triumphs over emissions discipline. The memory of what it feels like to lose initiative not because of a superior enemy weapon, but because of one's own invisible carelessness.

That memory was never erased. It was sharpened, institutionalized, and turned into a weapon — a relentless, disciplined vigilance that infused every Israeli operation across the electromagnetic, cyber, and information domains.

It was a lesson learned the hard way.
And it became a foundation upon which an entire philosophy of modern warfare was built.

The experience of 2006 had taught Israel that no force, however advanced, was immune to the invisible erosion of advantage. It taught that victory was not simply about the strength of weapons or the speed of maneuver, but about the discipline of perception — the ability to control what was seen, what was heard, what was believed, both by the enemy and by oneself.

From the shattered assumptions of that war grew a new way of thinking about conflict. A way that understood the electromagnetic spectrum not as a neutral environment, but as a terrain to be seized and defended. A way that treated emissions, signatures, and digital shadows as weapons and vulnerabilities of equal measure. A way that shaped not only movements on the ground, but the very space in which decisions were made, where battles began long before the first missile was launched.

This was the hard-earned awakening that redefined Israel's posture in the world — an awakening born not of theory, but of pain; not of prediction, but of experience; not of easy victories, but of failures that cut deep enough to demand change.

And in learning this, Israel joined a broader, unfolding reality — a reality where every nation, every force, every actor now lived in contested electromagnetic and informational space. A reality where the battles for initiative, tempo, and survival would increasingly be fought not only with physical arms, but with silence, deception, noise, and shadow.

A reality where those who learned from their vulnerabilities would shape the future.
And those who did not would find the future shaped against them.

# CHAPTER 8 — FROM LISTENING TO CONTROLLING: THE CYBER OFFENSIVE TURNS

The transition from passive defense to active control was not a single decision, nor the product of a single operation. It was an evolution that began in the wake of hard lessons, carried forward by necessity, and sharpened through the realization that in a contested information environment, waiting to be attacked was no longer viable. If survival depended on shaping what the enemy saw and heard, then control over those channels had to be seized, not merely defended.

Israel's earliest forays into communications dominance had been shaped by loss — the quiet harvesting of pager traffic during the Second Lebanon War, the slow bleed of operational rhythm through unsecured maintenance requests, the mapping of movement through analog emissions that had once seemed too mundane to matter. From these experiences came the first great operational truth: that interception was not merely a threat, but an opportunity.

If enemy emissions could be collected, they could be understood.
If they could be understood, they could be predicted.
And if they could be predicted, they could be shaped.

The first steps toward control were cautious. Initially, the focus remained on protecting Israeli emissions — tightening encryption, hardening networks, enforcing strict emissions discipline at every level. But as Israeli cyber and electronic warfare units matured, they began to ask a harder question: why should protection be the limit? Why only shield one's own signals, when it might be possible to infiltrate, to alter, to turn the enemy's communications into a weapon against him?

The answer came slowly, then all at once.

Early experiments focused on passive deception. Jamming and signal interference were employed selectively to disrupt enemy communications at critical moments, to create confusion and delay. But jamming was blunt, noisy, and easily detected. It revealed presence, invited countermeasures, and rarely produced more than tactical inconvenience. More sophisticated approaches were needed — techniques that would allow Israeli forces not merely to deny communications, but to co-opt them, to infiltrate enemy networks silently, to rewrite what was believed without ever triggering alarms.

Man-in-the-middle attacks became one of the first major operational tools in this new phase. Rather than simply listening to enemy communications, Israeli cyber operators sought to place themselves between communicating parties — intercepting, altering, and relaying messages in real time. The goal was not to block communication, but to subtly redirect it, to insert falsehoods that blended seamlessly into trusted channels, to shape adversary decisions from within.

This was a profound shift in doctrine. It demanded not only technical sophistication, but an intimate understanding of enemy operational rhythms, linguistic patterns, command structures, and decision-making behaviors. A clumsy insertion would be detected quickly. A well-crafted one could sow discord for hours or days before the enemy realized he was moving to orders he had never given.

Spoofing emerged as a complementary technique. Instead of intercepting live communications, Israeli cyber units sometimes generated entirely false communications streams, imitating the signatures of legitimate devices and networks. Spoofed orders rerouted enemy logistics convoys into kill zones. Spoofed evacuation signals induced premature withdrawals, leaving positions exposed. Spoofed command traffic fragmented enemy unit cohesion without requiring a single direct engagement.

Signal manipulation took many forms. Sometimes it was technical — altering transmission characteristics to create ghost units on enemy sensors, to mimic the emissions of large formations where none existed, to saturate adversary targeting systems with conflicting data. Sometimes it was psychological — crafting communications intended not to be trusted, but to be discovered and doubted, planting the seeds of operational hesitation and internal suspicion.

The origins of these techniques traced back to lessons learned from simpler systems. Pagers, once treated as trivial vulnerabilities, became early proving grounds for influence operations. During and after the 2006 conflict, Israeli signals intelligence units analyzed the traffic patterns of both friendly and enemy pager systems, identifying not only operational rhythms but social dynamics, unit structures, and command habits.

It became clear that pagers were not simply information leaks; they were maps of trust, hierarchy, and fear. They revealed who needed reassurance most often, who demanded immediate obedience, who hesitated, who panicked. Armed with this understanding, Israeli units began experimenting with ways to manipulate pager traffic — to insert false alerts, to simulate higher command instructions, to inject uncertainty into adversary command networks by exploiting their dependence on fast, trusted, unsecured communication.

These early efforts were crude by modern standards, but they laid the foundation for a doctrine that would expand dramatically as digital communications evolved. The core principle remained constant: trusted channels could be weaponized. The very communications that an enemy relied upon for cohesion could become the vectors of his unraveling if controlled with precision and patience.

The shift from passive interception to active control demanded new skills, new mindsets, new operational disciplines. It required operators who could think like enemy commanders, who could anticipate how information would be interpreted in the heat of battle. It demanded a fusion of signals intelligence, psychological operations, and cyber intrusion into a single, seamless function.

Training pipelines were reoriented accordingly. Cyber recruits were no longer taught only to find vulnerabilities or defend networks. They were taught to operate inside adversary communications loops, to see every message as both a source of intelligence and a potential tool of manipulation. They were drilled in the art of moving invisibly through hostile networks, shaping perceptions without triggering suspicion, crafting plausible deceptions tailored to the specific fears and assumptions of each target.

Operational planning incorporated communications shaping as a core phase. Before an attack, planners asked not only where and when to strike, but how to shape the enemy's understanding of the battlefield beforehand — how to open corridors, induce movements, fragment cohesion, and create exploitable hesitation through controlled emissions and false traffic.

This approach changed the nature of engagements. Battles were not fought only at the moment of kinetic contact, but in the hours and days preceding it — in the subtle war for the enemy's perception, in the crafting of a false operational picture that could be shattered at the decisive moment.

And it all began with the simple realization that in a world saturated with emissions, the side that controlled communications controlled not just information, but action, initiative, tempo, and ultimately, survival.

As the techniques matured, the gap between tactical

disruption and strategic influence began to narrow. What had started as localized deception — rerouting a convoy, sowing momentary confusion in a forward unit — grew into deliberate campaigns designed to reshape entire battlespaces before physical contact even occurred.

Israeli cyber and signals teams learned that subtlety was key. A false command that was too obvious would be quickly dismissed. But a slightly mistimed order, an altered resupply schedule, a fabricated sitrep introducing just enough doubt into an adversary's operational picture — these could snowball into hesitation, fragmentation, and paralysis without any need for jamming or overt cyber destruction.

The man-in-the-middle attacks that had once been technical achievements became operational art forms. In exercises and later in real-world operations, cyber operators inserted themselves between enemy command elements, not to block information, but to gently, imperceptibly distort it. A unit ordered to reinforce a position might find that order delayed by minutes at a critical moment. A resupply convoy might receive genuine movement instructions but on a different, more vulnerable route. Each manipulation, small by itself, aggregated into an adversary command environment that became increasingly disconnected from reality without knowing exactly when or how it had lost clarity.

Signal manipulation matured alongside these insertion techniques. During cross-border operations and limited conflicts, Israeli units began deploying electronic warfare platforms not simply to jam or confuse, but to create false images of force concentrations. Signature emitters mimicked tank formations where none existed. Communication nodes simulated headquarters traffic miles from the real location of command elements. Electronic feints suggested imminent assaults along one axis while masking real buildup along another.

These methods allowed Israel to regain a form of operational surprise that conventional wisdom had long assumed was dead in the modern, sensor-saturated battlefield. It was not achieved by hiding emissions completely — an impossible task in a contested electromagnetic environment — but by controlling what was emitted, when, and toward whom. It was not concealment by absence. It was concealment by misdirection.

Psychological shaping became inseparable from technical operation. By understanding how enemy commanders thought — their doctrinal biases, their risk tolerances, their likely reactions to different perceived threats — Israeli cyber-electronic units could craft deceptions that exploited not just technical vulnerabilities, but human cognitive patterns.

A formation commander accustomed to rapid Israeli maneuvers might be baited into premature redeployment by a spoofed fast-movement signature. A logistics officer operating under strict resupply timelines might overcommit resources to an axis of advance suggested by a manipulated maintenance order. A political commander with limited battlefield experience might hesitate fatally after receiving ambiguous or conflicting casualty reports, never realizing that the confusion was engineered.

The merging of these disciplines gave Israel a toolset for shaping adversary behavior across multiple layers simultaneously. It was no longer just about tactical wins — a disrupted convoy here, a delayed response there. It was about shaping the flow of an entire operation, about inducing structural hesitation in adversary command hierarchies, about making opponents doubt the reliability of their own internal communications and thereby slowing their cycles of action and reaction.

The foundations of this capability could be traced directly back to the study of pager systems and early interception practices.

What began as passive listening had evolved into active influence. What began as defensive emissions discipline had become offensive perception management. And what began as a narrow technical specialty had become a broad operational art, fusing signals intelligence, cyber exploitation, electronic warfare, and psychological shaping into a coherent, powerful mode of conflict.

Israeli doctrine increasingly treated the informational battlespace as one that had to be shaped continuously, not just at moments of crisis. Even during periods of relative quiet, cyber-electromagnetic operations continued, probing enemy communications, shaping expectations, conditioning behaviors, testing for seams and vulnerabilities. In this way, shaping became a permanent feature of operations, not a prelude to kinetic engagement but an ongoing contest in its own right.

Adversaries began to recognize — if not fully understand — that something had changed. Patterns of disruption, confusion, and delayed reactions became more common in forces facing Israeli operations. Commanders complained of lost synchronization, of units moving out of phase with each other, of intelligence that seemed accurate one moment and misleading the next. Few could trace these effects back to their true source. Fewer still could counter them effectively once trust in communications had begun to erode.

In a sense, the battlespace had tilted. It was no longer enough for adversaries to listen for Israeli movements or to guard against physical incursions. They had to defend against the invisible hand shaping their perceptions, against the erosion of clarity that began not with an explosion, but with a misrouted message or a delayed confirmation.

And for Israeli forces, the shift was profound. They no longer operated in an environment where surprise was assumed to be dead. They had rediscovered surprise — not by hiding physically, but by shaping informational realities so thoroughly that when movement came, it arrived inside the enemy's confusion, not against his readiness.

The future of conflict, they understood, would not belong solely to those who could maneuver fastest or strike hardest. It would belong to those who could shape the very decision spaces within which movement and striking took place.

And in that future, those who could listen were powerful.
But those who could control would be decisive.

With every new gain in operational control came an increase in risk. The further Israel pushed into the realm of information shaping, the more it had to account for the consequences of miscalculation. Once communications channels were not merely observed but actively manipulated, the potential for unintended escalation grew. A single spoofed command that landed incorrectly could trigger a panicked response, a collapse of cohesion, or a mistaken retaliation. The tools of influence carried with them an invisible weight — the burden of knowing that informational warfare, though bloodless in method, could have consequences as permanent as a kinetic strike.

Commanders and planners were forced to internalize a new kind of responsibility. The line between shaping and provoking was razor thin. Misinformation planted too cleverly might not just degrade enemy operations; it might trigger a humanitarian collapse, a retaliatory rocket barrage, or the death of civilians caught in the spiraling consequences of disoriented command structures. The more control one exerted over another's perception, the more one became accountable for how that perception unfolded into action.

This tension became clearest during engagements in densely populated areas, where adversaries such as Hamas relied on embedded command networks within civilian infrastructure. Israeli forces developed highly granular spoofing campaigns to trigger evacuations, to create safe corridors without declaring them, to mislead command nodes away from schools or hospitals. In theory, it was a precision humanitarian measure — moving hostile actors without striking them. In practice, the moment one inserted false traffic into a network of mixed military and civilian use, the outcome could not be predicted with confidence.

Even in military-only contexts, shaping enemy behavior raised strategic dilemmas. When an adversary begins to doubt the authenticity of their own orders, there is a chance they begin to ignore them altogether — including real ones. A force that ceases to respond predictably can quickly become dangerous in new and unintended ways. And in asymmetric warfare, where information spreads informally and discipline is uneven, deception can break structures rather than bend them.

The adversaries themselves began to adapt, even if unevenly. Hezbollah, long adept at using Israeli signals against them, began rethinking the openness of their own communications. Their units increasingly moved to analog fallback systems during high-stress periods. Orders were distributed in person, via runners or dead drops. Redundancy became a cultural norm, not merely a tactical plan. In places like Gaza, Hamas began separating logistical coordination from combat command, trying to isolate the systems most vulnerable to spoofing from those that mattered most during kinetic engagements.

These adaptations slowed their tempo, but they made deception harder. The more fragmented the adversary's network became, the more Israeli cyber planners had to study the social dynamics and human terrain behind the digital one. Manipulating the signal was no longer enough. To shape perception, one had to understand belief systems, hierarchies, tribal and ideological structures, levels of discipline, and the fracture lines along which misinformation would spread most efficiently.

Cyber and signals operations thus evolved again. Intelligence gathering expanded beyond metadata and protocol into linguistics, behavior, and sentiment analysis. In effect, every target network became a mirror of the people who used it — and shaping that network meant shaping those people, or at least their perceptions of each other. Misinformation ceased to be purely technical. It became social.

This presented its own dangers. Psychological manipulation, once confined to leaflets or broadcasts, now moved inside the opponent's trusted channels. False messages impersonating commanders didn't just give bad orders — they sowed doubt in the legitimacy of real orders. Units once cohesive began questioning their chain of command. In at least one instance, a Hezbollah logistics unit temporarily fractured after receiving contradictory instructions from what it believed to be different elements of senior leadership. Whether the disruption was the result of Israeli spoofing or internal confusion remains disputed. But the psychological impact was real. And Israel, for better or worse, had crossed a threshold: it was no longer merely degrading enemy operations. It was shaping enemy trust.

That line, once crossed, could not be uncrossed. Subsequent campaigns integrated information warfare from the outset. Spoofed messages were no longer just for tactical misdirection — they were used to fracture adversary confidence over time, to isolate more disciplined commanders from radical or less experienced ones, to create internal suspicion loops that would slow enemy decision-making before it ever reached the battlefield.

These techniques proved effective, but they also revealed a larger strategic question: how much influence is too much? At what point does shaping cross into dependency? What happens when an adversary's command structure becomes so degraded, so full of holes and second-guessing, that it ceases to function in ways that a shaping force can predict or control?

The Israeli answer was to build feedback loops. Every campaign included not only attack vectors, but real-time monitoring for unintended effects. Spoofed communications were triangulated against actual movement patterns. When adversary behavior diverged too far from expected models, shaping efforts were paused, recalibrated, or even rolled back. This wasn't mercy — it was control. Effective deception required confidence in the adversary's interpretive framework. When that framework cracked, so did the utility of influence.

The shift from listening to controlling, then, was not merely a technical evolution. It was a doctrinal one, an ethical one, and a psychological one. It transformed how Israel understood warfare. It transformed how adversaries understood their own vulnerability. And it transformed the informational domain from a support layer into a primary theater of combat — contested, shaped, and just as dangerous as any physical battlefield.

Control, once the end goal, became a condition to be maintained. A constant balance between pressure and legibility, between shaping and destabilizing, between knowing enough about the enemy to move them and not so much that they stopped moving predictably altogether.

This was the paradox of the cyber offensive turn.
To truly control, one had to resist the temptation to dominate completely.

As Israeli operations matured, the techniques of communications shaping expanded beyond tactical deception into full-spectrum strategic influence. What began as localized spoofing to disrupt a battle group or redirect a convoy grew into campaigns aimed at altering the broader operational posture of adversary organizations, even shifting the political and strategic calculations of hostile leadership.

The operational logic was simple but profound: if adversaries could be made to see the battlespace incorrectly, they could be maneuvered into strategic errors without the need for large-scale kinetic engagements. If a militant organization believed its logistics chain was compromised, it might slow or reroute operations unnecessarily. If political leaders believed that a critical commander had defected or been killed — even falsely — it could trigger internal purges, resource shifts, or delays in broader strategic planning.

These deeper influence operations required more than just technical cyber capabilities. They demanded a synchronized fusion of cyber intrusion, human intelligence, psychological profiling, and deep cultural understanding. Each message inserted, each distortion crafted, had to be calibrated not just to disrupt immediate operations, but to reverberate through the adversary's own structures of trust, authority, and fear.

Early experiments in strategic shaping were measured. During periods of low-intensity conflict with Gaza-based factions, Israeli cyber units infiltrated informal command structures — the networks by which lower-tier militants received their orders, coordinated safe houses, and managed logistics. By selectively corrupting certain communications — planting contradictory instructions, delaying confirmations, suggesting internal betrayal — they induced patterns of mistrust and operational caution that had cascading effects across entire units.

In some cases, the result was organizational paralysis. Commanders delayed movements awaiting confirmation that never came. Cells hesitated to regroup, fearful of compromised rally points. Tactical coordination broke down, not because of jamming or surveillance, but because the invisible scaffolding of trust had been quietly undermined.

At the same time, Israel learned that influence had to be carefully bounded. When doubt became too widespread, it ceased to shape predictable behavior and instead generated chaos. Militant groups that no longer trusted any communications became harder to manipulate and, paradoxically, sometimes harder to deter. Disconnected from centralized command, individual cells operated on initiative, improvisation, and ideological momentum. This made them less effective militarily, but also more unpredictable, more dangerous to civilians, and more immune to traditional deterrence.

The evolution of Israel's doctrine thus reflected a maturing understanding of influence warfare. It was not enough to simply degrade enemy networks. The goal was to manage enemy decision-making — to slow it, fragment it, channel it into less dangerous courses — without shattering it entirely unless prepared to absorb the consequences of an uncontrolled adversary.

In strategic campaigns against Iranian-aligned forces operating in Syria and Lebanon, this doctrine reached new levels of sophistication. Israeli cyber operations blended seamlessly with kinetic campaigns, diplomatic pressure, and information warfare. Shaping operations created ambiguities about the timing and objectives of Israeli strikes. False narratives were seeded into adversary command chains, suggesting internal betrayals, secret negotiations, or fictitious Israeli operational priorities.

Sometimes, the goal was to draw enemy forces into exposing themselves — moving assets prematurely, revealing command nodes, setting up hasty defenses that could be observed and targeted. Other times, the goal was simply to create paralysis, to buy time for other elements of national strategy to unfold without immediate military escalation.

Israeli planners understood that strategic shaping was not about forcing the enemy into a single desired action. It was about forcing them into worse choices — about narrowing their operational space, burdening their decision cycles, fragmenting their internal trust networks until even rational action became difficult.

Success in this domain did not look like dramatic enemy collapses. It looked like patterns of small errors accumulating over time: missed opportunities, mistimed attacks, misallocated resources, political infighting, broken alliances. Influence warfare, when done correctly, left no obvious fingerprints. It left adversaries bleeding momentum invisibly, wondering why initiatives stalled, why coordination faltered, why trust seemed harder to maintain.

At the technical level, Israel invested heavily in the tools needed to sustain this shaping doctrine. Real-time signals collection merged with automated linguistic analysis, social network mapping, behavioral pattern tracking. Cyber units operated less like traditional military formations and more like fusion centers, blending psychological insight, operational tempo analysis, and cyber intrusion techniques into a single stream of shaping options continuously updated in real time.

Targets were not just selected based on strategic value but on susceptibility to influence — commanders prone to indecision, political figures known for insecurity, mid-tier leaders vulnerable to perceived betrayal or professional humiliation. Communications shaping moved beyond disrupting logistics and battle orders into manipulating perceptions of loyalty, competence, and strategic outlook.

This approach required extraordinary discipline. Overreach — pushing too hard, crafting manipulations too crude — could harden adversary cohesion rather than erode it. Revealed deceptions could backfire, generating renewed solidarity against an external threat. Shaping campaigns had to move with a tempo matching the internal rhythms of the adversary, exploiting natural fault lines without appearing to create them.

The deeper truth behind Israel's success was that it no longer viewed communications solely as information channels. It viewed them as lifelines of organizational identity. Every message received or sent was a reinforcement of command, of unity, of operational purpose. Corrupting those lifelines subtly enough to fragment identity without shattering it outright was an art form — one that demanded patience, empathy for the adversary's point of view, and an almost ruthless commitment to operational ambiguity.

From listening, to spoofing, to controlling, and finally to strategic shaping, Israel's cyber and electromagnetic evolution revealed a broader truth about modern conflict: that survival and victory would increasingly belong not to those who could merely destroy the enemy's capabilities, but to those who could degrade the enemy's cohesion, disrupt his perceptions, and fragment his decision-making spaces without requiring constant kinetic confrontation.

And in this emerging form of war, the earliest proving grounds — the silent battles fought over pager signals, maintenance dispatches, and unsecured relay channels — had proven decisive in shaping the future.

What had once been vulnerabilities became weapons.
What had once been a lesson in listening became a doctrine of control.

The consequences of mastering communication shaping extended beyond the immediate battlefield. As Israel honed its ability to degrade adversary decision-making without necessarily firing a shot, it began to realize that these tools could have strategic effects in domains far removed from traditional combat zones. Influence at the tactical level could cascade upward, altering the political, diplomatic, and regional security environment without the need for visible confrontation.

Shaping operations against adversary militias and proxies in

Lebanon, Syria, and Gaza gradually expanded into shaping perceptions among state actors. Iranian-aligned commanders, made cautious by repeated disruptions and seemingly inexplicable failures, slowed their logistical coordination across the Levant. Hezbollah, traditionally aggressive in its posture, began hedging more carefully against the possibility of preemptive strikes it could neither predict nor fully explain. Militant political leaders began issuing more fragmented, contradictory statements to their own base populations, the result of strategic doubt planted slowly and patiently by an unseen hand.

Israel had, without formal declaration, extended its doctrine of information control into the regional balance of power. It no longer relied solely on kinetic deterrence — the threat of overwhelming military response to provocations. It complemented that deterrence with an invisible campaign of uncertainty, a low-pressure but constant erosion of adversary confidence in their own plans, their own alliances, even their own internal communications.

The objective was not to achieve peace through weakness, nor even to force adversaries into outright collapse. It was to maintain what might be called controlled instability — a condition in which hostile actors remained locked in cycles of doubt, hesitation, and internal tension, unable to mount coordinated strategic threats without revealing themselves or fragmenting under the strain. Yet this instability, if allowed to fracture too deeply, risked producing not docile adversaries but unpredictable actors beyond the reach of strategic deterrence.

This posture gave Israel greater freedom of action in the regional arena. Strikes against high-value targets in Syria, operations against weapons shipments intended for Hezbollah, counter-influence efforts in cyberspace — all unfolded within a shaped informational environment in which adversaries found it harder to react coherently, harder to mobilize unified responses, harder to frame Israeli actions as unprovoked or illegitimate in broader diplomatic forums.

Israel understood the dangers of this model. Influence was a dangerous form of control. It bred resentment, paranoia, and eventually counter-adaptation. No informational environment could be shaped indefinitely without risk of blowback. Indeed, by the late 2010s, signs of this adaptation were emerging. Iranian cyber units grew more sophisticated. Hezbollah restructured parts of its command network into decentralized cells less dependent on vulnerable communications streams. Hamas invested in low-tech fallback options, preparing for scenarios in which digital shaping would fail and resilience would depend on human trust chains, not network reliability.

Yet even as adversaries evolved, the strategic effect of Israel's doctrine remained. The electromagnetic and informational spaces that had once been taken for granted by both sides were now acknowledged as contested, fragile, and central to strategic survival. Every major conflict planning effort, whether Israeli or adversarial, now included cyber and communications considerations at the earliest stages. Every escalation cycle was fought not only over territory or military postures but over perception, initiative, and internal decision coherence.

The cyber offensive turn — the shift from listening to controlling — had changed not only how Israel fought wars, but how it thought about war itself.
Conflict was no longer a binary between war and peace, crisis and calm.
It was a continuous competition to shape the environment in which war might or might not occur — to stretch adversary decision cycles, to fragment unity before it could coalesce, to preempt initiative not with gunfire but with uncertainty.

It was a model that suited a small state surrounded by

persistent threats: efficient, asymmetric, and difficult for adversaries to counter directly without exposing their own informational weaknesses.

And it was a model born directly from the lessons of past vulnerability.
From the realization that being heard — once considered a trivial or manageable risk — could unravel the strongest operational plans, and that shaping what the enemy heard, believed, and feared could yield victories invisible to the untrained eye but decisive in their consequences.

This evolution — from passive listening, to active manipulation, to strategic shaping — marked the full arrival of information warfare as a central pillar of Israeli defense doctrine. Not an adjunct to kinetic power, but a co-equal force capable of reshaping adversary behavior, deterrence balances, and even the strategic architecture of regional conflict.

It was a power that demanded caution as much as ambition.
A weapon that demanded restraint as much as aggression.

And it was a path that, once begun, could not be walked backward.

The future of conflict would be fought not only with steel and fire, but with silence and noise, truth and illusion, fear and doubt — woven invisibly through the communications networks upon which every adversary, every ally, and every state increasingly depended.

The path from listening to controlling had been shaped not by theory, but by necessity. It was not a straight line of innovation, but a grinding, iterative evolution born of vulnerability, loss, and adaptation. Every step along that path — from the careless emissions of unsecured pagers to the deliberate shaping of strategic perceptions — had been paid for in lost initiative, in operational exposure, in hard lessons absorbed under fire.

Israel's mastery of communications shaping was not inevitable. It was the result of a profound cultural transformation, one that recognized that information could no longer be treated as an asset to be protected in isolation. Information was a battlespace in itself, a living, breathing domain that could be occupied, contested, degraded, or weaponized. It demanded continuous vigilance, constant shaping, and a willingness to think like the adversary — to anticipate not only what they might hear, but how they might interpret what they heard, and how their belief could be turned into an instrument of control.

The nature of warfare itself shifted under the weight of these realizations. Battles were no longer fought only when rockets flew and armor crossed borders. They were fought in the quiet hours before the first movement order was issued, in the whispered distortions of enemy communications, in the long, invisible campaigns to make sure that when confrontation came, it would come on terms shaped months or years before the first shot.

This was the true power of the cyber offensive turn.
Not simply the ability to disrupt systems, not merely the ability to insert false orders or confuse targeting networks, but the ability to wage war inside the mind of the enemy, to shift the terrain of decision-making itself, to erode the very certainty upon which coordinated action depended.

And yet, this power came with costs.
The more deeply information was shaped, the more fragile the entire informational ecosystem became. Misinformation, once seeded, could spiral into strategic miscalculations where rational signaling became impossible. Adversaries who doubted their own networks could become unpredictable, escalating based on false beliefs or worst-case assumptions rather than deliberate planning.

Israel understood these dangers. Its operators, its planners, its commanders lived daily with the knowledge that their mastery of shaping could not prevent every unintended consequence. The control they wielded was never absolute. It was conditional, contextual, temporary — a constantly shifting balance between influence and instability.

The final evolution of this doctrine was not arrogance, but humility.
A recognition that information control was a weapon of immense power, but one that could easily cut both ways.
A recognition that true mastery lay not in domination, but in continuous adaptation — in shaping just enough to hold the initiative without unraveling the very environment in which initiative could be exercised.

The road from passive listening to active controlling marked one of the most profound changes in the history of modern warfare. It reshaped not only how conflicts were fought, but when, why, and how adversaries thought they could win or survive.

And it left a lesson not just for Israel, but for every state, every force, every actor operating in the saturated battlespaces of the twenty-first century.

In a world where communications were the bloodstream of power,
the ability to listen was strength.
The ability to control was dominance.
But the ability to shape without losing balance — to mold without shattering — was survival.

# CHAPTER 9 — THE SYRIAN CIVIL WAR: A NEW LABORATORY

The collapse of Syria into civil war in 2011 created one of the most chaotic, information-rich, and operationally permissive environments modern cyber and electronic warfare units had ever encountered. For Israel, it presented not just a threat but an unprecedented opportunity — a living laboratory where new doctrines of cyber-electromagnetic shaping, influence, and targeted disruption could be refined in real-world conditions against a wide array of adversaries.

Unlike traditional state-on-state conflicts, Syria's fragmentation offered a complex, layered battlespace. Regular Syrian Arab Army units, Iranian Revolutionary Guard Corps elements, Hezbollah deployments, Iraqi militias, Palestinian proxy forces, Kurdish factions, Islamist insurgents, and global jihadist movements all operated within overlapping zones, often with incompatible communications systems, conflicting command structures, and wildly varying levels of cyber and signals discipline. No single adversary dominated the electromagnetic environment. Instead, it became a crowded, noisy ecosystem of emissions, ripe for exploitation by those disciplined enough to listen carefully, to map patiently, and to strike surgically.

From the beginning of the conflict, Israeli cyber and signals intelligence units positioned themselves to harvest this chaos. Every communication emitted within Syria — from military orders to maintenance requests, from courier relays to command net updates — became a potential vector for mapping, manipulation, or disruption. The collapse of centralized Syrian command structures meant that many factions fell back on ad hoc, decentralized communications methods: commercial satellite phones, cheap encrypted apps, analog radios, even unsecured digital walkie-talkie networks. Each of these carried weaknesses. Each presented an aperture through which shaping operations could flow.

Israel's highest priorities were clear: Iranian forces, Hezbollah units, and their associated proxy groups operating along the Syrian-Israeli frontier and the strategic corridor connecting Iran to Lebanon. These forces represented not merely tactical threats but the embodiment of a long-term Iranian strategy to encircle Israel through hardened, expeditionary paramilitary deployments. Every movement of weapons, every reinforcement of forward positions, every logistical buildup had to be monitored, disrupted, and if necessary, preemptively struck.

Cyber operations during this period mirrored and extended earlier doctrines. Malware implants were seeded into communications devices, command servers, and field systems wherever possible. The goal was not merely to collect intelligence but to enable real-time shaping of the operational environment. Malware designed for this theater focused less on traditional espionage and more on operational disruption: delaying orders, corrupting map data, falsifying logistics reports, scrambling maintenance schedules, misrouting reinforcements.

Signal spoofing campaigns evolved in sophistication. Rather than simply broadcasting false commands, Israeli units increasingly deployed precision spoofing — mimicking not only the technical signatures of trusted communications but the linguistic patterns, timing habits, and formatting conventions of specific enemy commanders. A unit receiving a spoofed message would have little reason to doubt its authenticity unless cross-checked against separate verification channels, which in the chaos of the Syrian theater were often absent or overwhelmed.

The distinction between cyber and kinetic operations blurred. Malware implants fed targeting data to kinetic strike forces. Communications disruptions preceded and shaped physical raids. Deceptive emissions created openings for rapid maneuver. Electronic warfare cells embedded into operational groups sowed confusion among enemy formations at the moment of attack, collapsing coordination and response before it could solidify.

One key innovation during the Syrian campaigns was the integration of tactical cyber-kinetic effects. In certain instances, malware implants were not used simply to disrupt communications but to create physical effects: disabling vehicle ignition systems, corrupting artillery targeting modules, crashing drone navigation software. These cyber-physical linkages allowed Israeli forces to achieve effects traditionally reserved for airstrikes or sabotage teams without exposing assets to direct contact or escalation risks.

Operational discretion remained paramount. Unlike broader cyber conflicts that played out in global forums, Israeli shaping operations in Syria were designed to be invisible wherever possible. Attribution was avoided. Effects were layered subtly into the fabric of battlefield chaos. A misrouted convoy, a failed resupply mission, a delayed reinforcement, a drone that crashed without explanation — these were the visible artifacts of an invisible campaign unfolding against adversaries often too consumed by their own internal chaos to recognize the full extent of their exposure.

The cumulative effect of these operations was profound. Hezbollah's logistical networks inside Syria became fragmented and risk-prone. Iranian command elements found their trusted communications degraded and intermittently compromised. Militia units grew hesitant, paranoid about movement orders, increasingly reliant on direct visual confirmation rather than electronic coordination. Each small shaping operation fed into a broader campaign of tempo control — preventing hostile forces from massing effectively, degrading their ability to synchronize, slowing their operational cycles until momentum itself became an elusive goal.

At the strategic level, Israel maintained plausible deniability. Official communications focused on kinetic red lines — weapons transfers, strategic base entrenchments, threats to Israeli territory. The shaping operations remained largely invisible to public scrutiny, their effects attributed either to operational incompetence among adversaries or to the natural chaos of a collapsing state. This invisibility preserved escalation control, allowing Israel to degrade adversary capabilities without triggering overt responses that might draw major powers or broader regional actors more deeply into direct confrontation.

The Syrian conflict thus became the proving ground for an integrated doctrine of continuous cyber-electromagnetic shaping — a doctrine that treated information dominance as a condition to be cultivated, not an event to be seized. A doctrine that wove cyber implants, spoofing, signal manipulation, and tactical cyber-kinetic effects into every level of operational planning.

It was an evolution that showed what modern information warfare could become when practiced not as an adjunct to combat but as a shaping force that preceded, enabled, and in some cases replaced traditional kinetic engagements. It was a glimpse into the future of contested environments where adversaries fought not merely for ground or for territory, but for the very ability to see, to decide, and to act coherently under pressure.

And in the broken, contested fields of Syria, that future was already unfolding, one intercepted message, one manipulated order, one shaped perception at a time.

The fractured landscape of Syria accelerated a style of

operational experimentation that would have been impossible in more orderly conflicts. Adversaries were diverse, their systems uneven, their command hierarchies in varying states of cohesion. Some forces operated on military-grade encrypted radios; others relied on consumer-grade apps running over unreliable cellular networks. Some units maintained hardened communications discipline; others transmitted location updates with reckless transparency, unaware or indifferent to who might be listening.

Israeli cyber units exploited these disparities ruthlessly. They understood that the complexity of the environment was an advantage. It was easier to hide shaping operations in noise. It was easier to introduce falsehoods when the truth was already fractured across a dozen overlapping narratives. It was easier to isolate targets when command coherence was already fragile and when paranoia, rivalry, and distrust were already latent within the adversary's ranks.

One particular focus was the Iranian supply chain operating through Syria into Lebanon. As Iran poured resources into the Syrian theater — weapons, advisors, proxy militias — its communications and logistics networks became targets not only for surveillance but for shaping. Malware implants inside logistic nodes allowed Israeli forces to monitor, and at times delay or misdirect, the flow of weapons shipments intended for Hezbollah. In some cases, false convoy orders were introduced into compromised systems, rerouting high-value assets into kill zones or away from critical handoff points. In others, supply vehicles arrived late, depleted, or fragmented, eroding the operational readiness of forward-deployed units without the need for overt kinetic interdiction.

Signal spoofing operations further degraded Iranian influence. Israeli units impersonated Iranian command elements at critical junctures, issuing misleading instructions to proxies, triggering defensive redeployments, and seeding doubt about whether commands originated from trusted sources or hostile infiltrators. The cumulative effect was to stretch Iranian command capacity thin, to fracture coordination between Iranian officers and their local militia partners, and to slow the tempo of operations until strategic opportunities — targeting, strikes, interdictions — could be executed with reduced risk of counteraction.

Hezbollah, more communications-savvy and hardened by decades of operational experience, proved a tougher target. Yet even among their ranks, signs of disruption emerged. Repeated targeting of Hezbollah logistical movements suggested patterns of exposure beyond traditional human intelligence. Field reports indicated instances of units receiving conflicting movement orders or encountering sudden jamming and signal confusion at critical moments. Though Hezbollah adapted — moving to hybrid communications methods, increasing physical courier usage, reinforcing verification protocols — the constant pressure degraded their ability to operate at the scale and speed they had achieved in earlier conflicts.

Israeli cyber units understood that not every shaping effort would yield perfect results. The objective was not perfection but pressure — a relentless campaign of small disruptions, cumulative doubts, incremental degradations that, over time, would make adversary operations more fragile, more cautious, and less synchronized.

At the tactical level, this often meant exploiting the seams between communications modes. A unit operating on military radios might still coordinate its logistics through unsecured mobile devices. A militia receiving formal orders through encrypted relays might rely on unencrypted local nets for immediate tactical coordination. Cyber units mapped these seams meticulously, looking for points where a single spoofed message or a delayed update could ripple across broader operational timelines.

At the operational level, timing was everything. Shaping efforts were carefully calibrated to enemy operational cycles — to hit logistics flows before offensives, to fracture command unity just prior to reinforcement movements, to degrade targeting networks just as Israeli air operations began. Shaping was no longer episodic. It was continuous, a background condition applied not randomly but with calculated rhythms to maximize disruption with minimal direct exposure.

The Syrian theater also allowed Israeli forces to refine hybrid cyber-kinetic operations. Malware was inserted not only to gather information but to pre-position options for kinetic strike support. In several cases, malware implants inside communication or targeting systems allowed for real-time updates on enemy movements, providing windows of opportunity for fast, precise kinetic action before the adversary realized it was exposed.

There are credible indications, based on open-source battlefield reporting, that in some instances Israeli cyber operations introduced latency into enemy air defense systems, degraded artillery targeting processes, or triggered misfires during moments of coordinated counterattack. These actions were rarely acknowledged officially. When observed at all, they were dismissed as equipment failures, operational errors, or simply the cost of waging war in a degraded environment.

In truth, the environment was not naturally degraded. It was shaped — continuously, patiently, surgically — by forces that understood the electromagnetic and informational terrain as intimately as the physical ground itself.

Israel's shaping campaign in Syria did not seek to control the entire battlespace. It did not attempt to dominate every frequency, every network, every channel. Instead, it focused on critical nodes — the vital arteries of coordination, supply, and command that, if disrupted selectively and repeatedly, would keep adversary operations fragmented, reactive, and incomplete.

This doctrine was built on a core principle: that in a chaotic battlespace, overwhelming control was unnecessary. Strategic advantage belonged to those who could shape friction — who could tilt the environment slightly, continuously, until the adversary's own efforts collapsed under the weight of compounded delays, doubts, and mistakes.

And in Syria, amid the ruins of a fractured state and the ambitions of foreign actors, Israel perfected the art of shaping without announcing itself, of breaking cohesion without direct confrontation, of winning time and space through the slow, relentless war of information.

The true measure of the Syrian theater as a laboratory for cyber and electromagnetic shaping came not from individual operations, but from the layered, compounding effects of sustained campaigns. Over time, patterns emerged that hinted at the scale of influence being exerted, even if attribution remained officially silent.

One such pattern appeared in the consistent degradation of Iranian weapons transfers through Syria into Lebanon. Public reports highlighted a string of failed convoys, late shipments, abandoned caches, and botched handoffs between Iranian handlers and Hezbollah recipients. Each incident could be explained individually — poor logistics, Syrian battlefield chaos, Israeli airstrikes. But the cumulative pattern suggested something deeper: a steady erosion of the adversary's ability to coordinate across long, vulnerable supply chains.

Communications compromise likely played a central role. Malware seeded into command devices, spoofed movement orders, and selective signal manipulation introduced friction precisely where it mattered most: in the invisible arteries that fed weapons, equipment, and reinforcements toward forward positions. Convoys were delayed not just by bombs from the air but by confusion within their own orders. Intermediate handoff points shifted without explanation. Trusted channels became suspect. Delivery schedules that had once operated on tight cycles stretched thin, brittle, vulnerable to kinetic exploitation.

Another pattern emerged in Hezbollah's shifting tactical posture. Traditionally adept at decentralized, resilient operations, Hezbollah forces inside Syria increasingly reverted to lower-emission movement — restricting communications, delaying transmissions, relying on in-person relays for coordination. While this adaptation enhanced operational security, it came at a cost: speed. Operations that once unfolded with rapid tempo bogged down under the need for verification, double confirmation, manual synchronization. The force that once prided itself on disciplined agility found itself slowed, encumbered by the very countermeasures necessary to survive in a shaped electromagnetic environment.

There were also indications that tactical cyber-kinetic effects had begun bleeding into air defense operations. During a series of Israeli airstrikes targeting Iranian positions and weapons depots near Damascus, multiple Syrian air defense batteries failed to respond effectively. Some launched late; others misfired or targeted false returns. While official narratives pointed to poor training, technical failures, or confusion, analysts noted anomalies consistent with cyber shaping: delayed sensor fusion, corrupted radar inputs, spoofed targeting data. Though no formal attribution was made, the pattern was consistent with the techniques Israel had refined during earlier shaping operations — injecting confusion not by destroying systems outright, but by distorting their perception of the battlespace at the decisive moment.

Even within Iranian command structures, cracks appeared. Reports surfaced of friction between Iranian officers and their Syrian counterparts, of mistrust among Iranian proxy militias operating across different sectors, of overlapping or conflicting orders that hinted at command disruption. Again, each instance could be dismissed individually. Together, they pointed to an adversary operating under sustained informational pressure — forced into reactive postures, unable to achieve strategic momentum.

The Syrian battlefield offered Israel something rare: a live-fire environment where cyber and electromagnetic shaping could be tested continuously against real adversaries without the political constraints of full-scale war. Every successful shaping operation fed back into doctrine. Every adversary adaptation refined the next iteration. The battlespace itself became a feedback loop — dynamic, self-correcting, constantly evolving.

By mid-decade, Israeli doctrine had fully embraced the concept of the "shaped environment" — an operational condition where adversary forces were not merely attacked or deterred, but molded, fragmented, and slowed through the persistent, low-signature application of informational pressure. In Syria, the doctrine proved its worth. Israeli forces retained operational freedom across the theater. High-value targets were struck with precision. Escalations were managed without broadening conflict. And adversaries, though adapting, operated at a tempo and cohesion level far below their theoretical potential.

Yet even as Israel succeeded, the experience of Syria underscored the limits of shaping operations. Control was never absolute. Adversaries learned. Proxy forces hardened their internal communications. Iranian cyber units grew more aggressive, seeking to disrupt Israeli collection efforts. Russia's intervention, while not directly hostile to Israeli objectives, complicated the electromagnetic environment with more sophisticated sensors, communications, and electronic warfare systems. The battlespace thickened, became noisier, more complex.

The lessons were clear.
Shaping provided extraordinary leverage.
But it demanded continuous vigilance.
Continuous adaptation.
Continuous investment in understanding not just enemy technology, but enemy psychology, enemy culture, enemy operational rhythms.

The Syrian Civil War did not offer a glimpse of a future where cyber operations would replace kinetic conflict.
It revealed a future where the two would merge completely — where information shaping would set the conditions for every engagement, where silence would be as strategic as fire, where influence over decision cycles would become a primary form of battlefield maneuver.

And it showed that the most powerful operations would not announce themselves with explosions.
They would unfold invisibly, subtly, persistently — like pressure on a fault line, building toward outcomes that adversaries would experience as chaos, never fully realizing that chaos had been engineered by those who understood the battlefield they could not see.

The operational success Israel achieved through shaping campaigns in Syria was not limited to tactical gains on the battlefield. Over time, it fed into a broader strategic recalibration — a realization that information dominance, when applied continuously and at scale, could reshape not just immediate conflicts but the regional balance of power itself.

The Syrian theater provided proof that adversaries could be corralled, slowed, and fractured without full-scale war. Supply chains could be degraded without mass bombardment. Proxy armies could be destabilized without needing to occupy territory. Strategic deterrence could be reinforced not only by the threat of visible kinetic response but by the invisible, persistent erosion of adversary confidence in their own operational environment.

This evolution marked a shift in Israeli defense thinking. Traditional deterrence models had relied on clear signals: a strike in response to a violation, an overt military operation to reset boundaries. Cyber-electromagnetic shaping introduced a more subtle, more durable layer of influence. Instead of reacting to threats after they materialized, Israel sought to shape adversary behavior continuously — to create conditions in which threats were less likely to materialize in the first place.

This was not deterrence by punishment. It was deterrence by friction.
By slowing the pace of hostile operations.
By degrading adversary coordination.
By ensuring that every move an enemy made was harder, riskier, more fraught with uncertainty than the last.

From the fields of Syria, a doctrine of strategic information shaping began to emerge — one that understood the region as a dynamic ecosystem of perceptions, capabilities, alliances, and rivalries that could be influenced not just by diplomacy or force, but by continuous, invisible pressure in the electromagnetic domain.

In practical terms, this meant expanding the toolkit beyond tactical malware implants and spoofed signals. It meant shaping media narratives, controlling what signals leaked into open-source collection, manipulating the timing of military actions to align with psychological and political vulnerabilities. It meant understanding not just enemy orders of battle, but enemy fears — the cultural, historical, and institutional biases that shaped how hostile actors perceived their options.

The Syrian experience taught Israeli planners that informational dominance was cumulative. A single shaping operation might achieve little. But a hundred shaping operations, layered over months and years, could bend the strategic environment itself. Hezbollah's caution along the Lebanese border. Iranian delays in entrenching new bases. Militia hesitations in coordinating multi-sector offensives. Each could be traced, at least in part, to years of sustained informational pressure — years in which every adversary move carried the hidden weight of doubt, delay, or dysfunction seeded by unseen hands.

It also revealed the critical importance of resilience. Shaping operations were not a one-way street. Israel's own informational environment was vulnerable. Russian, Iranian, and proxy cyber units adapted, probing Israeli systems, seeking to sow confusion in turn. Syria proved that the battlespace was never static. Every advantage demanded constant reinforcement. Every shaping campaign needed real-time assessment, recalibration, and sometimes withdrawal when effects risked backfiring or adversaries adapted faster than anticipated.

The Syrian Civil War, then, became more than a battlefield. It became a model — a prototype for twenty-first century conflict in contested environments where informational maneuver was as decisive as kinetic force, where wars were fought not just with weapons but with uncertainty, ambiguity, and the deliberate fracturing of the enemy's ability to act in coherent, synchronized ways.

This model was not universally transferable. Syria's chaos, its overlapping factions, its degraded state structures, created a permissive laboratory that might not exist elsewhere. In more structured environments — facing modern militaries with hardened cyber defenses, disciplined communications practices, and centralized control — shaping operations would face greater resistance. Signals might be encrypted, networks more resilient, organizational trust harder to erode.

But the core principle remained valid. Even sophisticated

adversaries were not immune to informational friction. Every system depended on assumptions about reliability, synchronization, verification. Every force, no matter how technologically advanced, relied on the perception that its communications, its logistics, its command rhythms could be trusted. Shaping doctrine recognized that no environment was too hardened to escape pressure. It simply demanded greater precision, greater patience, greater cultural and operational understanding.

And so Israel, having honed its doctrine in the fields of Syria, prepared for a broader stage. A stage where cyber-electromagnetic shaping would no longer be a tool of opportunity, but a deliberate pillar of national security strategy — integrated into every campaign plan, every escalation ladder, every strategic contingency.

The laboratory of Syria had not only proven that shaping was possible.
It had proven that shaping, when mastered, could alter the very character of conflict itself — slowing wars before they erupted, fracturing coalitions before they solidified, blunting threats before they coalesced into crises.

The future would not be decided solely by those who could strike fastest or hardest.
It would be decided by those who could shape earliest, most persistently, and most invisibly.
Those who understood that the real battlespace was not merely physical, but perceptual — fought in the minds of commanders, in the rhythms of decision cycles, in the shifting sands of trust and doubt.

And in the long, unfinished war unfolding across the Middle East, the laboratory of Syria stood as a living testament to that new reality.

The lessons of Syria did not remain confined to Israeli planners alone. Around the world, defense establishments, intelligence agencies, and strategic theorists watched the slow, grinding contest unfold, often without understanding the invisible battles that shaped its course. Many attributed Israel's operational successes to superior airpower, superior surveillance, superior intelligence. Few grasped that the decisive advantage was often quieter — embedded not in firepower, but in the erosion of enemy cohesion before shots were ever fired.

The doctrine that emerged from the Syrian campaign was not a blueprint for victory through technology alone. It was a recognition that technology, absent cultural and operational discipline, would always be fragile. That shaping the information environment required more than technical mastery; it demanded psychological insight, patience, and the ability to see conflict as a process of continuous pressure rather than episodic confrontation.

Israeli forces came to understand that every emission mattered. Every unsecured message, every pattern repeated too often, every assumption left unchallenged was an opportunity for an adversary to begin their own shaping campaign in reverse. Success depended not only on shaping the enemy's perceptions, but on hardening one's own — preserving internal trust networks, protecting command rhythms from external distortion, maintaining flexibility even when the information environment turned against expectations.

The Syrian Civil War, brutal and chaotic as it was, became the crucible in which the realities of cyber-electromagnetic shaping were tested at operational and strategic scales. It was there that Israel proved that shaping operations could sustain strategic advantage across years of conflict without triggering uncontrollable escalation. It was there that the limits of shaping were revealed — the constant threat of overreach, the need for recalibration, the inevitability of adversary adaptation. And it was there that the blueprint for future contests was drawn, not in the sand of seized territory, but in the electromagnetic spectrum, in the cognitive spaces where decisions are formed and trust is either maintained or shattered.

As the Syrian theater matured, Israel transitioned from experimental practitioner to seasoned architect of informational dominance. The techniques refined there — malware implants tailored for operational shaping, precision signal spoofing designed to fracture trust, tactical cyber-kinetic linkages to accelerate tempo control — became integral to national strategy, not only for immediate threats but for regional and even global contingencies.

What began with passive interception of careless pager traffic decades earlier had evolved into a doctrine capable of manipulating the battlespace itself — a doctrine that treated information as both terrain and weapon, both vulnerability and opportunity.

The laboratory of Syria had shown that the future belonged to those who could see war not merely as a contest of arms, but as a contest of perceptions.
Those who could listen more patiently.
Shape more precisely.
Influence more persistently.
And strike only when the enemy's ability to react had already been degraded beyond recovery.

This was the quiet revolution that unfolded in the Syrian shadows — a revolution invisible to most, but no less profound for its subtlety.

And as new conflicts loomed on distant horizons, those who had mastered the art of shaping knew that the first battles would be fought long before the world realized war had begun.

They would be fought in the signals no one noticed.
In the silences no one questioned.
In the fractures no one saw forming — until it was already too

late to stop them.

# CHAPTER 10 — PAGERS, RADIOS, AND THE PERSISTENCE OF THE UNSEEN THREAT

Despite decades of technological evolution, the vulnerabilities that once enabled Hezbollah to intercept Israeli pager traffic, and Israel to later weaponize adversary communications, have not disappeared. They have simply mutated, evolved, and spread across new conflicts. The electromagnetic spectrum remains contested, exploited, and fragile — a constant battlefield invisible to most, yet decisive in ways that few armies, even today, fully respect.

The persistence of insecure communications is not the result of ignorance alone. It stems from a tension that has haunted every military organization since the first radio crackled to life: the tension between speed and security. Encryption takes time. Verification introduces friction. Discipline demands training, constant reinforcement, and sometimes slower operational cycles. In the urgency of battle, in the shifting chaos of contested environments, the temptation to cut corners is ever-present. And adversaries who listen patiently, quietly, without needing to expose themselves, can reap enormous rewards from these moments of carelessness.

Nowhere was this more evident than in the war in Afghanistan. Despite the dominance of American military technology, despite years of investment in secure communications suites, unsecured or poorly secured radio traffic persisted. Taliban forces, operating with minimal technological sophistication, exploited these seams ruthlessly. Armed with nothing more sophisticated than commercial off-the-shelf scanners and tuned receivers, they monitored U.S. and coalition forces' battlefield communications, extracting patterns, learning movements, predicting operations. At times, they used intercepted traffic to stage ambushes, to avoid patrols, to target vulnerable supply lines. In some sectors, Taliban units understood American battlefield rhythms better than American planners understood theirs — not through superior firepower, but through the patient harvesting of undisciplined emissions.

The vulnerability was not limited to tactical radios. Satellite phone communications, unencrypted maintenance relays, even base logistical nets were intercepted and exploited. Each leak was small on its own. Together, they built a mosaic of operational exposure that insurgents could use to shape the tempo of the battlefield in their favor.

The same dynamic resurfaced with chilling clarity in Ukraine. During the Russian invasion of 2022, early stages of the conflict were marked by widespread communications failures on the Russian side. But it was the vulnerabilities in Ukrainian forces that highlighted the persistence of the unseen threat. Many Ukrainian units, particularly in the early months, operated on civilian-grade radios, unsecured mobile devices, and improvised digital platforms hastily adapted for wartime use.

Russian electronic warfare units, seasoned from prior conflicts in Georgia, Crimea, and eastern Ukraine, exploited these weaknesses aggressively. They intercepted frontline communications, triangulated unit positions, jammed coordination nets, and injected false traffic to confuse and disrupt Ukrainian operational cycles. Some Ukrainian units found themselves paralyzed when critical orders were jammed or misdirected. Others suffered casualties when positions were exposed through careless emissions.

The electromagnetic battlespace in Ukraine evolved rapidly. Ukrainian forces, with Western support, adapted — improving encryption, hardening nets, shifting to more disciplined emissions practices. But the first months of the war revealed a brutal truth: that no matter how much technology advanced, the human factors of communication — speed, friction, discipline — remained vulnerable. And where human weakness intersected with technical exposure, adversaries who knew how to listen and shape could strike without warning.

What was once true in southern Lebanon, what was proven again in Afghanistan, was reaffirmed in Ukraine: that information, once emitted, is irretrievable. That unsecured signals are gifts to any adversary patient enough to wait for them. And that the battle for control over the unseen spectrum is not ancillary to war — it is central to it.

The persistence of insecure communications is rooted also in structural and institutional realities. Modern militaries are sprawling ecosystems, blending professional soldiers, conscripts, contractors, foreign volunteers, and ad hoc paramilitary formations. Each brings different communications practices, different threat awareness, different levels of emissions discipline. Enforcing strict security across such heterogeneous forces is enormously difficult, especially under operational pressure.

Even when technology exists to secure every transmission, practical constraints intervene. Equipment shortages, power limitations, training gaps, and the simple pressures of speed all conspire to erode best practices. A soldier under fire is less concerned about the encryption status of his handset than about whether his request for support is heard in time. A logistician moving fuel convoys under threat prioritizes delivery schedules over emissions control. An artillery battery repositioning to avoid counterbattery fire may forego standard verification protocols if seconds mean survival.

Adversaries know this. They build their shaping operations around it. Patient collection teams map not only communications networks but the rhythms of stress, friction, and operational exhaustion that erode discipline. They wait for the seams to open — and then exploit them with ruthless efficiency.

Even the most advanced militaries remain vulnerable because human beings remain vulnerable. Because no matter how secure the radios, how sophisticated the ciphers, the choices made under pressure — the shortcuts, the assumptions, the momentary lapses — leave windows open that cannot be closed once exploited.

The unseen threat persists because it is woven into the fabric of human conflict itself. It is not a technological flaw alone. It is a human constant, magnified by the speed and saturation of the modern electromagnetic battlespace.

And as long as forces must communicate under fire, as long as speed must at times override security, as long as human beings must make split-second decisions under conditions of extreme uncertainty, the silent war for the spectrum will remain — a shadow conflict as decisive as any fought with tanks, missiles, or rifles.

The methods by which adversaries exploit unsecured communications have evolved in form but not in essence. In Afghanistan, Taliban interception efforts were simple, pragmatic, and devastatingly effective. Armed with inexpensive receivers, laptop-based software-defined radios, and the patience born of asymmetric warfare, Taliban units built their own picture of the battlefield from American emissions. Orders, supply updates, medical evacuation requests, artillery fire missions — all streamed across the spectrum, waiting to be harvested by anyone disciplined enough to monitor them.

The information extracted was not always comprehensive. Much of it was fragmentary, partial, confusing to the untrained ear. But insurgent forces did not need perfect intelligence to act. A pattern of repeated medevac requests from a particular sector suggested a weakening front. A sudden increase in logistical dispatches hinted at preparations for offensive action. A shift in radio net activity betrayed the movement of convoys or the repositioning of firebases.

Taliban commanders, often operating from cave systems, mountain ridges, or civilian buildings, learned to anticipate American movements by listening more carefully than their opponents spoke. They developed timing patterns for ambushes. They evacuated areas likely to be targeted. They set explosive traps in routes identified through traffic analysis alone. They did not need to break encryption when so much critical information was transmitted without it, or with forms of obfuscation so weak as to be meaningless under sustained collection.

This was not simply a failure of technology. It was a failure of habits.
A failure to recognize that the spectrum itself was an active battlespace.
A failure to adapt emissions discipline to the pressures and rhythms of real combat environments.

The same patterns recurred in Ukraine, but with new layers of complexity.
Russian forces deployed far more sophisticated electronic warfare assets than the Taliban could ever muster — directional jammers, broad-spectrum intercept platforms, advanced triangulation units capable of locating emitters with lethal precision. But the operational principle remained the same: harvest emissions, map rhythms, insert friction.

In the early phases of the 2022 conflict, Russian interception of Ukrainian military traffic was rampant. Ukrainian soldiers using unencrypted or lightly secured push-to-talk radios found their movements tracked, their orders intercepted, their positions targeted. Civilian cellular networks, hastily repurposed for military coordination in areas with degraded infrastructure, became easy prey for Russian cyber-electronic units.

Yet the Russian exploitation was not limited to listening. As the conflict matured, they began injecting false commands into Ukrainian nets, spoofing the voices and signatures of trusted commanders, sowing confusion about reinforcement orders, artillery targeting instructions, and evacuation corridors. Units, already under enormous stress, had to operate in an environment where every message carried the potential for deception, where every transmission risked betrayal.

The consequences were predictable. Hesitation spread. Orders took longer to verify. Initiative slowed. Commanders who once trusted their communication streams now second-guessed every instruction, every coordinate, every call for support. The friction introduced by informational shaping was not a side effect. It was the objective.

Yet the cycle of vulnerability and adaptation continued. Ukrainian forces learned. They hardened communications where possible. They shifted to burst transmission techniques, reducing exposure time. They adopted better field discipline, training soldiers to minimize emissions, to use pre-arranged codewords, to move rapidly after transmissions. They incorporated deception of their own — feeding false traffic into unsecured channels to mislead Russian intercept teams about their true movements.

Still, the underlying lesson remained harshly clear: in any conflict where communications are contested, the side that treats emissions discipline as a priority, not an afterthought, will survive longer, move faster, and strike with greater certainty. Those who fail to adapt will bleed information invisibly until their operational rhythms degrade into predictability and exposure.

The unseen threat persists not because militaries are unaware of it, but because the friction between ideal doctrine and real-world pressure is relentless. Units train for perfect emissions control under clean conditions, but war introduces chaos, fear, exhaustion, improvisation. In that chaos, discipline frays, shortcuts emerge, and adversaries who have the patience to listen quietly harvest the fruits of predictable human failure.

Efforts to solve the problem through technology alone — through better encryption, smarter radios, hardened networks — have failed to eradicate the threat because they misunderstand its root cause. The real vulnerability is not in the devices. It is in the patterns of human behavior that repeat across every battlefield, every generation, every war.

It is in the assumption that operational urgency can override basic communications security without consequence.
It is in the belief that speed must come at the cost of caution.
It is in the quiet erosion of best practices under the weight of real combat conditions, where survival trumps protocol and the enemy's ears are never imagined as close as they truly are.

This pattern, this cycle of exposure and exploitation, is not an accident. It is the natural byproduct of war conducted across an invisible, omnipresent battlespace — a battlespace where every signal, every burst of traffic, every unsecured call carries not just information, but risk.

And it is a battlespace that, even today, even after decades of bitter experience, remains the least understood, the least respected, and the most unforgiving arena in which modern conflict is decided.

Even elite forces, trained under the most rigorous emissions control standards, are not immune to the erosion that comes with operational pressure. The best radios, the strongest encryption, the most disciplined communications plans cannot fully counteract the raw reality of battlefield friction.

Special operations units, renowned for their technical

proficiency and operational security, have been compromised through electromagnetic exposure not because they lacked knowledge, but because combat conditions imposed conflicting demands. In several high-profile operations across the Middle East and Africa, radio emissions from otherwise covert teams were intercepted by adversaries using simple but patient methods.
Detection did not require the adversary to understand the content of communications — only the patterns, the bursts of transmissions, the timings between check-ins and exfiltration signals.
Silhouettes of operational cycles emerged not from decoding encryption but from observing rhythm.

The unseen threat is not merely about content. It is about metadata, timing, and predictability.
A unit that transmits every hour on the hour reveals more than its existence. It reveals its discipline, its tempo, its likely vulnerabilities.
A formation that maintains constant communications chatter while maneuvering under threat is broadcasting not only its location but its mental state — anxiety, pressure, urgency.

Adversaries who understand this terrain operate with a different mindset. They do not need to break into secure channels. They simply need to listen long enough, across wide enough bands, to build patterns of life.
Where are the dead zones? Where is the burst of activity? Where does silence break into noise?

The mastery of the electromagnetic battlespace lies in understanding that presence itself is a form of signature.
That a single misplaced transmission can collapse operational security as thoroughly as a captured prisoner or a compromised plan.

Modern conflicts have made this painfully clear.
In Syria, insurgent groups — many operating with limited

technological resources — learned to target forward operating bases by mapping their radio emissions profiles over time.
In the Sahel, jihadist groups tracked patrol routes not through direct observation, but by triangulating unsecured or poorly masked communications bursts.
In Eastern Ukraine, frontline units sometimes inadvertently exposed larger operational shifts — upcoming offensives, major rotations, supply movements — through anomalous traffic spikes that Russian intercept teams eagerly exploited.

And yet, despite these lessons, the cycle persists.
Because the operational pressures that drive emissions are real.
Because under fire, clarity often trumps caution.
Because commanders, faced with fragmented forces, chaotic environments, and incomplete information, revert to communications-heavy management to impose control.
Because in the moment, survival feels more urgent than stealth.

The persistence of the unseen threat is not just a technical problem or a training gap.
It is a structural feature of human conflict under stress.
And no amount of encryption, no doctrine of emissions control, no technological leap can fully eliminate the friction between the need to communicate and the need to remain unseen.

The result is an ongoing, evolving contest - between those who seek to communicate without revealing themselves, and those who seek to listen without being detected - between the visible movements of forces across terrain,and the invisible movements of information across the air.

This contest is older than the digital age. It traces back to the first armies using runners and signal fires, to the first telegraph wires humming with intercepted orders. It endures because it is bound to the nature of conflict itself — the need to coordinate, to command, to react faster than the adversary.

The electromagnetic battlespace is not an adjunct to war.
It is war, refracted through airwaves and signals, fought in bursts of noise and sudden silences.

And the forces that forget this — that treat their communications as background noise rather than foreground risk — invite a kind of slow defeat, death not by frontal assault but by the invisible erosion of initiative, surprise, and trust.

Every signal is a story told to the enemy.
Every pattern is a roadmap offered to those who have the patience to read it.

In the wars of the past, it was the unseen messages that often shaped the battlefield.
In the wars of the future, it will be the unseen listeners who decide whether battles are won before they even begin.

The battlespace of the unseen persists because it is built into the very architecture of modern existence. Every movement of troops, every supply chain, every airstrike, every shift in battlefield posture depends on communications. Every communication, no matter how fleeting, leaves a ripple. In an environment saturated with sensors, receivers, and patient adversaries, even the smallest ripple can be traced, mapped, and weaponized.

The future will not reverse this trend. It will accelerate it. As forces become more interconnected, as units rely increasingly on data fusion, real-time coordination, and digitally assisted command structures, the surface area of exposure grows. More devices mean more emissions. Faster decision cycles mean more urgency to communicate. The very systems designed to enhance military power — mesh networks, battlefield IoT, sensor-sharing architectures — create an electromagnetic fog dense enough to be harvested by anyone who knows where to listen.

This reality demands a shift not just in tactics or training, but in mentality.
Survivability will depend not simply on how much information can be gathered or how fast it can be shared, but on how little unintentional information is leaked in the first place.
The measure of discipline will no longer be only how well a force can maneuver physically, but how well it can maneuver informationally — masking its rhythms, blending its signals into the background, becoming indistinct against the electromagnetic terrain.

Commanders of the future will need to think like adversarial listeners.
They will need to ask not just, "What do I need to communicate?" but "What story does my communication tell, even when encrypted?"
They will need to treat silence as an active operational tool, not an accidental gap.
They will need to build forces that can operate under degraded or denied communications conditions, not as a contingency but as a primary mode of warfare.

And they will need to accept that no matter how sophisticated their tools, the unseen threat cannot be eliminated — only managed, mitigated, delayed.
Victory will belong not to those who seek perfect security, but to those who understand the imperfections of their own systems better than their enemies do.

The wars to come will not announce themselves with massed armies alone.
They will unfold first in the rising noise of emissions, in the shifting patterns of communications bursts, in the subtle exposure of operational intentions through unguarded signals. They will be shaped in the invisible exchanges of metadata, radio signatures, spoofed transmissions, and silent triangulations long before any missile is fired or any line is

crossed.

The forces that master this unseen domain — who respect it, who adapt to it, who learn to think in its logic — will move faster, strike deeper, and survive longer than those who treat communications security as a technical matter for specialists.

The forces that fail to adapt will find their movements preempted, their strategies eroded, their cohesion shattered — not through overwhelming physical attacks, but through the slow, persistent harvesting of what they gave away without knowing.

In this way, the lessons of the past — from the pagers of southern Lebanon, to the radios of Afghanistan, to the battlefields of Ukraine — are not relics.
They are warnings.
Warnings written in signals, broadcast across decades of conflict, ignored at the peril of those who believe that the electromagnetic spectrum is a neutral space rather than a terrain to be contested with the same seriousness as any physical ground.

The unseen threat endures because human nature endures.
Because the need to communicate under pressure endures.
Because the enemies willing to listen, to map, to shape through silence and signal, will always exist.

And so the battlefield remains open — a battlefield without front lines, without trenches, without monuments.
A battlefield measured not in meters gained, but in signals shaped, in rhythms disrupted, in doubts seeded invisibly into the enemy's mind.

It is the oldest kind of war, reborn in the newest spaces.
It is the war that never fully announces itself.
It is the war that, once lost, is almost impossible to win back.

# CHAPTER 11 — BUILDING A SHADOW SIGINT CAPABILITY: HEZBOLLAH'S CONTINUING EVOLUTION

The story of Hezbollah's growth from a guerrilla militia into a hybrid political-military entity is often told through the lens of its battlefield successes, its political influence inside Lebanon, and its asymmetric warfare against Israel. But less often explored, and perhaps more consequential over the long arc of regional conflict, is the parallel story of its evolution in the electromagnetic domain. Hezbollah, once merely a passive listener harvesting Israeli pager traffic and analog radio emissions, slowly began building a shadow signals intelligence capability — one that mirrored, in miniature, the functions of a national-level electronic warfare force.

The seeds of this transformation were planted in the aftermath of the 2006 Lebanon War. That conflict, though tactically costly to both sides, revealed a profound truth to Hezbollah's leadership: the side that could control information flow, harvest adversary signals, and disrupt enemy coordination held disproportionate power. Israel's temporary vulnerabilities — its exposed pager communications, its compromised analog radio systems — had given Hezbollah opportunities far beyond its traditional capabilities. Real-time access to Israeli logistical movements, casualty reports, and reinforcement orders had allowed Hezbollah forces to anticipate, reposition, and even launch targeted strikes based not on guesswork but on live operational intelligence.

This experience left a lasting imprint on Hezbollah's strategic thinking.

The ability to listen had proven more valuable than the ability to fire alone.
Information, if properly gathered and shaped, could extend survivability, multiply tactical opportunities, and compensate for material inferiority.

Iran recognized this lesson as well. In the years following the war, Iranian investment in Hezbollah's cyber and electronic warfare capabilities accelerated dramatically. Iran's Islamic Revolutionary Guard Corps (IRGC), particularly the Quds Force and elements of its own cyber-electronic command, saw in Hezbollah a proxy not merely for kinetic confrontation, but for regional intelligence collection and shaping operations.

Training pipelines were established quietly. Hezbollah operatives began rotating through Iranian signals intelligence and cyber warfare courses, receiving instruction not only in the interception of basic analog and digital communications but in more sophisticated techniques: signal triangulation, metadata analysis, spoofing, localized electronic jamming, basic malware implantation against low-security targets.

What emerged was not a mirror of Western SIGINT behemoths like the NSA or Unit 8200. Hezbollah lacked the resources, the infrastructure, and the global reach. But what it built was suited to its operational environment: a compact, resilient, decentralized SIGINT network optimized for battlefield shaping and regional influence operations.

By the early 2010s, field reports and captured materials indicated that Hezbollah units operating in Syria and southern Lebanon were equipped with interception kits capable of monitoring a broad range of frequencies — from military radio traffic to civilian cellular networks. Hezbollah units began deploying mobile signals collection teams alongside kinetic operations, sweeping for emissions that could betray the presence of hostile forces or civilian collaborators.

These teams were not simply passive collectors. Over

time, Hezbollah operators learned to fuse intercepted communications with tactical action. Intercepted position updates led to targeted mortar strikes. Harvested mobile phone metadata helped map Syrian rebel networks. In some cases, field units reportedly used simple spoofing techniques to impersonate friendly forces, luring enemy patrols into ambushes.

The sophistication of these operations remained limited compared to nation-state capabilities. Hezbollah did not field space-based SIGINT assets. It lacked the ability to conduct deep cyber exploitation against hardened targets. But within its operational tier — irregular warfare, asymmetric engagements, regional shaping — its capabilities grew steadily, fueled by Iranian technology transfers, technical advising, and battlefield experience.

Iran's influence extended beyond training and equipment. It shaped Hezbollah's doctrinal understanding of the electromagnetic domain. Hezbollah leaders internalized a key Iranian lesson: that information shaping was not merely an adjunct to kinetic operations but a strategic tool in its own right. Disrupting enemy cohesion, fragmenting decision cycles, seeding doubt and delay — these outcomes could be achieved through invisible operations long before bullets were fired.

Hezbollah's approach reflected a hybrid philosophy: aggressive information harvesting combined with conservative, disciplined operational security for its own forces. Units were trained to minimize emissions, to use hardened or obfuscated communications channels when possible, to operate under radio silence when necessary, and to treat every transmission as a potential exposure.

At the tactical level, this meant tighter control of battlefield communications. Hezbollah units increasingly shifted to encrypted digital radios, often commercially available systems modified for operational use. At the operational level, it meant building a layered communications infrastructure: blending analog fallbacks, cellular networks, satellite communications, and covert relay systems to ensure survivability even under heavy electronic warfare pressure.

At the strategic level, Hezbollah's growing SIGINT and cyber capability gave it new options. Not only could it shape battlefield engagements more effectively, but it could also extend influence into political, economic, and psychological domains. Intercepted materials could be weaponized not only for targeting but for propaganda, for internal disruption of enemy forces, and for selective leaks designed to fracture trust within opposing coalitions.

Speculating on what Hezbollah has learned from being "the listener" reveals sobering possibilities. They have learned that information exposure can break stronger enemies without requiring overwhelming force. They have learned that trust is as fragile as armor under electromagnetic pressure. They have learned that the invisible battlefield of signals, once entered, can reshape physical battles before they even begin.

Most dangerously, they have learned that shaping the perception of an enemy's own environment — through spoofing, disinformation, selective exposure — is a force multiplier no less potent than rockets or fortified bunkers.
And they have been trained to view information not as a static resource to be defended, but as a dynamic terrain to be contested, manipulated, and turned against adversaries at every level.

The transformation of Hezbollah's SIGINT and cyber capabilities represents more than a technical evolution.

It is a cultural evolution — a shift from seeing communications as a tool of coordination to seeing the electromagnetic spectrum itself as an operational front, a weapon to be wielded as actively and aggressively as any rifle or missile.

This shadow capability remains imperfect, constrained by resource limits, technological gaps, and the realities of asymmetric force structure. But it is persistent, adaptive, and dangerous precisely because it grows in the spaces between major powers' attention spans — in the gaps left by conventional militaries too focused on kinetic dominance to police their own emissions vulnerabilities.

In the next conflict, Hezbollah's shadow SIGINT capability may not decide the outcome alone. But it will shape the battlespace invisibly, harvesting, manipulating, degrading enemy cohesion one signal at a time.

And those who fail to recognize the enemy's invisible ears until after the first engagements may find themselves fighting a war whose outcome was already shaped long before the first shot was fired.

The Syrian conflict offered Hezbollah the operational breathing room to refine and test its emerging signals intelligence capabilities under real battlefield conditions. Unlike the tightly surveilled environment of southern Lebanon, Syria's fractured battlespace provided a messy, chaotic arena where interception, spoofing, and communications shaping could be practiced against a range of adversaries — Sunni Islamist groups, Syrian rebel factions, and even other Iranian-aligned militias competing for influence and resources.

In Syria, Hezbollah's signals collection teams operated with growing sophistication. Field reports indicated that Hezbollah elements not only intercepted adversary radio traffic but began correlating that data with patterns of movement, logistical resupply, and artillery deployments.

Intercepted conversations were mapped against drone surveillance feeds. Captured metadata from seized devices was used to reconstruct social networks within hostile groups.

Entire sectors were monitored not only for immediate threat indicators but for longer-term analysis of operational tempo and command rhythms.

The importance of this shaping cannot be overstated.

Where Hezbollah previously relied on physical reconnaissance and human intelligence for battlefield awareness, it increasingly supplemented these traditional methods with electromagnetic collection — harvesting the invisible environment for signals that revealed not only where the enemy was, but what they feared, how they moved, and how quickly they adapted to pressure.

Spoofing operations, though more limited in scope, evolved alongside passive interception.
Instances were reported where false orders were injected into rebel communications nets, leading to premature withdrawals, abandoned positions, or even friendly fire incidents between loosely coordinated insurgent groups.

In a conflict where alliances were fluid and communications discipline often lax, Hezbollah's ability to sow confusion through invisible means represented a significant force multiplier, allowing them to conserve strength while adversaries exhausted themselves against phantom threats.

At the same time, Hezbollah continued internal hardening.

Battlefield communications shifted increasingly to encrypted commercial radios customized with operational codes and discipline protocols tailored for the Syrian environment.

Low-tech fallback systems remained in place for resilience, but the emphasis was clear: emissions were a liability, and every transmission was to be treated as a potential source of exposure.

This dual track — harvesting enemy signals while shielding their own — reflected a maturation in Hezbollah's doctrinal approach to information warfare.

They no longer saw interception as a lucky advantage or a passive windfall. They treated the electromagnetic battlespace as a living, contested domain — one where active shaping, denial, and exploitation occurred constantly, regardless of whether kinetic engagements were underway.

Beyond the Syrian theater, Hezbollah's evolution hinted at even broader ambitions.

Captured materials, intelligence leaks, and rare field disclosures suggested that Hezbollah's cyber capabilities were expanding beyond tactical communications interception into more traditional cyber operations.

Reports indicated attempts to infiltrate Lebanese government systems, to target rival political factions with cyber espionage, and even to probe regional infrastructure networks linked to adversary intelligence and military assets.

These efforts remained embryonic compared to the capabilities of major nation-state actors, but the intent was clear: to extend influence operations beyond the immediate battlefield, into the strategic, political, and psychological realms where information manipulation could alter outcomes without a single rocket launch.

Iran's hand was visible in this shift. The IRGC had long advocated a doctrine of layered influence: kinetic, psychological, informational.

Hezbollah, drawing from its Iranian sponsors, was adapting that doctrine into a regional context, using cyber operations not just for espionage but for strategic shaping — seeding doubt within hostile populations, undermining trust in government institutions, disrupting coalition formation among its adversaries.

In this vision, the electromagnetic spectrum was merely one axis among many — part of a broader operational philosophy that saw perceptions, decisions, and social cohesion as legitimate targets for shaping operations.

Cyber operations blurred into SIGINT; SIGINT blurred into psychological operations; and all of it fed into the broader goal of extending Hezbollah's strategic reach without exposing itself to direct confrontation.

The consequences of this evolution were profound. Hezbollah, once a local militia with strong religious identity and limited technical capacity, was emerging as a proto-hybrid force — blending irregular warfare, political operations, and increasingly sophisticated information warfare into a resilient, adaptive model of regional influence.

Speculating forward, it is reasonable to assume that Hezbollah's leadership sees signals intelligence and cyber operations not as temporary advantages, but as permanent pillars of its survival strategy.

Every Israeli movement, every Lebanese political realignment, every Syrian security shift presents an opportunity — not necessarily for immediate action, but for collection, mapping, positioning.

Information, once gathered, need not be used immediately. It can be stored, correlated, and weaponized at moments of strategic choice, turning latent knowledge into decisive leverage.

The listener has learned not just to hear, but to interpret. Not just to observe, but to shape.

And as Hezbollah's operational environment grows more complex, its mastery of the invisible battlespace — the realm of signals, metadata, perception, and doubt — will become not merely an asset, but a central determinant of its ability to survive, to strike, and to shape outcomes in conflicts yet to come.

Looking forward, Hezbollah's trajectory suggests a steady continuation of its investment in the electromagnetic and cyber domains, driven by both opportunity and necessity.

The operational environment is evolving, and Hezbollah's leadership understands that survival against stronger, faster, and often better-equipped enemies requires preemption in the information sphere as much as it requires readiness on the ground.

One plausible area of evolution is deeper integration of cyber and SIGINT capabilities into kinetic targeting cycles. Already, there are indications that Hezbollah has moved beyond simply intercepting enemy communications toward fusing harvested data with direct action. Future iterations could involve real-time exploitation of compromised networks to support precision strikes, high-value individual targeting, and even the disruption of enemy command rhythms during escalatory phases.

Imagine a scenario in which a Hezbollah cyber cell quietly injects malware into the communications infrastructure of a forward-deployed enemy unit, subtly degrading response times, introducing delays in targeting confirmations, and creating windows of exposure at the tactical edge.

Such operations would not require mass cyber attacks or headline-grabbing hacks.
They would require only patience, access, and a deep understanding of the natural rhythms of military operations under pressure.

At the same time, Hezbollah's increasing access to Iranian and possibly Russian technical expertise raises the possibility of enhanced electronic attack capabilities — moving from passive interception and shaping toward active disruption.

Localized jamming, selective signal denial, and false flag communications could become standard tools in its operational arsenal, enabling Hezbollah to sow confusion at the micro-tactical level without inviting massive retaliation.

The urban battlefields of the future, particularly in southern Lebanon and the outskirts of Beirut, favor such methods.

Dense electromagnetic environments, civilian infrastructure intermingled with military movements, and a saturation of digital devices create fertile ground for low-signature, high-impact shaping operations. A single manipulated burst of traffic in such environments could trigger premature defensive movements, misdirect incoming strikes, or fracture coordination among hostile forces attempting complex maneuvers.

Beyond the immediate battlefield, Hezbollah's political and information warfare arms are likely to increasingly fuse cyber and electromagnetic methods into broader strategic campaigns. Selective leaks of intercepted communications to discredit political opponents, cyber-enabled psychological operations aimed at eroding the morale of opposing forces, and even social media shaping operations synchronized with real-world battlefield shaping efforts are all within the realm of possibility.

In a future conflict, Hezbollah could intercept enemy orders, spoof reinforcement signals, jam critical nets, seed political doubt through curated leaks, and selectively paralyze key portions of enemy digital infrastructure — not aiming for total collapse, but to fracture cohesion precisely where adversaries depend most on speed and trust.

Such operations would require coordination, investment, and discipline. But Hezbollah's history suggests that it is capable of exactly this kind of gradual, persistent adaptation — especially when the returns on investment directly amplify its core strategic advantages: survivability, influence, and asymmetric leverage.

Critically, Hezbollah's embrace of information warfare is not a betrayal of its original asymmetric ethos. It is a natural extension of it. The same principles that guided its early reliance on decentralized cells, its emphasis on psychological endurance, and its strategic patience now apply to its engagement in the electromagnetic battlespace. Victory is not defined by territorial conquest or overwhelming force but by the slow, deliberate erosion of enemy initiative, cohesion, and certainty.

The future iterations of Hezbollah's shadow SIGINT and cyber capabilities will likely prioritize a few core goals. They will pursue persistent collection across all accessible domains — military, political, and civilian communications alike. They will refine the targeted shaping of adversary perceptions, focusing less on spectacular cyber attacks and more on inducing small, cumulative errors of judgment.

They will invest in resilience against counter-cyber operations through compartmentalization, obfuscation, and the use of mixed civilian-military infrastructures designed to complicate attribution and retaliation. And they will cultivate an environment where every signal — every burst of radio traffic, every encrypted message, every misrouted packet — carries potential strategic leverage.

The ultimate ambition, whether articulated openly or not, is clear. It is to become not merely a tactical irritant to Israeli or regional adversaries, but a persistent, shaping force in the broader regional information environment. It is to erode the ability of conventional powers to operate with confidence in the electromagnetic spectrum. It is to fracture the fragile synchronization that modern military operations depend upon. And it is to achieve, through the invisible shaping of perception and decision, what cannot always be achieved through firepower alone.

In this vision of conflict, Hezbollah does not need to defeat Israel or other adversaries on the battlefield in the traditional sense. It needs only to degrade them steadily — to slow their operations, fragment their coalitions, and seed enough doubt and friction that their superior resources and capabilities cannot be brought to bear decisively.

From intercepting pager signals in the hills of southern Lebanon to training shadow cyber units in the ruins of Syria, Hezbollah's journey through the electromagnetic domain tells a clear story. The listener has evolved. The shaper has emerged. And the battles yet to be fought will unfold not only in ruined cities and contested borderlands, but in the silent, contested space between transmissions — where every signal is both a lifeline and a liability, and where every misstep in the spectrum can turn the tide of war before the first rocket leaves its rail.

# CHAPTER 12 — HOW TO HACK A PAGER: A TECHNICAL INTERLUDE

Before the world encrypted its messages and shielded its transmissions behind layers of cryptographic protection, there was a simpler kind of trust: the assumption that the air itself was safe. Early wireless communication systems, including pagers, operated on this principle. They broadcast their signals freely, without encryption, without authentication, and without much concern for interception. In the world of analog radios and slow, expensive scanning receivers, that assumption was rarely challenged.

The first generation of paging protocols — most notably POCSAG (Post Office Code Standardization Advisory Group) — embodied this mindset. Developed in the 1970s and widely adopted in the 1980s, POCSAG prioritized efficiency. It allowed thousands of users to receive messages through centralized high-power transmitters, distributing vital information to medical staff, emergency services, logistics workers, and technical personnel with extraordinary speed for its time. FLEX, developed by Motorola later in the 1990s, built on these principles, offering improved bandwidth efficiency and lower battery consumption but inheriting the same basic flaw: no expectation that the transmission itself needed to be protected.

The idea was simple. Pagers were one-way devices. They received, they did not transmit. If no response was possible, and if messages could only be seen by those holding the correct physical device, why worry about eavesdroppers? The technical and financial barriers to interception seemed high. Specialized receivers were expensive. Scanning pagers capable of operating across multiple frequencies were rare. Radio scanners existed, but were legally restricted and technically limited. The wireless environment appeared inhospitable to interception not because interception was impossible, but because it was impractical.

By the late 1980s and early 1990s, however, those barriers were already beginning to erode. Enthusiasts and researchers with access to radio scanners and simple decoding software could reconstruct pager traffic, even with analog equipment. Law enforcement agencies quietly used pager monitoring in surveillance operations. Private security firms exploited pager interception in corporate espionage cases. Yet these activities remained fringe, rarely discussed publicly, and often dismissed as irrelevant to operational security.

The critical flaw remained hidden: POCSAG and FLEX were open protocols. The structure of their transmissions was published, standardized, and well understood. A message broadcast over a pager network was a plain-text radio emission. Anyone with the right equipment, properly tuned and connected to the right decoding tools, could capture and read it without the sender or recipient ever knowing.

For militaries, critical infrastructure providers, and emergency services, this open-air vulnerability was a time bomb — one few recognized and fewer addressed. Assumptions of physical security ("we control the towers"), procedural security ("we trust our users"), and obscurity ("no one is listening") replaced technical security. By the time adversaries in asymmetric conflicts began exploiting these vulnerabilities seriously, the operational damage was already inevitable.

The Second Lebanon War in 2006 shattered these illusions publicly. Hezbollah's disciplined interception of Israeli pager and radio traffic — conducted with patient, methodical monitoring using relatively simple equipment — allowed them to map Israeli troop movements, anticipate logistics flows, and prepare ambushes with a precision that stunned traditional military planners. The flaw was not that Israeli pagers had been hacked. It was that they had been trusted in the first place.

Today, those early assumptions persist in legacy systems still in operation. Hospitals, energy facilities, transportation hubs, and emergency services across the world continue to use pagers, often unaware — or willfully ignorant — that their emissions are as open now as they were forty years ago. The air, once assumed to be silent and secure, remains an open conduit for those who know how to listen.

The story of pager interception is not one of hacking complex encryption algorithms or exploiting software vulnerabilities. It is the story of assuming that because a message vanishes into the air, it also vanishes from reach. It is the story of invisible exposure, and of how complacency in wireless trust became the quiet prelude to catastrophic operational failures.

In many ways, the act of building a passive pager interception station today is the most tangible demonstration of how little has changed since the earliest vulnerabilities were exposed. What once required specialized government equipment and technical teams now requires nothing more than patience, commodity hardware, and publicly available software. The barriers to entry have collapsed. The vulnerabilities remain.

The heart of a modern interception station is a Software Defined Radio (SDR) receiver. The most commonly used device for this purpose is the RTL-SDR, a USB dongle originally manufactured for digital television reception, later repurposed by the open-source community into a general-purpose radio scanner. For less than fifty dollars, an RTL-SDR dongle can monitor frequencies from approximately 25 MHz to 1.75 GHz, covering the entire range used by most pager systems worldwide.

More sophisticated alternatives exist. Devices like the Airspy Mini, HackRF One, or SDRplay offer wider bandwidth, higher sensitivity, and better signal-to-noise ratios. In operational environments where capture fidelity is critical — for instance, when monitoring weak or heavily congested paging carriers — these more advanced receivers offer a tangible advantage. But for basic interception, the humble RTL-SDR suffices.

The antenna is the second critical component. Most pager networks operate in the VHF range, typically around 138–174 MHz. A simple telescoping whip antenna, tuned roughly to the midpoint of this range, can capture pager traffic in urban and suburban environments with minimal difficulty. In rural areas or hardened operational environments, directional antennas such as Yagi arrays or even home-built tuned dipoles can dramatically increase reception range and signal clarity.

Software completes the build. SDR# (SDRSharp) is a widely used Windows-based program that interfaces with the SDR hardware, allowing visualization of the radio spectrum through a dynamic waterfall display. Frequencies can be scanned manually or swept systematically to locate active pager carriers, which appear as narrow, constant signals with characteristic pulse patterns.

Once a carrier is identified, the SDR is locked onto the frequency. Gain settings must be adjusted carefully. Insufficient gain will cause weak signals to vanish into the noise floor. Excessive gain will overload the receiver, distorting the demodulated output and rendering decoding unreliable. Environmental noise — from nearby electronics, urban RF clutter, or poor shielding — must be accounted for.

The raw audio output from the SDR software is then piped into a decoding program. On Windows, PDW (Pager Decoder Windows) remains the most popular tool for decoding POCSAG and FLEX pager transmissions. On Linux systems, multimon-ng provides similar capabilities. The decoder listens for the distinctive framing patterns that define pager messages, reconstructs the bitstreams, and translates them into human-readable alphanumeric text.

The result is unsettling in its simplicity. Patient monitoring updates from hospitals. Dispatch orders from emergency services. Maintenance requests from industrial control systems. Without a single password guessed, without a firewall bypassed, the operational lifeblood of entire organizations flows onto the screen of anyone who chooses to capture it.

In practice, professional passive interception setups employ further refinements. Bandpass filters tailored to the target frequency can clean up noisy signals, increasing decoding accuracy dramatically. Low-noise amplifiers (LNAs) positioned close to the antenna — before signal loss through long cables — can enhance weak signals without introducing excessive distortion. Wideband SDR receivers with sufficient storage capacity can record entire swaths of spectrum for later forensic analysis, allowing the interception of multiple pager networks simultaneously without the need for real-time tuning.

Even without such enhancements, however, the operational capability is devastating. A single fixed receiver, strategically placed, can monitor hospital traffic across an entire city. A mobile setup — mounted in a vehicle with GPS correlation — can triangulate pager transmitter locations over time, revealing network layouts, transmitter redundancies, and operational perimeters.

The most chilling aspect is how little technical skill is required. All necessary tools are open-source. The protocols are documented and standardized. The airwaves themselves are obligingly filled with information that, in any rational security environment, should never have been left unprotected.

Constructing a passive interception station is not merely an academic exercise. It is an act of operational reenactment — proof that the vulnerabilities this book describes are not relics of historical negligence, but active, living failures. It requires no privilege escalation, no malware deployment, no clandestine infiltration. It simply requires listening where others assumed no one would bother.

In the electromagnetic domain, assumptions are operational liabilities. And the simplest interception station — built with a laptop, a fifty-dollar receiver, and publicly available code — is a weapon against those who forgot that the air has no loyalty.

The vulnerabilities of pager networks are not theoretical artifacts from a bygone era; they are active operational risks that have been repeatedly exploited in the modern world with disturbingly little effort. In 2020, cybersecurity researchers conducted passive monitoring campaigns across several major North American cities, focusing specifically on hospital pager traffic. Using basic SDR setups assembled with inexpensive hardware and freely available software, they captured thousands of live messages over the course of several weeks. The intercepted content revealed a staggering array of sensitive information, including patient names, diagnoses, room assignments, treatment plans, and even detailed surgical updates. Particularly alarming were the Code Blue alerts — urgent signals indicating patients in full cardiac arrest — which often included personal identifiers and explicit descriptions of emergency response procedures. In some cases, researchers were able to reconstruct internal hospital triage timelines purely by correlating the pager messages as they flowed across the airwaves.

When confronted with these findings, many hospital administrators acknowledged the existence of the problem but cited legacy system dependence, budget constraints, and operational inertia as barriers to immediate remediation. Although encryption overlays for pager systems do exist, their adoption has been sporadic, and even where implemented, gaps persist. Administrative messages, maintenance alerts, and fallback systems often continue to operate without protection, leaking operational details into the electromagnetic spectrum despite efforts to secure critical patient data.

The problem extended beyond healthcare. In 2021, security researchers broadened their monitoring efforts to critical infrastructure sectors, including water treatment facilities, energy distribution nodes, and transportation networks. The results were no less troubling. Pager broadcasts routinely carried operational alerts concerning pump status, transformer failures, chemical treatment processes, and maintenance dispatches. Although no single message necessarily constituted a critical breach, the aggregation of this operational telemetry over time revealed detailed insights into system vulnerabilities, maintenance cycles, and response protocols. In one documented instance, researchers captured a sequence of pager messages that effectively mapped the maintenance schedules and system health of a regional water treatment facility, information that could have enabled a malicious actor to time physical sabotage or cyberattacks for maximum disruptive effect.

These exposures were not the result of complex exploits or sophisticated cyberattacks. They were the inevitable consequence of legacy systems continuing to operate in an environment that had fundamentally changed. The old assumptions — that radio traffic was difficult to intercept, that specialized knowledge was required, that obscurity provided sufficient protection — no longer hold. Software-defined radio technology, open-source decoding tools, and widespread public knowledge of paging protocols have democratized the capability to intercept and exploit pager communications. The very design features that once made pagers efficient — simple broadcast architecture, one-way communication, lack of encryption — now render them vulnerable in an environment where interception is cheap, undetectable, and devastatingly effective.

Every unsecured transmission is an opportunity for a patient adversary. A maintenance dispatch reveals not just a fault but a location where personnel will be stretched thin. A sequence of Code Blue alerts indicates not just medical emergencies but organizational strain under crisis. The aggregation of operational signals, even when individually mundane, allows an observer to reconstruct internal rhythms, identify vulnerable periods, and predict the behavior of complex organizations under stress. The vulnerabilities exposed by hospital pager traffic and industrial maintenance messages are not isolated anomalies. They are systemic operational failures, silently broadcast every day to anyone who chooses to listen.

The air, once thought empty and harmless, has become a reservoir of critical information. The cost of harvesting that information is low, the tools are accessible, and the strategic advantage it provides is immense. The organizations still relying on legacy pager systems are not merely clinging to outdated technology. They are broadcasting their vulnerabilities openly, continuously, and often unknowingly, surrendering operational security with every unguarded message that vanishes into the spectrum.

While a simple SDR receiver capturing a single frequency can reveal sensitive information, serious passive interception operations rarely limit themselves to such narrow monitoring. Wideband SDR systems, capable of capturing hundreds of megahertz of spectrum simultaneously, elevate interception from opportunistic listening to systematic surveillance. Instead of targeting individual frequencies manually, these systems record entire slices of the spectrum continuously, preserving every transmission, heartbeat, and maintenance ping for forensic analysis. This comprehensive capture allows adversaries to shift their focus from individual messages to broader operational patterns, reconstructing the unintentional rhythms of critical organizations over time.

The aggregation of these emissions creates a strategic map far richer than any isolated intercepted message could provide. By timestamping every captured burst of pager traffic and correlating their timing, a patient observer can infer operational tempos that are otherwise invisible. Hospital shift changes, maintenance surges at infrastructure facilities, emergency mobilizations, and even unusual activity patterns surrounding special events or crisis responses become discernible through careful analysis of raw transmission timing and intensity. Over days or weeks, a passive surveillance effort can build an increasingly detailed portrait of an organization's functional rhythms, identifying vulnerabilities that would be invisible through conventional means.

More sophisticated interception efforts expand further, employing multiple geographically dispersed receivers to enable triangulation of transmission sources. By measuring relative signal strength or calculating time difference of arrival (TDOA) across synchronized receivers, an interceptor can roughly geolocate the origin of transmissions without ever transmitting a signal themselves. Even mobile assets, such as ambulances, utility maintenance vehicles, and temporary command centers, can be tracked if they routinely communicate over unsecured paging systems or other broadcast channels. Over time, adversaries can reconstruct movement patterns, operational deployment strategies, and likely command and control nodes, all from emissions that defenders assumed were harmless background noise.

This kind of passive mapping is devastating precisely because it is invisible. No active probing occurs. No alerts are triggered. There is no malware, no login attempts, no system logs to review after the fact. The defenders never know they have been observed. Every unsecured transmission becomes another breadcrumb in the adversary's growing map of the battlespace. In cumulative form, these breadcrumbs reveal far more than any single incident ever could. They expose the assumptions and habits that structure real-world operations, offering insights into not only what a target is doing today, but how they are likely to react tomorrow under pressure.

Historical examples reinforce how catastrophic this passive leakage can become. During the Second Lebanon War, Hezbollah's disciplined monitoring of Israeli pager and radio traffic allowed them to predict Israeli troop movements, massing points, and logistical patterns well before kinetic engagements occurred. They did not need to hack complex networks or deploy sophisticated cyber attacks. They simply needed to listen patiently, harvest the patterns that unsecured transmissions revealed, and act with precision based on the operational intelligence thus gathered.

Today, this methodology is even more accessible. Modern SDR hardware, open-source software, and low-cost storage solutions mean that the kind of wideband interception and passive battlespace mapping that once required national-level resources can now be conducted by small, disciplined teams operating with little more than laptops and carefully placed antennas. The strategic threat is no longer defined by the complexity of the interception operation, but by its simplicity and deniability.

Those who continue to broadcast into the electromagnetic spectrum without discipline — trusting legacy systems, relying on obscurity, or assuming that no one is listening — are not merely exposing operational data. They are shaping the battlefield against themselves, creating invisible vulnerabilities that can be harvested methodically, silently, and catastrophically by those who recognize the spectrum for what it truly is: a battlespace where patience, not intrusion, wins the first phase of conflict.

# CHAPTER 13 — MISINFORMATION, SPOOFING, AND PSYCHOLOGICAL WARFARE

The evolution from interception to deception was inevitable. Once the ability to listen was mastered, the next logical step was to speak with a stolen voice. In an environment where signals themselves had become weapons, it was no longer sufficient to merely harvest information passively. The greater advantage lay in shaping the information space of the adversary, manipulating what they heard, what they believed, and how they responded.

Misinformation campaigns and signal spoofing did not require advanced technology. They required understanding human psychology under stress, operational rhythms under pressure, and the subtle weight that a familiar signal, even slightly twisted, could carry on a battlefield. A copied format, a familiar call sign, a sequence that seemed legitimate enough to trust — these were the tools that turned interception into active psychological warfare.

In early conflicts where unsecured communications were rampant, simple tactics often proved devastatingly effective. Radio operators impersonated enemy units by mimicking cadence, jargon, and call-and-response structures learned from intercepted transmissions. Entire patrols were diverted by fake orders transmitted from mobile signal vans mimicking the correct frequencies. Commanders, overwhelmed by the chaos of fast-moving battles and often reliant on unsecured or poorly authenticated messaging systems, found themselves responding to enemy-designed narratives, believing them to be legitimate operational directives.

The psychological impact was profound. Units began to doubt their own communications nets. Orders were second-guessed. Coordination frayed not because the enemy was stronger, but because the enemy had infected the decision-making loop itself. Trust, once eroded, degraded combat effectiveness faster than any direct kinetic engagement could. The weapon was not firepower. It was doubt.

Modern adaptations of these early spoofing methods have become more sophisticated but remain rooted in the same principles. In the electromagnetic battlespace, authenticity is often inferred, not verified. Systems built on speed and expediency — pagers, field radios, even battlefield texting platforms — were often designed without strong authentication layers. When emissions security collapsed, so did the ability to trust that any given signal was genuine.

There are credible accounts from asymmetric conflicts where spoofed communications led enemy units into pre-positioned ambushes. In some cases, the deception was subtle: an order for a slight repositioning of a patrol, a re-tasking of a supply column to a different route. In others, it was more dramatic: false evacuation orders prompting panic withdrawals, or fabricated emergency alerts forcing commanders to divert forces unnecessarily. Each fake message had a ripple effect, magnified by the inherent friction and confusion of combat.

The methodology was straightforward. First, intercept enough legitimate traffic to build a model of how real orders looked and sounded. Identify gaps in authentication procedures, vulnerabilities in signal discipline, or simple human fatigue points. Then inject plausible but false orders into the system, trusting that the enemy's own command-and-control inertia would carry the deception further than any single transmission could.

The use of pager-like systems only made this easier. Their

broadcast nature meant that once a signal was transmitted, it reached everyone within range without discrimination. A single spoofed pager alert could send ripples of confusion through multiple layers of command. If a logistics coordinator received an urgent, seemingly authentic resupply request, they moved. If a battlefield medic received an emergency extraction request with familiar identifiers, they responded. Speed, the same virtue that made pagers effective tools for coordination, became the channel through which deception propagated almost effortlessly.

Psychological operations did not stop at tactical misdirection. They expanded into the realm of strategic shaping. If a unit could be made to believe it was isolated, outflanked, or abandoned, its operational resilience degraded dramatically. Spoofed messages warning of encirclement, exaggerated casualty reports broadcast through compromised channels, or false alerts of enemy breakthroughs all served to fragment morale and sow panic at scale.

In conflicts where lines were fluid and situational awareness was already fragile, these information attacks magnified the fog of war into a paralyzing blindness. Leaders found themselves trapped in decision loops where every signal carried the potential to be a lie, where hesitation was as dangerous as action, and where trust in the electromagnetic environment — once an invisible foundation of command — collapsed entirely.

The technological arms race that followed was predictable. Stronger authentication protocols, encrypted communications, challenge-response verification systems, and multi-channel cross-checking measures were all introduced to counter the growing threat of signal spoofing. But none of these measures were absolute. Every system hardened for security became a new target for adversaries willing to invest time and resources into studying its weaknesses.

Even today, in battlefields layered with encryption and network authentication, the principle remains intact. If an adversary can insert doubt into the communications process, they can shape outcomes without firing a shot. The method may have evolved — from voice impersonation to protocol-level forgery to cyber-augmented social engineering — but the goal remains the same. Own the signals, and you own the battlefield's psychology.

Spoofing operations have extended beyond traditional military contexts. In cyber-enabled conflicts, false messaging has been used to trigger political crises, fabricate battlefield victories, or erode public trust in institutions. In some instances, attackers have used public radio bands, satellite messaging systems, or even hacked civilian alert systems to broadcast false emergency warnings. The principle that once shaped tactical maneuver on small battlefields now scales into national and even global arenas, with information shaping operations designed to alter perceptions at the level of entire societies.

Pagers, with their broadcast simplicity and lack of validation, were an early proving ground for these techniques. But the lesson they taught remains critical. Control over the signal is control over the mind of the adversary. The power to inject a falsehood with enough plausible structure to be believed is the power to redirect decisions, fragment unity, and dismantle operational cohesion from within.

Misinformation campaigns built on signal spoofing exploit not just technological vulnerabilities, but human cognitive biases. In high-stress environments, individuals are more likely to accept information that aligns with their fears or expectations. An isolated unit already fearing encirclement is more susceptible to believing a false message confirming their worst anxieties. A command post already overwhelmed by contradictory reports is more likely to act on the first clear signal received, even if its authenticity is uncertain.

The adversary's job is not to create a perfect lie. It is to create a lie plausible enough to survive the first seconds of scrutiny — long enough for its effects to ripple outward, amplified by the chaos of operations. It is to create conditions where doubt is paralyzing, action is disjointed, and leadership is stripped of its ability to coordinate coherent responses.

Spoofing attacks do not need to be technically perfect. They need only to be psychologically effective.

The vulnerabilities exposed by early pager spoofing experiments laid the groundwork for modern exploitation techniques. In today's battlefields and contested environments, misinformation and signal manipulation have expanded into more sophisticated, multi-layered operations. Yet the core principle remains unchanged. Insert false signals into a trusted communication channel, allow human cognitive biases to do the rest, and reshape reality without a kinetic strike.

In the Syrian conflict, numerous reports emerged of tactical deception using false radio orders, text message alerts, and localized spoofing of battlefield communications. Militias and state actors alike used low-cost signal jammers and injectors to mimic official Syrian army broadcasts. Rebel units, already fragmented and operating under conditions of limited trust, were susceptible to fabricated retreat orders, warnings of imminent airstrikes, and feigned requests for ammunition resupply that never materialized. In the chaos of irregular warfare, the authenticity of a signal often mattered less than its urgency.

Similar patterns played out in Ukraine, where Russian-backed forces demonstrated a sophisticated understanding of electromagnetic shaping. Ukrainian soldiers reported receiving text messages on their personal phones warning them to abandon their positions to avoid artillery strikes — messages that often preceded real bombardments, amplifying the psychological impact. Some units received spoofed calls appearing to originate from friendly command centers, giving withdrawal instructions or falsely claiming that reinforcements had been captured. The goal was not simply to confuse. It was to paralyze. To insert hesitation at the exact moment decisive action was needed.

The technical methods varied. In some cases, sophisticated IMSI-catchers mimicking cell towers were used to inject fake messages into soldiers' phones. In others, localized signal repeaters rebroadcast altered versions of legitimate communications. Sometimes it was as crude as jamming the real signal while broadcasting an impostor version on a nearby frequency. The technological layer mattered less than the psychological exploitation underneath. The victim needed only to believe, for a few critical seconds, that the falsehood was true.

The consequences of successful signal spoofing in combat environments are disproportionate to the technical effort required. A single false order leading to an unnecessary retreat can collapse a defensive line. A faked casualty report can trigger a breakdown in morale far beyond the immediate tactical space. A fabricated supply shortage can cause commanders to make desperate, irrational decisions that ripple outward across entire operational zones.

Even outside formal military engagements, spoofing operations have proven devastating. In 2018, residents of Hawaii received a terrifying push notification on their mobile phones warning of an incoming ballistic missile attack. "THIS IS NOT A DRILL," the message emphasized. Although the false alert was attributed to operator error rather than malicious action, the incident exposed a critical truth: trusted channels, once compromised or mishandled, create instant mass psychological effects.

Imagine if such a broadcast had been engineered deliberately.

A single false missile alert injected into the emergency alert infrastructure of a major city could trigger mass panic, economic disruption, and cascading political consequences — all without a single bomb being dropped. The power of signal control extends far beyond battlefield units. It reaches into the fabric of civilian society, financial systems, governance stability.

This is not hypothetical. Adversarial state actors have explored methods to compromise or spoof civilian emergency alert systems, public warning networks, and even air traffic control communications. The goal is not always immediate destruction. Often, it is strategic conditioning — eroding public trust in the reliability of alerts, fraying the social contract between institutions and populations, preparing the ground for broader psychological destabilization.

Military forces are not immune. No amount of encryption or hardened infrastructure can fully compensate for human vulnerability to shaped information. In training environments, red teams routinely demonstrate how misinformation injected into communications nets can fracture even highly disciplined units. A simulated false order, a fabricated casualty report, or a fake signal about a chemical threat can derail operations in minutes. If it works in controlled exercises, it works even more effectively under the real stresses of combat.

Modern defensive strategies acknowledge the risk. Cross-channel authentication — requiring confirmation of critical orders through multiple independent systems — is now standard in high-value military operations. Behavioral training emphasizes skepticism of unexpected signals, encouraging operators to challenge unusual orders, verify independently, and fall back on established decision frameworks when in doubt. Yet these defenses rely heavily on time, bandwidth, and human judgment — luxuries often unavailable in fluid combat or crisis conditions.

Spoofing operations exploit precisely these gaps. They aim for the pressure points where time constraints, operational stress, and the instinct to act quickly create opportunities for manipulation. They do not seek to defeat systems technologically. They seek to defeat operators psychologically.

The future evolution of spoofing will likely blend even more seamlessly into the broader cyber and electromagnetic battlespace. With artificial intelligence capable of generating synthetic voices, crafting convincingly formatted digital communications, and mimicking known traffic patterns, the difficulty of discerning real from fake will only increase. In coming conflicts, the signals that adversaries intercept and inject may be so finely tuned to the target's expectations that even sophisticated operators will struggle to distinguish them.

Pagers were merely the first, crude example of this vulnerability. Open, unencrypted, unauthenticated broadcasts taught early practitioners how easily operational rhythms could be mapped, mimicked, and manipulated. What began with simple fake orders in unsecured radio environments now extends into a future where every node of communication — every phone, every command net, every alert system — must be assumed contested unless proven otherwise.

The battles of tomorrow will not just be fought over territory, resources, or access to digital systems. They will be fought over perception itself. Over the ability to shape what the enemy believes, what they fear, what they hesitate to do. Over the invisible battlefield that exists not in the code of a hacked server or the encryption of a radio transmission, but in the choices made by humans under pressure.

And in that battlefield, the art of spoofing — the ancient art of speaking in the enemy's trusted voice — will remain as decisive as ever.

The tools and technologies that enable spoofing will continue to evolve, but their foundation rests on something older and far more immutable: human trust. In every system built for speed, efficiency, and coordination, there remains an underlying assumption that the source of a message can be known, that the chain of custody for information is intact. When this assumption is undermined, the system collapses not through external force, but through internal doubt.

Spoofing attacks aim precisely at this weakness. They do not need to destroy communications infrastructure to win. They need only to pollute it. They need to make every signal suspect, every directive questionable, every order a potential trap. The strength of a military, a corporation, a government is built on the ability to act decisively on trusted information. Spoofing erodes that decisiveness, replacing it with hesitation and second-guessing at the moments when clarity is most needed.

In the operational domain, this translates into real and measurable effects. Units pause before executing orders. Commanders delay critical decisions seeking verification. Staff officers overload already saturated networks with redundant authentication requests. The tempo of operations slows, cracks widen, adversaries exploit openings created not by superior firepower, but by superior manipulation of perception.

Strategically, the implications are even greater. In future conflicts, the contest for information authenticity will not merely be a supporting activity to kinetic operations. It will be a primary theater of war in its own right. Victory will not necessarily go to the side with the strongest encryption, the fastest weapons, or the deepest cyber arsenals. It will go to the side that maintains internal coherence under informational assault — that preserves trust inside its own decision-making cycles while injecting doubt into the enemy's.

The lessons of early pager spoofing, primitive as they were, foreshadowed this future. They demonstrated that even in the absence of technical sophistication, control over the appearance of authenticity was enough to cause chaos. A fake resupply order, a fabricated withdrawal request, a falsified emergency alert — all were sufficient to disrupt the enemy's internal synchronization, forcing decisions that benefited the attacker without requiring a single kinetic engagement.

Modern military planners increasingly acknowledge that the electromagnetic spectrum is not just a technical resource but a contested battlespace in its own right. Control over emissions, signal discipline, and authentication are recognized as critical pillars of operational security. Yet even with encrypted radios, multi-factor authentication, and satellite-based command nets, the underlying human reliance on perceived authenticity remains a vulnerability that cannot be patched with technology alone.

Spoofing exploits the gap between technical assurance and human belief. It operates in the psychological space where urgency, fear, fatigue, and assumption collide. In environments saturated with information, where milliseconds matter and the cost of hesitation is measured in lives, adversaries who master the art of timely, plausible deception will hold disproportionate power.

No system is immune. Even the most hardened, disciplined forces are vulnerable in moments of exhaustion, under the pressure of cascading crises, or facing information saturation designed to overwhelm verification procedures. Spoofed signals do not have to be perfect; they have to be timely, plausible, and injected into the right pressure point at the right moment. Like a wedge driven into a fault line, their force is magnified by the fractures already present.

The battle for trust, once abstract, is now operationally decisive. It is fought not just through cybersecurity measures and encryption upgrades, but through culture, training, and organizational resilience. Forces must be conditioned to operate under informational uncertainty, to recognize when communications may be compromised, and to rely on decentralized decision frameworks when the reliability of central command is in doubt.

Resilience to spoofing does not mean perfect detection of every deception attempt. It means the ability to recognize when doubt must be accepted, when redundancy must be leveraged, when action must proceed even in an environment where some signals cannot be trusted. It demands a shift in mindset from blind reliance on communications systems to a more adversarial, skeptical, and layered approach to decision-making.

The invisible war for control over trusted signals will define the operational environments of the future. It will not be fought with massive armies clashing head-on, nor solely with cyber weapons disabling infrastructure. It will be fought inside the minds of commanders and operators, in the split-second between receiving an order and deciding whether to believe it.

Spoofing is not merely a tactical threat. It is a strategic method for eroding the fundamental cohesion of adversary forces. By sowing distrust at every level — between commanders and subordinates, between operational centers and frontline units, between national leadership and civilian populations — an attacker can achieve strategic paralysis long before a single shot is fired.

The pager systems of yesterday taught that communications could be intercepted, mimicked, and weaponized even with primitive tools. Today, the tools are more advanced, the stakes are higher, and the battlespace extends from foxholes to fiber optics to satellites. Yet the principle endures. He who controls perception controls action. He who controls action controls outcomes.

In the coming conflicts, victory may hinge less on who has the largest arsenal and more on who can speak most convincingly in the enemy's voice — at the right time, with the right signal, shaped perfectly to exploit the moment of doubt that always lies just beneath the surface of even the most disciplined operation.

And it will not be enough to intercept the enemy's communications. It will not be enough to defend one's own. The decisive advantage will belong to those who understand that war itself is a contest of trusted signals, and that every transmission, every order, every whispered alert is a potential battlefield unto itself.

The history of warfare is filled with examples where perception, not strength, determined the outcome. In ancient battles, false retreats lured enemies into ambushes. During World War II, entire phantom armies were created with inflatable tanks, fake radio traffic, and fabricated operational orders to mislead enemy intelligence services. In each case, the manipulation of information created opportunities far disproportionate to the resources required. Spoofing in the electromagnetic era is merely the latest incarnation of this timeless principle.

The invisible terrain of trusted communications has become as real and decisive as any physical high ground. Where once armies sought to dominate hills and choke points, today they seek to dominate belief — to seize the cognitive terrain of their adversaries before the first missile launches or the first tanks cross a border. The actors who master the shaping of signals, the timing of deceptions, and the implantation of hesitation will hold advantages that raw numerical superiority can no longer guarantee.

There is a certain elegance in this form of conflict. It requires an economy of force, a precision of understanding about the enemy's psychology, an intimate knowledge of operational processes and how to disrupt them subtly, invisibly. Spoofing is not about overwhelming systems; it is about surgically inserting falsehoods that magnify internal friction until cohesion fractures naturally under pressure.

In the future, strategic victories may not be won by conquest, but by the systematic corrosion of trust. A war could be lost before the main forces ever engage if command centers fall into a recursive loop of second-guessing, if frontline units hesitate at the critical moment, if political leadership can no longer distinguish reality from manipulated perception.

Spoofing is an accelerant to that corrosion. It provides the toolset to reach inside the decision cycles of adversaries, to insert poisoned signals at key points, to push small, almost invisible wedges that will, under the stress of operational tempo, split cohesion apart. The best deceptions will not appear fantastical or absurd. They will look almost ordinary — small anomalies introduced at just the right time to tilt entire chains of action off course.

As the technological barriers to spoofing decrease, the demand for resilience against it becomes a strategic imperative. Secure communication channels are necessary but insufficient. Forces must cultivate an adversarial awareness within themselves, training operators to recognize when the environment has shifted from merely contested to actively manipulated. Organizations must assume that every system — no matter how encrypted or hardened — is subject to compromise at the perception layer.

Crisis decision-making must evolve to function even when certainty cannot be guaranteed. Redundancy, cross-verification, fallback protocols, and mission command principles that empower decentralized, trust-based leadership will become central pillars of operational survival. Trust will need to be redefined — not as blind faith in signals, but as trust in disciplined processes, hardened judgment, and trained skepticism under pressure.

Spoofing is not an aberration. It is the natural consequence of any environment where trusted signals exist and where adversaries have the opportunity to contest them. As operations move increasingly into complex, multi-domain battlespaces — blending cyber, electromagnetic, kinetic, and psychological dimensions — the control and manipulation of communications will be inseparable from the broader art of war itself.

The pager systems of the late twentieth century were early warning signs, not just of technical vulnerabilities but of the enduring human vulnerabilities that technology can amplify. Their failures were primitive by modern standards, yet they exposed a truth that remains relevant: that information, once compromised, can be more devastating than physical defeat.

Spoofing, when executed with precision, operates below the thresholds that traditionally trigger response. It undermines without revealing itself. It shifts decisions without leaving immediate forensic evidence. By the time its effects are visible, by the time units are routed or coalitions fracture, the seeds have long since been planted, watered by doubt and accelerated by the enemy's invisible hand.

Victory in the wars of the future will require more than superior firepower or faster cyber capabilities. It will require institutional cultures that understand trust as both a weapon and a vulnerability. It will require leaders who can operate amidst contested truths, who can maintain unity of purpose even when signals are ambiguous, and who can recognize that hesitation, once introduced into the bloodstream of an operation, is often fatal.

Spoofing will not always be decisive on its own. But it will always be present — a low, continuous pressure applied against the seams of trust, waiting for stress, fear, or confusion to create the first cracks.

In an environment where every message could be genuine or poisoned, the ultimate contest will not be over bandwidth, encryption strength, or network architecture. It will be over mental resilience — the ability to act decisively in an atmosphere of uncertainty, to operate with partial information without falling prey to adversary manipulation, to understand that in the domain of trusted signals, the greatest strength is neither silence nor shouting, but disciplined judgment shaped under fire.

The battle for perception is already underway. The question is no longer whether adversaries will attempt to shape it. The question is how ready forces are to survive and prevail when every signal — every page, every order, every call for help — may already be a contested space, and when the enemy's greatest weapon is not the bullet, but the doubt embedded inside the message.

Spoofing, at its core, is not merely a tactical trick or an opportunistic hack. It is the deliberate engineering of cognitive terrain. It is the recognition that the battlefield extends beyond geography and systems into the minds of those tasked with making decisions under duress. Every communication becomes an avenue for influence, every signal an opportunity to shape perception subtly, invisibly, decisively.

As forces across the world race to harden their networks and encrypt their channels, they risk missing the deeper truth. The contest is not about who can build the most technically secure infrastructure. It is about who can maintain operational coherence when infrastructure is compromised, when signals are contested, and when the ground truth is obscured behind layers of engineered noise.

Future conflicts will not begin with clear declarations or visible massing of forces. They will begin with the slow erosion of trust, seeded months or even years in advance through the quiet manipulation of communications environments. Spoofing will be one of the primary tools — not as isolated stunts, but as a sustained campaign to disorient, fragment, and disable an adversary's decision-making ability before kinetic operations ever commence.

In such a landscape, victory will belong to the side that treats the integrity of decision-making as a primary objective. This demands more than securing radios or segmenting networks. It demands cultivating decision-making cultures that are resilient to informational ambiguity, that are suspicious of perfect clarity delivered too easily, and that train leaders to recognize when they are being manipulated through the very systems designed to enable action.

The old assumptions — that an authenticated-looking signal is genuine, that a familiar format implies a familiar origin, that a system behaving normally is a system behaving truthfully — must be abandoned. In their place must rise a more adversarial mindset, one that sees every communication channel as a contested resource, and every unverified signal as a potential shaping operation.

Spoofing at scale — targeting civilian communications, public warning systems, financial transaction platforms, and critical infrastructure — will likely become a feature of future major conflicts. It will not be limited to soldiers and field commanders. It will extend to populations, leadership structures, and international alliances, sowing confusion, panic, and mistrust at every level.

The most dangerous aspect of spoofing is that it weaponizes trust itself. It uses the very systems designed to preserve order against their owners. The more critical the channel, the more devastating its compromise. A forged withdrawal order to a battalion is dangerous. A forged missile alert to a civilian population is catastrophic. A forged diplomatic communique to an ally could fracture coalitions that took decades to build.

The future battlespace will be saturated with signals, both genuine and false, constantly overlapping, constantly contesting each other. Adversaries will invest as much effort in studying an opponent's operational habits, communications formats, and procedural rituals as they do in building kinetic weaponry. The goal will not be to defeat forces through attrition, but to fracture them from within, using their own systems as delivery mechanisms for distrust.

Resilience will depend on more than better encryption. It will depend on training operators to think adversarially about information, to cross-verify, to trust but constantly validate, to develop instincts for when operational signals feel "wrong" even if technically they appear correct. It will depend on building command structures that can function in environments where perfect information is impossible, and where every action must be weighed not only against enemy kinetic capabilities but against enemy cognitive operations.

Spoofing reminds us that the center of gravity in modern conflict is not merely control over terrain or systems. It is control over belief — over what units believe about their situation, what populations believe about their leadership, what alliances believe about each other's commitments. Shaping that belief subtly, persistently, and decisively is the highest form of influence. Spoofing is simply one of the sharpest tools to accomplish it.

The war for trusted signals is not a side campaign. It is the campaign.
Control the signals, and you control decisions.
Control decisions, and you control outcomes.

In an age where the electromagnetic spectrum is as contested as the air, land, sea, and cyberspace, where every frequency carries both lifelines and vulnerabilities, the mastery of spoofing — and more importantly, the mastery of resilience against it — will separate those who endure from those who fracture.

The lessons are ancient, but the applications are immediate.

In every pager chirp, in every battlefield radio call, in every emergency alert, there lies a simple, brutal truth:
Trust is a weapon.
Belief is a battlespace.
And victory belongs to those who know how to fight there first.

# CHAPTER 14 — OLD TECH, NEW THREATS: LEGACY IN CYBER CONFLICT

In an age defined by machine learning, zero-click exploits, and autonomous weapon systems, there is a certain temptation to believe that modern conflict will be won or lost solely in the arena of cutting-edge technology. Governments and corporations alike spend billions securing cloud infrastructures, building resilient AI models, and racing to harden the most advanced edges of their digital footprints. Yet beneath this shimmering surface of technological innovation, a shadow battlefield persists — one built not on tomorrow's breakthroughs, but on yesterday's forgotten architectures. The old vulnerabilities, quietly ignored, remain not only present but exploitable. And in many cases, they represent the softest, most strategically significant targets available.

Legacy systems inhabit a strange space in cybersecurity discourse. They are understood intellectually to be a risk. Their known weaknesses are cataloged in compliance checklists and technical debt reports. Yet operationally, they persist, embedded deep within critical infrastructures and industrial systems. They remain because they work. They remain because replacing them is expensive, disruptive, and fraught with uncertainty. They remain because no one wants to explain why a vital system that has functioned for decades must suddenly be ripped out and replaced simply to satisfy abstract security models.

As a result, national critical infrastructures are laced with legacy components — unpatched control servers, outdated operating systems, serial-connected field devices, wireless communications using protocols never designed for authentication or encryption. Water treatment plants rely on PLCs older than most of their operators. Power grids depend on SCADA systems first installed when internet access was a luxury, not a given. Transportation hubs coordinate logistics over radio networks vulnerable to trivial interception and spoofing. These systems do not sit at the bleeding edge of technology. They sit at the heart of operational viability. And they are increasingly exposed not because they are weak in principle, but because the world around them has changed while they have remained still.

The problem is not simply technical obsolescence. It is cultural inertia. In many industrial and government environments, reliability is prized above all else. A system that functions without error for twenty years is seen not as a risk, but as a success. Security retrofits, where they are implemented, are often layered superficially onto these systems — firewalls at network edges, VPNs wrapping insecure protocols, segmentation strategies that assume the underlying nodes can be trusted. Yet attackers understand that the deeper vulnerabilities do not lie at the perimeter. They lie inside the trusted core, waiting for an adversary who is patient enough to work laterally, quietly, and with an eye toward the systems least capable of defending themselves.

The romance of zero-day exploits and AI-driven attacks has, in some cases, distracted defenders from the simpler, quieter threat: that access can be gained not through sophisticated hacking, but through the exploitation of forgotten, unmonitored systems operating on assumptions of trust forged decades ago. An unpatched Windows NT server running a critical database. A serial modem still listening for remote maintenance commands. A broadcast pager system coordinating logistics without authentication. These are not hypotheticals. They are common, persistent realities in industries ranging from energy to healthcare to defense logistics.

Attackers have long recognized the value of these soft targets. Nation-state operations, in particular, have demonstrated a preference for patience over glamour. Campaigns attributed to advanced actors have consistently shown a willingness to use old vulnerabilities, to burrow into legacy systems where defenses are weakest, to compromise trusted communications and management planes that defenders forgot to harden because they seemed too old to matter. In many ways, the sophistication of the attack lies not in the technical complexity of the exploit, but in the strategic vision to pursue pathways most defenders assumed were irrelevant.

The myth that legacy equals safety — that obscurity, age, or operational obscuration provide protection — is perhaps the most dangerous cultural vulnerability still prevalent in critical infrastructure security. An industrial controller installed before cybersecurity was a field does not benefit from ignorance of modern threats. If anything, it is more vulnerable, built without the basic design principles that newer systems take for granted. It expects trust. It assumes command channels are clean. It cannot distinguish between a legitimate operator and an adversary who has learned the command syntax and network topology through lateral reconnaissance.

The presence of these legacy systems transforms the risk landscape. It shifts the center of gravity away from hardened endpoints and into the shadow zones where forgotten devices, old protocols, and outdated assumptions still govern essential operations. A modern power station may be protected by redundant firewalls, real-time monitoring, and anomaly detection systems tuned to detect sophisticated attacks against its primary network. But a thirty-year-old auxiliary control module, reachable through a maintenance network overlooked during modernization, may provide a quiet, uncontested entry point to disrupt core operations.

The same logic applies across industries. In transportation, outdated signaling systems still govern rail networks. In healthcare, legacy imaging equipment transmits unencrypted patient data across internal hospital networks. In manufacturing, supervisory control systems speak Modbus or DNP3 without authentication, trusting that segmentation will prevent outsider access — a trust that evaporates the moment an attacker breaches a less-protected adjacent environment.

Legacy systems are not just operational risks. They are strategic liabilities. In a contested cyber environment, they become the equivalent of undermanned outposts on a critical flank — tempting targets for adversaries looking not for direct confrontation, but for quiet, sustainable footholds from which to launch future operations.

The persistence of these systems creates opportunities for asymmetric attack strategies. Advanced actors need not defeat the strongest parts of a network. They need only to compromise the weakest nodes, pivoting quietly, moving laterally, and accumulating control over time. This approach reduces the need for high-risk, high-visibility exploits. It enables operations that prioritize longevity, persistence, and control over shock and awe.

Even as defenders invest in AI-powered detection systems and predictive analytics, the quiet gravitational pull of legacy vulnerability grows stronger. New systems must coexist with old ones. Modern cyber defenses must wrap around infrastructures built before cyber was a consideration. And in this coexistence, cracks form — cracks wide enough for patient adversaries to slip through unnoticed.

The threat is not theoretical. It is operational, it is structural, and it is growing.

Real-world incidents have already illustrated how legacy systems, overlooked in the rush toward modernization, can become critical vulnerabilities. In 2015, during the now-infamous attack on Ukraine's power grid, attackers leveraged not some exotic zero-day exploit, but basic lateral movement through trusted, under-secured networks. Legacy industrial control systems, reliant on decades-old communications protocols, provided the crucial openings. Once inside, adversaries did not need to defeat modern cybersecurity defenses head-on. They operated through the seams, the places where old systems connected to new ones, where assumptions about trust had never been revisited.

The breach was not an anomaly. It was a demonstration. Infrastructure sectors across the world operate under similar conditions. Air traffic control systems in many nations still rely on radar installations and telemetry links built on foundations older than the internet itself. Water treatment plants manage flow control through serial devices that can be hijacked remotely if an adversary navigates past perimeter defenses. In some cases, life-critical systems still depend on wireless or leased-line communications that lack even the most basic encryption or authentication because they were never designed for a contested environment.

When attackers seek to establish long-term presence inside a network, legacy systems offer more than just initial entry points. They provide durable footholds, places to hide, to maintain persistence even when defenders perform incident response on the more modern surfaces of the network. Old control servers, forgotten maintenance interfaces, outdated backup systems — these artifacts of technological archaeology allow attackers to survive clean-up operations, to reinsert themselves into operations even after major remediation efforts.

Nation-state actors have shown particular skill in exploiting these opportunities. The campaigns attributed to groups like Sandworm, APT33, and others consistently display a strategic patience that favors finding legacy targets over chasing headline vulnerabilities. They understand that a system abandoned by active maintenance is a system abandoned by active defense. They understand that the easiest way into a hardened fortress is often through the crumbling side gate no one remembers exists.

The problem extends beyond industrial control environments. Legacy enterprise systems — unpatched Active Directory servers, end-of-life VPN concentrators, aging email servers — remain scattered across corporate and government networks. These systems often coexist with newer, well-defended assets, creating hybrid environments where the security posture is defined not by the strongest component but by the weakest overlooked link. Even as organizations migrate to cloud infrastructures, on-premises legacy systems often remain for reasons of regulatory compliance, data residency, or simple operational inertia.

In one case, a major financial institution suffered a breach not through its front-line digital banking platform, but through an ancient employee management portal that had been migrated across successive generations of infrastructure without ever undergoing fundamental security hardening. The portal, running on a decade-old version of a web application server, became the unguarded alleyway into a system that had otherwise been heavily fortified. The breach was not prevented by the institution's expensive next-generation firewalls or its AI-powered fraud detection systems because the legacy portal operated outside the perimeter assumptions baked into those defenses.

This pattern repeats itself across sectors. The larger and older the organization, the more likely it is to carry within it a hidden skeleton of legacy systems — operationally indispensable, poorly documented, and difficult to modernize. These systems are not just technical artifacts. They are strategic vulnerabilities disguised as operational conveniences. They persist because removing them is expensive, disruptive, and politically difficult. Yet their presence reshapes the risk landscape in ways that even sophisticated defenders often underestimate.

Attackers do not need to compromise the crown jewels immediately. They need only to compromise enough legacy infrastructure to gain persistence, observation, and influence. From there, access can be escalated slowly, methodically, across months or even years. In hybrid environments, where cloud-native assets coexist with on-premises legacy servers, attackers can use the trust assumptions built into authentication and identity management frameworks to pivot between old and new seamlessly.

Defending against this class of threat requires more than traditional perimeter hardening. It requires a relentless, often politically difficult program of discovery, risk assessment, and decommissioning of legacy systems. It requires acknowledging that every old server left online, every forgotten control panel still reachable, every unauthenticated communications link still active is not a benign operational artifact but a potential bridgehead for an adversary.

This kind of remediation is unglamorous. It rarely fits into glossy cybersecurity marketing campaigns or political talking points. It is slow, tedious, expensive, and often resisted by operational teams focused on uptime and continuity. Yet it is one of the most strategically important forms of cyber defense available. It denies adversaries the quiet, persistent footholds they need to turn minor initial compromises into major operational effects.

Ignoring legacy systems in the name of focusing on "future threats" is an invitation for strategic failure. Cyber conflict is not defined solely by cutting-edge attacks on cutting-edge systems. It is defined by the exploitation of the entire operational footprint, old and new alike. Legacy systems are part of that footprint, and in many cases, they are the weakest, most inviting parts.

The broader strategic community is slowly awakening to

this reality. National cybersecurity strategies increasingly emphasize asset visibility, supply chain integrity, and the need to treat legacy technology as part of critical risk management. Yet the gap between policy acknowledgment and operational execution remains large. The inertia of legacy persists, embedded not just in technology stacks, but in budgets, procurement practices, and cultural attitudes toward risk.

Until that gap is closed, old technology will continue to pose new threats.

And in the next major cyber conflict, the deciding blow may not come through a sophisticated AI-crafted exploit or a quantum-enhanced attack. It may come through a decades-old system no one thought worth protecting, compromised quietly, patiently, and at a moment of the adversary's choosing.

Adversaries do not stumble into legacy vulnerabilities by accident. They seek them deliberately, integrating their discovery and exploitation into the early phases of campaign planning. While defenders often think of attacks in terms of technical signatures or tactical exploits, sophisticated actors view infrastructure holistically, studying the operational environment for weak points, unmonitored systems, and aging nodes that no longer fit into the current security model. Legacy systems, often treated as afterthoughts by defenders, become primary targets for those who recognize their strategic leverage.

A legacy server may not contain crown-jewel data or offer obvious pivot points on its own, but it offers something more valuable: quiet access. An unmonitored node allows adversaries to observe operational rhythms, to harvest credentials over time, to map internal trust relationships without triggering alarms tuned to watch the modern perimeter. From there, they move patiently, escalating privileges, extending reach, and planting artifacts that will persist even through partial remediation efforts.

This approach transforms the legacy system from a simple vulnerability into an operational anchor — a beachhead inside the defender's infrastructure. And because legacy systems are often less scrutinized, less actively monitored, and less regularly patched, they offer a durability that attackers value deeply. In environments where every new alert triggers investigation and incident response, a quiet foothold on an old, semi-forgotten system provides a base of operations immune to many of the detection methods modern cybersecurity relies upon.

The strategic value of such footholds is not limited to espionage or quiet reconnaissance. In the event of a full-scale conflict or escalation to destructive cyber operations, pre-positioned access through legacy systems offers an adversary the ability to degrade, disrupt, or disable critical infrastructure with speed and plausible deniability. It allows for precise targeting of key operational nodes without the need to mount high-risk, high-visibility attacks against better-defended modern systems.

Shadow systems — legacy components no longer formally documented, outside the scope of active defense plans — compound this risk. These systems persist not because of conscious malice, but because of the inherent complexity of large-scale infrastructure environments. Over time, mergers, acquisitions, emergency deployments, and evolving operational requirements leave behind technical sediment — servers whose original owners have moved on, control systems bypassed by newer automation, communication links maintained for redundancy but no longer central to daily operations.

In a world where asset visibility is still a persistent challenge even for the best-resourced organizations, these shadow systems form the uncharted zones of critical infrastructure. And in those zones, adversaries find opportunities to maneuver undetected.

The operational blindness created by shadow systems is not merely a technical oversight. It is a strategic vulnerability. It means that defenders cannot accurately model their own attack surface. It means that risk assessments, no matter how rigorous, are incomplete by definition. It means that security investments, however sophisticated, may be aimed at the wrong targets while the real point of entry sits unmanaged and unseen.

This asymmetry — between what defenders know and what adversaries can discover — has already shaped the outcomes of multiple major cyber operations. It is not simply a matter of patching faster or responding better. It is a matter of fundamentally rethinking how infrastructures are managed over their entire lifespan, acknowledging that every device, every system, every node left online carries an operational risk profile that changes over time.

In modern conflict, where time horizons extend beyond immediate engagements into campaigns of years or even decades, the patience to exploit legacy vulnerabilities offers outsized strategic returns. While defenders cycle through news-driven priorities — hardening against the latest ransomware technique, deploying the newest AI threat detection model — adversaries can operate on slower, deeper timelines, investing in mapping and maintaining access to legacy components until the political or operational conditions align for decisive action.

The broader problem is compounded by organizational factors. Budgets are often allocated for new initiatives, not for remediating old systems. Executive attention gravitates toward visible innovation, not the hidden, grinding work of decommissioning legacy architectures. Risk reports prioritize threats that can be clearly articulated and mapped to active compliance frameworks, leaving diffuse or undocumented legacy exposures in the margins where they are easier to ignore.

The adversary operates differently. They do not need the permission of a budget cycle. They do not need to justify their actions to oversight committees or auditors. They move through the environment with an eye toward what is not secured, what is not monitored, what is not prioritized. Legacy systems, from their perspective, are not technical debt. They are strategic opportunities.

As the global cybersecurity community intensifies its focus on supply chain risk, software bill of materials transparency, and the resilience of emerging technologies, the need to grapple seriously with legacy exposure becomes even more urgent. The backdoors of tomorrow will not be installed only through compromised updates or advanced persistent threats embedded in firmware. They will be maintained quietly through systems left online by inertia, by bureaucracy, by the human tendency to prioritize new construction over the dismantling of what has been left behind.

National adversaries understand this dynamic intimately. Their doctrine reflects it. Their campaigns show a consistent bias toward patient, methodical exploitation of systemic weaknesses rather than high-risk confrontation. They win not by overwhelming defenses in dramatic engagements, but by finding and exploiting the quiet corners defenders have abandoned — by making the old, the forgotten, and the operationally invisible into vectors for influence, persistence, and, when necessary, attack.

Legacy systems do not age gracefully in a contested environment. They either evolve through active maintenance and reintegration into the defensive architecture, or they decay into liabilities waiting to be triggered. And once triggered, the damage they enable can be massively disproportionate to their apparent importance.

The wars of the future will not be won purely through superior algorithms, faster processing, or more resilient cloud architectures. They will be shaped in part by the contest over legacy — over who can better manage, secure, or exploit the technological remnants of prior eras now embedded in the critical infrastructure of modern life.

The adversaries who understand this — who treat the entire operational footprint, old and new alike, as part of the battlefield — will enjoy a profound asymmetric advantage. The defenders who continue to overlook legacy risk, who treat old systems as afterthoughts rather than attack surfaces, will find themselves vulnerable at precisely the moment they believe themselves most secure.

The implications of legacy system exposure extend beyond individual organizations or isolated critical sectors. They shape national security environments at a strategic level. In an interconnected world, where energy grids cross borders, supply chains span continents, and communications infrastructure underpins both civilian life and military readiness, the persistence of legacy vulnerabilities creates systemic risks that cannot be easily isolated or contained.

When old technology lingers in essential services, it creates interdependent fragility. A compromise in one sector — a breach of an outdated water treatment control system, a disruption of a hospital's unencrypted paging network, a compromise of a regional power distribution substation — can cascade across other domains, multiplying effects far beyond the original point of failure. In modern national infrastructure ecosystems, no system is truly isolated. Everything connects eventually, often through precisely the legacy interfaces least prepared for adversarial exploitation.

This interconnected fragility creates opportunities for adversaries to engineer effects with strategic patience. Rather than striking hardened national defenses directly, they can chip away at the peripheries, exploiting legacy exposures to build pressure, destabilize confidence, and create cumulative effects that, over time, erode national resilience without triggering the clear thresholds that would provoke conventional responses.

In this environment, national adversaries do not need to bring down entire grids or networks to succeed. They need only to create persistent low-grade disruptions — localized blackouts, regional supply shortages, communication failures in critical response units — seeded through the exploitation of legacy components and leveraged to sow doubt in the reliability of national institutions.

The psychological effects are as significant as the operational ones. Populations accustomed to stable, reliable services begin to lose confidence when infrastructure falters unpredictably. Businesses rethink investment decisions. Political leadership faces mounting pressure to respond to disruptions whose root causes remain obscure or deniable. Trust in national competence erodes — not through spectacular cyberattacks or public acts of digital sabotage, but through the slow, grinding exploitation of vulnerabilities no one prioritized fixing until it was too late.

Legacy systems thus become not only technical liabilities but instruments of political and social destabilization. Their persistence enables adversaries to engage in strategic shaping operations that weaken a nation's internal coherence over time. They provide the access points for adversarial campaigns aimed not merely at infrastructure disruption but at broader erosion of confidence, unity, and resilience.

The danger is magnified by the way modernization efforts often coexist uneasily with legacy dependencies. Even as nations roll out next-generation 5G communications networks, modernize defense command systems, and deploy cloud-native infrastructure for government services, they remain anchored by critical legacy components too costly, too complex, or too risky to replace fully. Modern systems increasingly depend on the operational reliability of their oldest, least secured counterparts.

Adversaries understand this duality. They design operational campaigns around it. Penetration of hardened cloud environments might be difficult, but finding an unmanaged legacy VPN endpoint, an unmonitored SCADA interface, or a forgotten telemetry link offers paths to the same outcomes — more quietly, more reliably, and often without detection.

In this sense, legacy exposure becomes a force multiplier for adversaries. It reduces the cost, complexity, and risk of mounting effective operations. It offers asymmetric pathways to strategic effects traditionally achievable only through high-end, resource-intensive cyber capabilities. And because these operations often fall below the threshold of overt conflict, they complicate attribution, response planning, and escalation management for defenders.

Closing the gap between legacy reality and modern defense requirements demands more than technical upgrades. It demands national strategies that integrate asset discovery, phased decommissioning, aggressive segmentation, and layered hardening of legacy infrastructure into core security planning. It demands a cultural shift away from treating old systems as untouchable relics and toward treating them as active components of a contested operational environment.

This is not a one-time project. It is a continuous operational discipline — an acknowledgment that in a world of persistent contestation below the threshold of declared war, every unmanaged device, every legacy communications path, every old control system left online by inertia becomes a vector for strategic exploitation.

Nations that treat legacy management as a peripheral issue will discover, too late, that their most sophisticated defensive systems are only as strong as the oldest, least-defended elements they continue to depend upon. Those that build sustained programs to eliminate, secure, or meaningfully harden legacy components will deny adversaries a critical avenue of advantage — not by outmatching them in technical sophistication, but by closing the vulnerabilities patience and strategic vision seek to exploit.

The shape of future conflict will not always be determined by who fields the newest weapons or the most advanced algorithms. It will be determined in part by who masters the long, grinding work of hardening the operational terrain against exploitation — old and new alike.

In that contest, legacy is not just a technical problem. It is a strategic battlefield. And it is one that few nations, even now, are fully prepared to defend.

The persistence of legacy vulnerabilities is not ultimately a failure of technology. It is a failure of imagination. It is the belief, often subconscious, that systems designed in an earlier era can continue indefinitely without adaptation, that what once served reliably can do so forever in a world that has changed beyond recognition.

This blindness is not unique to any one nation or industry. It is systemic, rooted in human habits of comfort, familiarity, and resistance to change. Infrastructure that fades into the operational background, functioning quietly year after year, ceases to feel urgent. It becomes invisible through repetition. Its risks, however well documented, are rationalized away in the daily calculus of budgets, operational continuity, and perceived trade-offs.

Adversaries thrive in this blindness. They map it, study it, exploit it not because they are more technologically advanced, but because they are often more disciplined in their long-term thinking. They understand that security is not a static achievement but a dynamic contest. And they recognize that the parts of a system least visible to defenders are the parts most vulnerable to attack.

The mythology of modern cyber conflict — with its emphasis on advanced persistent threats, exotic malware strains, and AI-driven attacks — risks perpetuating this blindness. It draws attention upward and outward, toward the gleaming edges of innovation, away from the rusted foundations that continue to support critical national functions. It teaches defenders to fear the improbable and neglect the inevitable.

Legacy systems are inevitable. Their vulnerabilities are inevitable. And unless confronted directly, their exploitation in future conflicts is inevitable.

The shift required is not purely technical. It is cultural. It demands that organizations, sectors, and nations treat legacy management as a core pillar of operational resilience, not as a side task to be deferred until funding, attention, or political will permit. It requires an uncomfortable reckoning with the fact that resilience is not built through adding new layers atop old weaknesses, but through the painstaking, often unglamorous work of eliminating those weaknesses at their roots.

This reckoning must extend across the entire operational landscape. Every facility relying on control systems older than the networks they now connect to. Every emergency response organization still coordinating through insecure legacy communications. Every cloud-migrated enterprise that leaves shadow infrastructure tethered to modern systems through forgotten interfaces and orphaned credentials.

The adversary's map of the battlefield will not be based on the public diagrams of hardened defenses. It will be built from the invisible terrain — the legacy systems, the obsolete links, the unguarded pathways that defenders have allowed to persist through neglect, denial, or simple operational inertia.

In that map, the vulnerabilities are not distributed evenly. They cluster around sectors, regions, and nations that have allowed the gap between technological modernization and operational security to widen over time. They cluster where budgets favor new projects over maintenance. They cluster where governance structures separate cybersecurity from operational risk management, treating them as parallel, rather than integrated, disciplines.

The future of strategic resilience will not be decided solely by who invents the most powerful new technologies. It will be decided by who can see clearly the parts of their own operational environments they have forgotten to protect. It will be decided by who can close the doors they did not even realize were still open.

In this future, legacy is not merely technical debt. It is strategic debt, accumulating interest in vulnerability every day it remains unpaid. Nations that invest in clearing this debt — systematically, ruthlessly, without allowing operational convenience to override strategic necessity — will build resilience that no adversary can easily fracture.

Those that delay, deny, or distract themselves with visions of a future unmoored from the realities of their own infrastructure will discover that their vulnerabilities are not theoretical artifacts. They are active weapons, lying dormant until the moment they are needed most by those who seek to do harm.

Old technology remains embedded at the heart of modern life. Old assumptions remain embedded at the heart of modern security thinking. In the contested battlespaces of the future, both will be tested.

Those who survive will be those who learn to see the old not as a comfort, but as a battleground. And who act accordingly.

# CHAPTER 15 — SIGNAL SHADOWS: LESSONS FOR MODERN CYBERSECURITY

The story of the pager wars is not simply a historical curiosity. It is a warning encoded in experience, a signal from the past meant for those willing to listen. In the rush toward advanced cyber defense, it is easy to believe that the threat landscape is defined by the latest vulnerabilities, the newest exploits, the most recent disclosures. But the lessons that matter most are often older. They are embedded in the patterns of failure that emerge whenever trust is misplaced, whenever visibility is lost, and whenever assumptions about security outrun the realities of technology.

Modern cybersecurity environments are larger, faster, and more complex than anything that existed during the early days of wireless interception. Yet the underlying dynamics have not changed. Systems that cannot be seen cannot be defended. Communications that are not authenticated cannot be trusted. Technologies that operate on outdated assumptions about isolation, obscurity, or insignificance are not simply artifacts of a prior era. They are active liabilities.

The first lesson drawn from the era of pager interception is simple: know what exists. Asset inventories are not a bureaucratic exercise. They are the foundation of operational security. Every unknown system is a potential blind spot. Every undocumented device is a potential avenue of exploitation. Without a comprehensive, living understanding of the operational environment, defenders are not defending a known terrain. They are defending an imagined one, a map missing key features that adversaries will inevitably discover and use.

In the pager era, systems broadcast into the air with the implicit assumption that no one was listening. The absence of visible threat was mistaken for the absence of actual threat. Today, the same mistake is made when organizations assume that devices connected only internally, or buried behind multiple layers of network infrastructure, are immune to adversary attention. Attackers do not operate under these assumptions. They map exhaustively. They inventory more thoroughly than the defenders themselves. They understand that persistence depends not just on penetrating hardened targets but on inhabiting the forgotten corners of the network, the operational equivalents of unsecured pagers quietly leaking sensitive data.

Modern defenders must approach their environments with the same thoroughness. Asset discovery is not a one-time project. It is a continuous operational discipline. Networks change daily. Devices are added, modified, abandoned, or repurposed in ways that formal change management often fails to capture fully. Shadow systems emerge not from malice but from human nature, from operational expediency, from the simple fact that in complex environments, entropy favors the creation of unmonitored nodes. The only counter to this is constant, active inventory — not just of what is supposed to be there, but of what is actually there.

The second lesson is equally stark: unencrypted communications must be treated as exposed communications. Pagers operated under the assumption that low visibility equated to security. Messages were short, technical, and presumed uninteresting to anyone outside the operational audience. Yet interception revealed how even mundane operational data could be leveraged for strategic advantage. Movement patterns, logistical rhythms, organizational hierarchies — all of these were visible through analysis of seemingly trivial messages.

Today, systems still operate under dangerous assumptions

about the value of data in transit. Internal communications between servers, telemetry traffic from IoT devices, maintenance interfaces for industrial equipment — all are often left unencrypted because they are perceived as being inside a trusted boundary. Yet boundaries are porous. Compromise one device, one pathway, and the attacker inherits the same trust. Encryption must be a default, not a selective afterthought applied only to outward-facing systems. Anything sent across a network must be assumed to be potentially observable by an adversary. Encryption, authentication, and verification are not luxuries. They are necessities for operational survival.

The third lesson is a deeper, structural one: realistic threat modeling must account for the adversary's perspective, not merely the defender's assumptions. In the pager wars, defenders believed certain communications were beneath the threshold of interest. They misjudged the cost-benefit calculus from the attacker's side. To an adversary facing asymmetry in conventional capabilities, every scrap of operational insight, every fragment of decision-making tempo, every leaked logistical detail offered leverage.

Modern threat modeling must operate on the same principle. Defenders must recognize that adversaries often derive value from data that defenders consider low-priority. Metadata, telemetry, error logs, legacy credentials, system version disclosures — these are not meaningless. They are puzzle pieces. They are indicators of posture, readiness, and vulnerability. They provide adversaries with the building blocks to craft more precise, more devastating attacks.

Realistic threat models must also recognize that adversaries are patient. They do not need immediate access to the crown jewels. They seek footholds, observation points, lateral movement pathways. They are willing to operate below detection thresholds for extended periods, harvesting low-level data until conditions are right for escalation. Defensive models built solely around the protection of high-value assets, without regard to how low-value assets can be weaponized as stepping stones, are incomplete and insufficient.

The fourth lesson is cultural. Trust assumptions must be continually challenged. In the pager era, operational trust was implicit. Messages were broadcast because they were believed to be harmless, or at least harmlessly opaque to outsiders. When that assumption was broken, when adversaries demonstrated that trust could be exploited through interception, the entire structure of operations had to adapt.

Modern organizations often operate on similarly implicit trust — in internal communications, in segmented network zones, in authentication methods inherited from less hostile eras. But in a contested environment, trust must be earned, maintained, and validated continuously. Communications must be authenticated not because it is convenient but because it is necessary. Devices must prove their identities. Users must verify their access rights. Systems must operate under the assumption that compromise is not a distant possibility but a present and persistent reality.

Trust is not the default condition of secure operations. It is the output of disciplined, adversarially aware processes that assume signals can be spoofed, identities can be forged, and boundaries can be crossed without warning.

These lessons are not theoretical abstractions. They are operational imperatives drawn from real failures — failures that cost lives, that disrupted operations, that handed adversaries advantages disproportionate to the simplicity of the attacks that enabled them. They are reminders that the complexity and sophistication of modern cybersecurity must not blind defenders to the enduring vulnerabilities rooted in visibility, authentication, encryption, and trust.

The pager wars ended not because pagers became

invulnerable, but because operational cultures adapted. Communications hardened. Assumptions about invisibility were discarded. Threat models evolved to recognize that what could be heard could be exploited, and that what could be exploited could, with patience, become decisive.

Modern defenders face a battlefield orders of magnitude more complex, but the principles remain the same. Visibility. Authentication. Encryption. Realistic threat modeling. Cultural humility in the face of evolving adversary capabilities.

The shadows that signal vulnerabilities are not confined to the past. They still move across modern networks, hidden by operational complexity, shielded by outdated trust models, waiting for those moments when defenders, distracted by the chase for the newest threats, forget the enduring lessons written in the compromises of the past.

The difference now is scale. A missed signal, a forgotten device, an unencrypted channel can ripple outward through global systems in ways unimaginable to those first caught unprepared in the hills of southern Lebanon or the crowded hospitals of 1990s urban centers. The consequences of forgetting the lessons of visibility, trust, and encryption are no longer local. They are systemic.

Cyber defense must begin with remembering. And remembering must begin with seeing clearly the invisible vulnerabilities we would rather not acknowledge.

Translating these lessons into practical cybersecurity doctrine requires more than acknowledgment. It demands operationalization. Visibility, for instance, cannot remain a conceptual goal. It must become a measurable discipline, embedded in daily security operations. Asset inventories must not be static spreadsheets created for audit purposes once a year. They must be dynamic, continuously updated through active discovery mechanisms that sweep environments for anomalies, unknown devices, and new connections without relying solely on manual reporting.

Discovery cannot be limited to managed devices. It must extend aggressively into the unmanaged, the embedded, the assumed. Rogue wireless devices, forgotten engineering workstations, outdated printers, vendor-supplied management consoles — every system with an electronic heartbeat must be accounted for or treated as hostile until proven otherwise. In a landscape where attackers prioritize the discovery of what defenders have forgotten, leaving even a single device unmonitored creates an unacceptable risk surface.

Modern cybersecurity architectures must treat the failure of visibility as an operational outage. If an organization cannot definitively enumerate what is connected, it cannot claim to control its environment. And if it cannot control its environment, it cannot hope to resist a patient, methodical adversary.

Encryption, too, must cease being treated as a performance trade-off or a perimeter defense. It must be endemic, layered into every point of communication, applied not because an external auditor demands it but because operational reality demands it. Every byte transmitted across a network should be encrypted unless there is a compelling, rigorously justified reason otherwise — and even then, the exceptions must be viewed as vulnerabilities to be mitigated, not conveniences to be normalized.

Authentication must be treated with the same severity. Legacy systems that cannot authenticate securely must be isolated, segmented, monitored, or replaced. The days of assuming that a device or user inside a trusted zone is safe must end. Zero trust is not a marketing slogan. It is the operational expression of the reality that compromise is not an if but a when — and that communications, identities, and transactions must prove themselves trustworthy at every interaction, not once at initial connection.

Realistic threat modeling must evolve beyond regulatory compliance matrices and tick-box risk assessments. It must begin with the assumption that adversaries are already studying the environment, looking for the forgotten, the unencrypted, the unauthenticated, the assumed-to-be-safe. It must account for human error, for operational shortcuts, for systems left in transitional states longer than intended. It must assume that breaches will happen not necessarily through the latest vulnerability disclosed at a security conference, but through the oldest system forgotten during the last merger, acquisition, or technology refresh cycle.

Organizations must train themselves to think like their adversaries. Not just in red-teaming exercises staged once or twice a year, but in daily operational mindsets. Every time a new system is deployed, defenders must ask: how will an adversary discover this? Every time a device is decommissioned, they must ask: what artifacts, if left behind, will create new footholds? Every time a communication pathway is configured, they must ask: if compromised, how could this be weaponized against us?

Defensive strategies must move beyond detection and response toward resilience. Detection assumes a defender will recognize a breach quickly enough to contain it. Resilience accepts that breaches will occur and designs systems that can absorb, survive, and recover from compromise without catastrophic failure.

Resilience starts with minimizing the impact radius of a breach. Segmentation is critical — not just logical network segmentation but operational segmentation. Systems should be architected so that the compromise of one node, one zone, or one communication pathway does not cascade uncontrollably into broader operational paralysis.

Authentication contexts must be tightly scoped. Devices

and users should have the minimum privileges required to perform their functions, no more. Access rights should be time-limited, audited continuously, and revoked aggressively when no longer necessary.

Monitoring must shift from reactive event logging to behavioral baselining. Knowing when something is wrong requires knowing what normal looks like at a granular level. In modern environments flooded with telemetry, signal-to-noise ratios must be actively managed. Detection strategies must emphasize deviation from known baselines, not just signature matching for known threats.

Most critically, defenders must cultivate the mental discipline to resist the cultural gravity of technological optimism. It is tempting to believe that new technologies will erase old risks, that innovations in encryption, authentication, AI, or blockchain will somehow compensate for operational blind spots left untouched. They will not. Old vulnerabilities remain until they are addressed. Shadow systems persist until they are found. Trust assumptions remain exploitable until they are challenged and re-engineered.

The lessons of the pager wars are lessons about human nature as much as technology.
They are lessons about the consequences of treating invisibility as security, about the dangers of believing that what we do not see cannot hurt us. They are lessons about how adversaries do not need to defeat our strongest systems; they need only to find our weakest ones. And they are lessons about how those weaknesses often exist not because we lacked technology, but because we lacked the operational will to see, to authenticate, to encrypt, and to distrust by default.

The organizations that thrive in the contested information environments of the future will not necessarily be those with the biggest cybersecurity budgets, the most advanced detection algorithms, or the flashiest defense-in-depth diagrams. They will be the ones that remember the simplest truths: that security begins with visibility, that trust must be earned continuously, that every signal carries risk, and that the human tendency to forget, to assume, and to defer is as dangerous as any adversary waiting on the other side.

These are not new lessons. They are old lessons. Older, even, than the first pager message intercepted from the air and turned against its sender. And they are lessons we can afford to forget only if we are willing to accept the consequences again — consequences that will not wait to announce themselves loudly, but will arrive quietly, patiently, as a shadow moving through a signal, unnoticed until it is far too late to stop.

Examples of the cost of forgotten visibility are not confined to the past. They are recent, ongoing, and deeply instructive for any serious defender. Major breaches over the past decade have repeatedly traced their origins not to the failure of front-line defenses, but to the exploitation of unmonitored, underprotected, or entirely unknown systems lingering at the edges of complex environments.

In the breach of a major retail corporation, attackers gained access not by penetrating the company's hardened point-of-sale networks directly, but by compromising a third-party HVAC vendor whose credentials granted limited but sufficient access into the broader environment. The vendor's connection, intended for remote monitoring of environmental systems, was old, poorly segmented, and insufficiently monitored. It was not malicious insiders or cutting-edge exploits that brought down defenses. It was the exploitation of trust assumptions and forgotten pathways — the modern equivalent of a broadcasted pager signal, left open and unguarded because it was seen as peripheral, unimportant.

The SolarWinds compromise that shook the cybersecurity world was not executed through a direct frontal assault on hardened government and enterprise systems. It was achieved by exploiting trust in the software supply chain, injecting poisoned code into an update mechanism that defenders had no reason to distrust. Yet beneath the technical sophistication, the success of the operation was rooted in the same principle exposed during the pager wars: the attacker moved not against what was defended, but against what was assumed to be safe. The update channel, like the pager message, was trusted implicitly, authenticated superficially, and insufficiently scrutinized.

In healthcare, repeated breaches of hospital networks have originated through legacy medical devices — imaging equipment, patient monitoring systems, wireless infusion pumps — operating on unencrypted, unauthenticated protocols because they were deployed in eras before cyber threat models accounted for patient data as a strategic target. These devices, invisible to many asset inventories, unpatched due to regulatory complexity or operational necessity, provide attackers with footholds from which to observe, map, and ultimately escalate privileges within environments where the protection of life-critical systems depends on speed and certainty.

In every case, the breach did not begin with a dramatic penetration of front-line defenses. It began with a gap in visibility, a failure of inventory, a misplaced trust.
It began with a signal shadow — a system left outside the active field of defensive focus — exploited by an adversary who understood that the path to victory lay not through confrontation, but through exploitation of what defenders had chosen, consciously or unconsciously, to overlook.

Defenders must internalize that in the contested cyber environments of today and tomorrow, attackers map differently. They do not begin with the strongest points of the network. They begin by asking: what have the defenders forgotten? What have they assumed safe? What have they left visible, unguarded, or unquestioned?

The answer to these questions defines the true attack surface. And in an environment where perimeter defenses, detection algorithms, and response playbooks are growing ever more sophisticated, it is the exploitation of the forgotten, the neglected, and the assumed that offers adversaries their surest paths to operational success.

Cyber defense strategies must shift accordingly. Visibility programs must not be constrained by current operational maps. They must hunt actively for what is not yet documented, for what has drifted into shadow over years of operational churn.

Threat models must not prioritize only the high-profile assets but must recognize the cumulative strategic value of exploiting low-profile, low-visibility systems.

Incident response plans must assume that attackers will move through these forgotten spaces, using them as platforms for lateral movement, persistence, and escalation.

This shift demands uncomfortable choices. It demands investment in asset discovery, in segmentation of legacy environments, in hardening of systems that were never designed for a contested threat landscape. It demands accepting that no system, however peripheral it may seem, is free of strategic value to an adversary. It demands the ruthless prioritization of reducing the invisible, the undocumented, the untrusted — even when doing so carries operational disruption, political resistance, or cost.

The price of neglect is visible not only in the breaches we know about, but in the breaches still undiscovered — compromises that began with a forgotten device, a shadow connection, a hidden signal, exploited by an adversary patient enough to wait until conditions favored decisive action.

Every device left out of inventory, every communication

channel left unencrypted, every assumption of trust left unchallenged is an opportunity created for the adversary.

The only counter to this quiet erosion of security is a culture that treats visibility, authentication, and skepticism not as compliance artifacts but as operational imperatives.
A culture that remembers the lessons of the pager wars — that what is invisible to defenders is not invisible to adversaries, that what is assumed safe is often most at risk, and that trust, once broken through exploitation of the overlooked, can take years to rebuild.

Cybersecurity will not be won by better dashboards alone. It will not be secured by monitoring only what is easy to see or by hardening only what is high-profile. It will be won by those who map their environments as adversaries do — relentlessly, exhaustively, without assumption. It will be secured by those who encrypt every signal not because it is convenient but because it is necessary. And it will endure among those who remember that the shadows cast by forgotten systems are not relics of the past, but active battlefields of the present and future.

Victory in this contest will not be announced. It will be measured in the attacks that fail because no foothold could be found, no assumption could be exploited, no overlooked system could be quietly turned against its owner.

In the silence of unexploited signal shadows, true security will be found.

The challenge ahead is not simply technical. It is cultural, philosophical, and ultimately existential for any organization that seeks to survive in an environment where invisibility no longer protects, where assumptions no longer shield, and where the adversary sees more clearly the vulnerabilities defenders refuse to confront.

Modern cyber defense must evolve into a discipline of adversarial vision. It must train itself to see not only what systems claim to be doing, but what they could become under adversarial control. It must recognize that every forgotten device, every unchecked trust relationship, every unexamined communication channel is a signal shadow — a potential weapon, a future compromise written into the present architecture.

Resilience will belong to those who refuse to be lulled into comfort by the sophistication of their surface defenses. It will belong to those who resist the optimism that new technology erases old liabilities. It will belong to those who understand that the battles for system integrity, operational trust, and organizational survival are fought daily, invisibly, in the spaces between monitoring, between policy, between assumptions.

Asset discovery must not be treated as an initiative. It must be a continuous operational function, as central as patching or logging or response readiness. Every new discovery, every new inventory correction, must be seen not as an embarrassment, but as a victory — one less shadow for the adversary to hide in, one less forgotten signal that could be turned against its source.

Encryption must not be rationed according to perceived threat or exposure level.
It must be applied universally, reflexively, without question, because the alternative is to rely on hope — hope that unencrypted data will not be intercepted, hope that lateral movement will be noticed before it is too late, hope that the adversary is less patient than the defender is inattentive.

Authentication must be a living process, not a static control. Devices and users must continually re-earn trust. Context must be evaluated constantly. Anomalies must be weighted with suspicion, not dismissed with convenience. And systems that cannot meet these standards must be isolated or decommissioned, no matter how operationally painful the transition.

Threat modeling must begin from the perspective that defenders are operating inside a partially known, partially understood environment. It must assume that there are always shadows. It must assume that there are always overlooked vulnerabilities. And it must train defenders to think like adversaries, to move through their own infrastructures with the ruthlessness and imagination of those who would exploit them.

Above all, organizations must build cultures that revere operational humility.
Not in the sense of defeatism, but in the disciplined acknowledgment that complexity creates blindness, that trust is fragile, that security is a continuous, unfinished struggle against human tendencies toward assumption, convenience, and forgetfulness.

The battle for signal dominance is no longer a distant contest among nation-states alone.
It plays out every day inside corporations, utilities, hospitals, transportation networks — anywhere that electronic systems sustain human life and institutional continuity.

Those who win will not necessarily be those who deploy the most powerful artificial intelligence, or the most sophisticated behavioral analytics. They will be those who remember that security begins with the simplest, hardest disciplines: seeing what is really there; trusting nothing without verification; protecting every signal, not just the ones deemed most valuable; treating every device as a potential entry point until proven otherwise. And never assuming that yesterday's defensive architectures are sufficient for today's adversarial patience.

The lessons of the pager wars are not nostalgic anecdotes about a simpler time.
They are mirrors, held up to modern defenders, reflecting uncomfortable truths about the risks that still endure — not

because technology has failed, but because human nature has not changed.

Those who learn from these signal shadows will build environments where attackers find no foothold, where trust must be earned at every step, and where every attempt to weaponize the unseen is met not with blindness, but with vigilance sharpened by hard-won experience.

Those who forget will find themselves breached not by overwhelming force, but by quiet patience. Not by new vulnerabilities, but by the oldest ones left unheeded. And not by inevitable technological superiority, but by the careful, relentless exploitation of the shadows they allowed to remain.

In cybersecurity, there are no perfect shields. There is only the contest of vigilance and erosion, of discipline and decay, of remembering versus forgetting.

Victory belongs to those who choose to see.

# CHAPTER 16 — ASYMMETRIC POWER: HOW A CHEAP RADIO CAN CHANGE A WAR

Wars are not won solely by the side with the greatest stockpile of tanks, missiles, or satellites. They are won by those who understand the terrain better — not just the physical landscape, but the informational, electromagnetic, and cognitive dimensions of the conflict. Throughout history, whenever a smaller or weaker actor survived, or even triumphed, against a seemingly superior force, it was because they exploited gaps — operational, technical, or conceptual — that their adversaries failed to protect. Often those gaps were technological in nature, but the technologies exploited were not always those admired in defense journals or showcased in military parades. They were the overlooked, the underestimated, the invisible artifacts of operational environments that no one respected until they became instruments of disruption.

The saga of intercepted pager traffic is more than a historical curiosity. It represents a foundational truth about conflict in the information age: asymmetric actors do not require technological parity to impose meaningful costs on stronger adversaries. They require only a disciplined understanding of where visibility fails, where security assumptions falter, and where operational habits leave exploitable seams. A cheap radio, a basic receiver, and a rudimentary knowledge of electromagnetic environments were sufficient to harvest information that could shape battles, affect troop movements, and expose logistical patterns. It was not the technical sophistication of the interception that mattered, but the operational discipline it represented — the willingness to listen where others assumed silence, and to see value where others saw irrelevance.

Pager signals, considered trivial by those who used them, betrayed operational rhythms, command hierarchies, and even geographic concentrations of forces. The very simplicity of the medium created blind spots; the short, technical messages appeared too insignificant to protect, too fragmented to exploit. Yet patient adversaries who gathered, correlated, and analyzed these fragments uncovered patterns invisible to their better-equipped opponents. Their advantage did not come from matching the enemy's strength but from identifying the weaknesses created by routine, habit, and neglect.

The lesson is not confined to history. In every era, the tools of asymmetric warfare have evolved, but the principles remain. Today's equivalent of the cheap radio may be a software-defined receiver picking up unencrypted telemetry from industrial devices, or a modest server mapping forgotten cloud storage. It may be a compromised third-party contractor whose limited access creates a vector into larger, more fortified systems. The same strategic logic applies: small technological advantages, patiently and intelligently applied, can create outsized effects by exploiting gaps left by overconfidence, operational complexity, or simple human oversight.

In modern environments, superior technological capability often creates its own vulnerabilities. Militaries and corporations alike tend to assume that because their primary systems are well protected, the entire environment shares that same level of defense. Hardened endpoints, encrypted command channels, and monitored infrastructure give the illusion of security while legacy interfaces, unmonitored pathways, and default configurations quietly persist beneath the surface. In asymmetric conflict, it is not the strongest part of a system that determines survivability — it is the weakest part, the neglected corner that an adversary can quietly claim and use as a base of operations.

The exploitation of neglected technologies requires neither brilliant innovation nor enormous resources. It requires patience, operational imagination, and an understanding that in every complex environment, some systems will always be forgotten, poorly monitored, or assumed to be of little consequence. A simple antenna tuned to the right frequency, a passive listening post configured to harvest emissions over weeks or months, a modest foothold established through forgotten credentials or outdated maintenance channels — these become the asymmetric tools that disrupt operations, seed confusion, and fracture decision-making cycles.

Complacency is the hidden enemy of technologically advanced powers. When forces control airspace, sea lanes, and terrestrial routes, it becomes tempting to believe that invisible spaces — the electromagnetic spectrum, metadata trails, unguarded internal communications — are less worthy of defensive attention. When millions are spent on sophisticated encryption systems, it becomes easy to dismiss the unprotected auxiliary channels as inconsequential. When network segmentation diagrams present clean, logical barriers, the messy realities of legacy backdoors and cross-domain leaks are often overlooked.

Adversaries operating asymmetrically do not prioritize prestige or complexity when choosing targets. They prioritize survivability, accessibility, and the opportunity to create cascading effects. The quiet harvesting of operational data from unsecured signals, the lateral movement through underprotected legacy systems, and the shaping of decision environments through cumulative advantage matter far more than head-on engagements with hardened perimeters.

In modern cyber conflict, the equivalent of the cheap radio is everywhere. It is the abandoned development server still exposed to the internet. It is the unencrypted sensor transmitting operational data over insecure protocols. It is the vendor access portal left open because decommissioning it was politically inconvenient or operationally risky. And as in previous conflicts, these are not the systems that defenders celebrate for their sophistication. They are the systems defenders forget exist until they are used against them.

Small technological advantages, patiently applied against neglected vulnerabilities, can offset enormous disparities in raw power. The side that maps its environment relentlessly, understands its adversary's operational habits deeply, and identifies not just the hardened fortresses but the unguarded alleyways, holds the advantage. In asymmetric contests, knowledge and patience, not hardware superiority, define strategic success.

The battlefield beneath the battlefield — the landscape of assumptions, trust relationships, unmanaged systems, and invisible emissions — is where these contests are decided. It is a battlefield invisible to most defenders, yet fully visible to those disciplined enough to look for it.

History shows that wars are rarely won by the side with the best technology alone. They are won by the side that understands the true structure of the conflict, including the invisible structures others ignore. The cheap radio is not an artifact of the past. It is a reminder that every environment, no matter how advanced, contains vulnerabilities rooted not in technology, but in human assumptions.

Victory belongs to those who are willing to listen in places others assume silence. Victory belongs to those who map what others forget to see.

The principle of asymmetric exploitation has only deepened as systems have grown more interconnected, layered, and dependent on external trust. Modern cyberwarfare is not a clash of giant technical constructs battering each other openly, but a quiet war for influence, presence, and cumulative advantage beneath the surface of visible operations. The same logic that allowed simple radios to collect life-altering intelligence during the pager wars now allows small footholds in forgotten servers, neglected devices, and misconfigured services to act as levers of disproportionate power.

Strategic patience remains the defining virtue of successful asymmetric operations. Adversaries do not need to breach the most heavily fortified systems on day one. They need only to find a way inside, however modest, and build quietly. They map not just networks but organizational behaviors, identifying when maintenance windows occur, how remote access is granted, which legacy systems are least monitored. They are not seeking immediate destruction. They are seeking persistence, the ability to gather information, shape decisions, and ultimately achieve effects disproportionate to their initial investment of resources.

One of the most critical lessons drawn from these patterns is that modern conflict is increasingly about information friction. Small, seemingly innocuous actions — the interception of unprotected telemetry, the spoofing of low-trust communications, the quiet establishment of secondary command paths — can introduce hesitation, mistrust, and operational confusion at scale. In battle, a few seconds of uncertainty can shatter synchronization. In strategic campaigns, months of harvested low-level intelligence can yield vulnerabilities that high-level surveillance would never reveal.

The cheap radio metaphor persists because complexity breeds shadows. In every large organization, whether military, industrial, or governmental, there exist systems that no longer align cleanly with the primary architectures. These are the fragments of prior generations — legacy VPNs, old backup services, forgotten authentication methods — kept alive by operational inertia and forgotten by most defenders. They are invisible to official network diagrams, yet fully real to an adversary willing to map patiently, infer connections, and find those corners where defenses grow thin.

When nations invest heavily in cutting-edge technology while leaving these shadow systems operational, they create the perfect environment for asymmetric exploitation. Every sophisticated command system is only as strong as the most vulnerable component connected to it, however indirectly. Every encrypted primary channel can be undermined if an unsecured auxiliary channel provides access to the same decision processes. Adversaries understand that direct assaults on core systems are unnecessary when persistence can be achieved through these forgotten vectors.

What emerges from this environment is a strategic model where cyberwarfare is fought not only with the most advanced tools available but also through the systematic harvesting of vulnerabilities born of neglect. It is fought through the careful observation of systems others have abandoned to operational obscurity. It is fought by leveraging the psychological effects of disruption: the erosion of trust, the paralysis of decision-making, the corrosion of operational rhythm. A cheap radio may not win a war alone, but it can deliver the critical information or disruption needed to create cascading failures across entire infrastructures.

Modern examples abound. In the cyber domain, attackers have compromised entire enterprise environments through unsecured cloud storage buckets left misconfigured, granting access to sensitive data with no need for malware or sophisticated intrusion. State-sponsored groups have pivoted into industrial control systems through forgotten remote access platforms initially deployed for vendor maintenance years earlier and never fully retired. Ransomware gangs have leveraged default administrative credentials left in embedded systems, quietly indexing networks until they found the moment to strike with maximum leverage.

These operations are not technologically overwhelming in their execution. They are devastating because of their precision, patience, and understanding of human operational tendencies. The defenders' failure to see the environment in full — to recognize not just their high-value assets but the overlooked, low-trust pathways that interconnect them — is what gives asymmetric actors their power.

The discipline to defend against such attacks does not come from technological supremacy alone. It comes from operational realism, from the hard and continuous work of reducing the attack surface not just through adding new defenses, but by systematically eliminating unneeded exposures. It comes from treating every system, however old or peripheral, as part of the active security environment. It comes from recognizing that in the eyes of an adversary, no signal is meaningless, no device insignificant, no pathway truly forgotten.

In asymmetric cyberwarfare, victory belongs to the side that is willing to map its own weaknesses with the same tenacity that adversaries bring to the task. It belongs to those who understand that no part of an operational environment is too small to matter. It belongs to those who respect the terrain of shadow systems as seriously as they respect the terrain of primary operations.

The cheap radio is a symbol of this mindset: humble in its appearance, devastating in its application. It reminds defenders that technology alone does not create superiority. Discipline, understanding, and the refusal to ignore what lies just beneath the surface of daily operations — these are the true sources of resilience in a world where asymmetric threats are not hypothetical, but active and evolving.

The future of conflict will not be defined solely by the arms races of high technology. While artificial intelligence, quantum computing, and next-generation encryption will undoubtedly shape parts of the battlefield, the fundamental dynamics of asymmetric exploitation will persist. As complexity grows, so too does the ecosystem of forgotten systems, of poorly understood interactions, of legacy artifacts embedded within the infrastructure of modern operations. The gap between what defenders believe they control and what actually exists will widen, and in that gap, adversaries will continue to find space to maneuver.

Emerging technologies will create new opportunities for asymmetric actors precisely because they are layered atop architectures still riddled with old assumptions. Cloud-native deployments will coexist with fragile authentication practices. Autonomous systems will interface with control networks that still harbor unencrypted telemetry channels. Machine learning models will draw their training data from environments vulnerable to subtle poisoning through peripheral access points. In every case, the sophistication of the front-line technology will be undermined by the quiet persistence of the neglected, the forgotten, the assumed.

The cheap radio of the next decade may not be a physical device at all. It may be a lightweight algorithm designed to scrape, correlate, and interpret emissions from public-facing APIs. It may be a small implant placed in a supply chain component, collecting low-frequency telemetry until it can be aggregated into operational insights. It may be an attacker leveraging edge devices — sensors, cameras, industrial controls — not for disruption, but for information harvesting at the margins of visibility. The principle remains unchanged: small technological efforts applied consistently against overlooked vulnerabilities yield strategic dividends far beyond their immediate appearance.

Adversaries who understand this will design campaigns around persistence, patience, and cumulative effect. They will avoid the highly visible frontal assaults that trigger immediate detection and response. They will build long-term presence within environments where defenders have grown blind to their own operational complexity. They will leverage not just technological vulnerabilities, but human ones — complacency, assumption, trust misplaced by habit rather than by verification.

For defenders, the counter to this emerging reality cannot be reliance on technology alone. New tools will be necessary, but insufficient. Asset discovery must become relentless. Vulnerability management must extend beyond compliance to operational ruthlessness, seeking out not just exploitable configurations but the hidden trust relationships that bind old systems to new ones. Communications security must be enforced universally, without exception, recognizing that partial protection creates disproportionate risk.

More fundamentally, defenders must cultivate adversarial awareness as an organizational discipline. They must train themselves to see their own infrastructures not through the lens of intention, but through the eyes of a patient attacker. They must ask not whether a system is useful to them today, but whether it offers advantage to an adversary tomorrow. They must understand that the battlefield extends into spaces they do not wish to look at, spaces they have rationalized away, spaces deemed too small, too old, or too complicated to matter.

Every operational environment carries its own field of shadows. Some are technical — forgotten systems, unmonitored links, insecure protocols. Some are procedural — outdated access practices, poorly documented dependencies. Some are cognitive — assumptions about trust, about insignificance, about the nature of threat itself. In the wars to come, these shadow fields will be where the first, most critical battles are fought and often decided.

The history of asymmetric power shows that it is not technological parity that shifts the balance in conflict. It is the ability to exploit structural weaknesses that larger forces either cannot see or refuse to acknowledge. It is the discipline to focus not on overwhelming the enemy's strengths, but on hollowing out their foundations, one unnoticed signal at a time, one neglected device at a time, one misplaced trust at a time.

A cheap radio, collecting pager traffic from the hills of southern Lebanon, demonstrated this principle decades ago. The tools have evolved, but the dynamics remain constant. Visibility is the beginning of security, not its conclusion. Trust is the result of continuous verification, not a default granted by familiarity. Complexity is not a shield. It is a battleground.

The contests of the future will not be decided solely by who fields the most powerful machines. They will be decided by who masters the shadow terrain of neglected systems and unexamined assumptions. They will be won by those who understand that even the smallest foothold, patiently leveraged, can shift the course of a campaign, a strategy, or a war.

The enduring reality of asymmetric power is that it does not require dramatic victories to achieve strategic success. It requires only the ability to impose steady, compounding costs on a stronger adversary, to erode their operational tempo, to disrupt their internal trust, and to force adaptations that draw disproportionate resources away from their primary objectives. The tools to accomplish this are rarely celebrated. They are not the hypersonic missiles or the dazzling cyberweapons unveiled at international summits. They are the simple receivers, the quietly maintained footholds, the low-cost operations that remain undetected until their effects become undeniable.

Strategic influence emerges not from overwhelming force alone, but from shaping the environment in which decisions are made. Adversaries who master asymmetric exploitation shape the tempo and character of conflict, forcing larger powers into reactive postures, into cycles of uncertainty, into endless layers of countermeasure and control. They seize initiative not through direct confrontation, but through the systematic denial of coherence. They turn the defender's own complexity into a source of friction, transforming operational strength into vulnerability.

In modern cyberwarfare, this shaping occurs invisibly at first. It happens in the compromises of systems deemed peripheral, in the unnoticed deviations of communications flows, in the subtle distortion of situational awareness. A breached telemetry feed. A compromised maintenance channel. A shadow credential that allows just enough access to monitor, to influence, to disrupt at key moments. These footholds accumulate quietly, forming the architecture of future leverage.

Resilient organizations understand that asymmetric threats cannot be defeated by technology alone. They understand that defense is a living discipline, one that requires constant humility, constant visibility, and a relentless willingness to confront the parts of their environments that feel too small, too complex, or too uncomfortable to address. They understand that every system left unexamined, every signal left unencrypted, every trust relationship left unquestioned is not just a gap, but a deliberate invitation to adversary influence.

Victory against asymmetric exploitation is not achieved by building higher walls around primary assets. It is achieved by eliminating the blind spots adversaries rely upon to bypass those walls. It is achieved by seeing what is usually ignored, by monitoring what is assumed benign, by questioning what is assumed safe. It is achieved by understanding that in contested environments, the absence of attack is not proof of security. It is often evidence of an adversary's patience.

There is no final victory in this contest. Visibility must be renewed daily. Trust must be earned continuously. Complexity must be managed ruthlessly. Organizations that embrace these disciplines will not eliminate risk, but they will deny adversaries the easy victories, the persistent footholds, the quiet shaping opportunities that asymmetric actors rely upon.

The cheap radio is a reminder that technology's power lies not in its cost or sophistication, but in how it is applied. The simple act of listening, of gathering fragments, of mapping what others leave unguarded, has the potential to shape conflicts, to alter outcomes, to defy expectations.

In the coming years, the cheapest tools — the ones based on disciplined observation, patient collection, and intelligent exploitation of overlooked spaces — will continue to offset even the most dazzling advances in defense technology. They will continue to remind us that power in conflict is not measured only by what is built or bought, but by what is understood, leveraged, and shaped quietly from the margins.

Those who prevail in future conflicts will not be those who rely solely on superior weaponry or greater resources. They will be those who refuse to leave parts of their environment invisible. They will be those who respect the small, the forgotten, the assumed. They will be those who understand that in modern war, knowledge is asymmetry, and asymmetry is power.

In every conflict, there is a second battlefield — not the one measured in ground held or forces destroyed, but the one fought in the silent space between emissions, between forgotten devices, between signals that once seemed too trivial to matter.
It is there, in that contested, invisible space, that wars are increasingly won and lost.
And it is there that a cheap radio, patiently listening, still has the power to change the course of history.

# CHAPTER 17 — OPERATION GRIM BEEPER: THE RETURN OF ELECTRONIC SHADOWS

For a time, it seemed that the lessons of the pager wars had been internalized. Israel hardened its battlefield communications. Hezbollah moved away from reliance on open wireless protocols. Electronic warfare became a background concern, managed through discipline and technological upgrade. Yet war is not static, and neither are its assumptions. In the shadows of the Syrian Civil War, and again during the rising tensions along the Israeli-Lebanese border in 2023 and 2024, the patterns once thought relegated to history began to reemerge.

The invisible battlefield of signals and emissions, once defined by crude pager bursts and analog radio chatter, evolved but never disappeared. It simply grew more complex, more embedded within the operational fabric of modern irregular warfare. Hezbollah expanded its communications infrastructure, investing in encrypted push-to-talk radios, satellite uplinks, commercial mobile networks, and ad hoc battlefield relays. Yet the fundamental vulnerabilities remained: signals had to be transmitted, systems had to trust identity, and human operators, under stress, would revert to expedient practices.

As border skirmishes escalated in late 2023, it became clear that Israel's electronic warfare units had not forgotten the lessons of southern Lebanon. Reports began to surface of signal disruption campaigns targeting Hezbollah's tactical communications. Open-source intelligence documented sudden failures of handheld radios used by Hezbollah field commanders. Civilian mobile networks, particularly in southern Lebanon, experienced unexplained outages in areas close to Israeli surveillance assets. In the fog of rising tension, there were indications of something more deliberate: not just jamming or denial of service, but precision spoofing, interception, and psychological shaping conducted through the electromagnetic domain.

Multiple sources suggested that Israeli forces, likely through elements of Unit 8200 and affiliated EW units, had begun targeting Hezbollah's ad hoc networks with tailored electronic operations. In some cases, intercepted traffic from low-priority systems — logistical coordination, rear-echelon messaging — was used to infer movement patterns and supply routes. In other instances, spoofed communications were allegedly injected into Hezbollah command channels, creating confusion about orders, timing, and operational intent.

The sophistication of these operations stood in stark contrast to the blunt-force jamming campaigns of earlier decades. Rather than flooding the spectrum indiscriminately, modern Israeli tactics appeared to focus on selective manipulation. Spoofed withdrawal orders, false reports of Israeli troop movements, fabricated casualty notifications — these techniques mirrored, in spirit, the same dynamics that Hezbollah had once exploited against Israel's own pagers. The tools had evolved, but the battlefield logic had not: sow doubt, fracture cohesion, exploit the reliance on trusted signals.

Most striking were the reports — unconfirmed but consistent across multiple independent observers — that Israel had reactivated techniques targeting unsecured or lightly secured paging and radio systems used by Hezbollah's support infrastructure. Logistics hubs, resupply teams, and secondary command layers were allegedly monitored through legacy wireless transmissions, some of them no more secure than the pager messages of twenty years prior. It appeared that in the rush to expand and sustain forces across multiple theaters, Hezbollah had created its own version of the blind spots it once exploited.

In this sense, the electromagnetic battlefield completed a grim circle. The actors had changed roles, but the vulnerabilities persisted. Information leaked through the same fundamental mechanisms: emissions that could not be fully concealed, trust that could not be fully enforced, operational rhythms that could not be fully hidden. Even in an era of encrypted apps and hardened radios, the human reliance on speed, improvisation, and operational convenience recreated old risks in new forms.

Israel's electronic operations against Hezbollah in 2023 and 2024 demonstrated not only technical proficiency but strategic patience. The goal was not immediate battlefield collapse. It was shaping: conditioning Hezbollah's forces to question their own communications, slowing decision-making at critical junctures, injecting enough uncertainty into the tactical picture to erode confidence over time.

Yet the shaping did not end at confusion and delay. In September 2024, it evolved into something far more irreversible — a direct attack that turned Hezbollah's own trusted communication devices into weapons against them.

The quiet shaping of Hezbollah's communications environment through spoofing and interception was violently escalated during what would later be reported as "Operation Grim Beeper." In a coordinated series of explosions across southern Lebanon and parts of Syria, Hezbollah operatives were struck not by conventional airstrikes or artillery, but by the very devices they relied on to communicate. Pagers, walkie-talkies, and other portable communications equipment detonated nearly simultaneously, killing dozens and injuring thousands.

Investigative accounts revealed that the devices had been compromised well before their deployment. Small quantities of PETN explosive were embedded in battery compartments during manufacturing, concealed from ordinary inspection methods. The compromised devices were seeded into Hezbollah's logistical networks through shell companies operating in Europe and Asia, exploiting supply chain trust at its deepest levels.

The explosives were remotely triggered, though the precise mechanism remains classified. When the detonation signals were sent, the result was instantaneous: chaos, confusion, and devastation among Hezbollah's field units and support personnel. The operation demonstrated not only technical prowess but the extraordinary strategic patience necessary to infiltrate supply chains, maintain operational silence, and strike with precision timing.

Strategically, the impact extended far beyond the immediate casualties. Trust in Hezbollah's logistical and operational backbone was shattered. Every device became suspect. Every message carried the shadow of mortal risk. Hezbollah was forced to question not only the integrity of its communications but the very security of its procurement networks. Psychological paralysis set in, amplifying the already corrosive effects of earlier signal disruption operations.

The operational doctrine behind Operation Grim Beeper represented a convergence of information warfare, supply chain subversion, and kinetic force — a direct evolution of the silent battles waged through intercepted pager traffic decades earlier. Where the old pager wars sowed doubt, the new electromagnetic wars sowed destruction from within.

The ethical implications of embedding physical lethality within information tools were not lost on observers. Critics warned that the deliberate targeting of personal communications devices blurred lines of distinction between combatant and civilian, raising questions under the laws of armed conflict. Yet defenders of the operation pointed to

Hezbollah's own history of embedding within civilian systems, arguing that the responsibility for this erosion of norms rested equally on those who had militarized the infrastructure of everyday life.

In strategic terms, Operation Grim Beeper mirrored earlier evolutions in cyber warfare, most notably the Stuxnet operation against Iranian nuclear facilities. In both cases, patient infiltration of trusted systems led not to immediate exposure but to carefully calibrated, precisely targeted physical effects. Where Stuxnet silently spun centrifuges into destruction while reporting false data to operators, the exploding pagers silently infiltrated Hezbollah's operational space before erupting into visible chaos. In both cases, trust was weaponized — not just the trust in technology, but the trust in the very fabric of operational normalcy.

The deeper lesson was not about technology. It was about dependency. As forces increasingly intertwine their effectiveness with electronic and informational infrastructures, their vulnerabilities multiply invisibly alongside their capabilities. The stronger the dependency, the greater the opportunity for asymmetric exploitation by disciplined adversaries willing to think over the horizon of conventional engagements.

The psychological aftermath of the exploding pagers may prove to be the operation's most enduring legacy. For Hezbollah, the betrayal of trusted tools shattered not only operational confidence but the mythology of invulnerability. Every pager, every radio, every unsecured device became a vector of fear, slowing movement, fracturing decision-making, and eroding the organizational cohesion that irregular forces depend upon for survival.

Victory in modern conflict does not always announce itself through grand battles or territorial gains. Increasingly, it announces itself through silence — through decisions delayed, actions hesitated, plans doubted. The battle for initiative, once fought at the visible level of maneuver warfare, now unfolds invisibly within the contested space of trust and communications. And in that contest, the side that listens longer, that moves more precisely through the electromagnetic shadows, holds the advantage even before the first kinetic shot is fired.

Strategically, these operations revealed a deeper shift. Israel no longer viewed electronic warfare solely as a tactical support tool for kinetic operations. Instead, it became an independent axis of competition, capable of shaping the broader operational environment through the gradual erosion of the adversary's internal trust mechanisms. Electronic attacks were timed not only to battlefield maneuvers but to political cycles, public perception management, and strategic signaling. By undermining Hezbollah's communications credibility internally, Israel subtly reinforced external narratives about Hezbollah's vulnerability, its lack of operational control, and its exposure to modern surveillance and exploitation.

The asymmetry lay not merely in technological superiority, but in the strategic patience with which it was applied. Hezbollah, despite its modernization efforts, remained bound by the realities of irregular warfare: it could not fully abandon wireless communications, it could not encrypt every layer of its operations without unacceptable loss of flexibility, and it could not prevent human error in environments saturated with stress and friction. These limitations, universal to all forces operating in contested environments, created opportunities that disciplined adversaries could exploit over time.

From an operational perspective, the return to signal-centric shaping operations highlighted the criticality of controlling the cognitive space of conflict. Modern battlefields are decided not only through firepower but through perception

— the perception of command integrity, the perception of situational awareness, the perception of initiative. By targeting Hezbollah's communication chains, Israel was not simply degrading battlefield effectiveness. It was degrading the psychological cohesion necessary to sustain coordinated resistance over time.

The lessons of the past have returned, not as relics, but as sharpened tools. The cheap radio, the intercepted pager, the unguarded emission — all have evolved into an ecosystem of vulnerabilities waiting for those with the discipline and vision to exploit them. The contest is no longer merely about who has the most powerful weapons, but about who can best see and shape the invisible terrain where trust, coordination, and initiative are forged or broken.

Victory in this domain belongs not only to those who can deny the adversary's communications, but to those who can erode the adversary's will to trust their communications at all.

In that contested space, the cheap radio has not disappeared.
It has evolved.
And those who forget its enduring power to change the trajectory of conflicts do so at their peril.

# CHAPTER 18 — EPILOGUE: THE LAST UNENCRYPTED MESSAGE

History does not always hinge on grand battles or sweeping offensives. Sometimes it turns on a single overlooked signal, a single moment of carelessness, a fragment of information floating in the electromagnetic ether, waiting for someone with the patience and discipline to hear it. In an age saturated with communications, where the flow of information is constant and overwhelming, it is tempting to believe that any single message, any single transmission, is too small to matter. But in war, as in every human endeavor that depends on uncertainty and timing, the smallest cracks often yield the greatest consequences.

In the southern hills of Lebanon, during the summer of 2006, a simple pager transmission — no more sophisticated than a note passed across a classroom — revealed the movement of an Israeli patrol. It was not a high-level order or a strategic directive. It was a routine logistical update, the sort of thing transmitted hundreds of times a day without a second thought. But it was enough. Hezbollah's listening posts caught the signal, decrypted it not through any technical wizardry but through the simple fact that it was never protected to begin with, and reacted. The ambush that followed was not the result of strategic brilliance or technological mastery. It was the product of discipline, patience, and the willingness to see value where others saw noise.

One intercepted pager message set off a chain of events that culminated in the capture of two Israeli soldiers, the deaths of several others, and the eruption of a war that neither side had intended to ignite at that moment. The initial act was invisible, unremarked, almost mundane. Its consequences reshaped the operational landscape for years to come. One unguarded signal. One unencrypted fragment of operational truth released into the open air. And a war was born.

The story is not an outlier. Across conflicts ancient and modern, the pattern repeats: small information leaks accumulate, unnoticed until they coalesce into decisive fractures. The battlefield is never composed solely of terrain and force; it is also composed of information, of perceptions, of the invisible architecture of trust that binds movements into plans and plans into victories. In this architecture, every signal matters, and every act of transmission is an act of risk. The complacency that creeps into routine — the belief that some communications are too minor, too low-value to protect — is not a neutral habit. It is an invitation.

The modern battlefield, cluttered as it is with encrypted radios, satellite uplinks, mesh networks, and digital command systems, is no less vulnerable than the pager grids of twenty years ago. In fact, it is more vulnerable precisely because of its complexity. Each device, each connection, each handshake between nodes, carries not just data but assumptions about trust, visibility, and control. Each emission, however fleeting, is a potential vector for exploitation. The illusion that any signal can be harmless persists not because it is true, but because acknowledging the full risk is exhausting.

But adversaries are not exhausted. They do not operate on the defenders' timelines of fatigue and assumption. They operate with patience, with a willingness to sift through oceans of noise for the one signal that matters. They understand that the decisive message is rarely labeled as such. It arrives buried in the ordinary, transmitted without ceremony, dismissed by its sender as inconsequential. And yet it shapes the field of battle as surely as any missile or mortar.

The last unencrypted message is not a relic of the past. It is a certainty of the future. Somewhere, in the contested spaces of modern conflict, a transmission will leave its point of origin without encryption, without authentication, without serious thought. It will pass through the air like a breath. It will be collected by someone listening carefully enough. And it will change the outcome of a skirmish, a battle, perhaps a war. It will not be recognized for what it is at the moment of transmission. It will be recognized only in retrospect, when the consequences have already hardened into history.

The warning for the future is simple, and it is absolute: there is no such thing as a harmless transmission. Every signal is a statement of trust — in technology, in process, in operational discipline. Every signal is an opportunity for adversaries to see what was not meant to be seen, to infer what was meant to remain obscure, to exploit what was meant to be routine. The war for control of the electromagnetic terrain is not a future possibility; it is an ongoing reality, unfolding invisibly every moment systems breathe life into the air with information.

Defenders who fail to grasp this reality will find themselves fighting with half their battles already lost. They will respond to attacks whose roots they cannot see. They will patch holes they never perceived opening. They will lose operational initiative not through lack of firepower or courage but through the steady erosion of trust in their own information architecture.

The invisible battlefield demands the same rigor as the visible one. It demands encryption not as a technical afterthought but as an operational imperative. It demands authentication not as a bureaucratic checkbox but as a discipline of survival. It demands an understanding that every convenience — every shortcut in securing communications — carries a cost, a risk that may manifest not today, but inevitably.

In this future, the victors will not be those who build the tallest walls or the fastest networks alone. They will be those who understand that the quiet spaces between transmissions, the marginal details of signal discipline, are not margins at all. They are the front lines. They are the points of first contact in wars that will be fought not only with weapons but with the unseen movements of information across contested air.

The last unencrypted message is always waiting. It waits in every system built without full knowledge of its exposures. It waits in every rushed deployment, every "good enough" compromise, every decision to trust in obscurity rather than in defense. It waits because human nature, not technology, creates the spaces in which it lives. And it will continue to shape the future of conflict as long as those spaces remain.

To imagine that such messages belong only to the past is to repeat the mistakes that filled the air with unguarded signals during the pager wars. To believe that technology alone, unaided by discipline and vigilance, can close the vulnerabilities of the electromagnetic battlefield is to invite defeat in its next evolution. Victory will belong to those who remember the lesson: that every signal is a battlefield, every transmission a decision, every emission a declaration of operational posture — whether intended or not.

And somewhere, sometime, in some future conflict already forming beyond today's horizon, a simple, unencrypted message will again shape the course of history. Perhaps it will be a maintenance update, a logistic note, a hurried confirmation between commanders. It will seem too small to matter. It will seem harmless. And someone will be listening.

The technology itself will continue to evolve. Encryption algorithms will grow more sophisticated. Authentication protocols will deepen in complexity. Zero-trust architectures will stretch across networks like webs spun by cautious architects who have seen too many breaches slip through overconfidence. But none of it will erase the human factors that leave the first cracks exposed. Rushed operations, field improvisations, outdated equipment pressed into service because it still works, a technician's shortcut to meet a deadline — these are not anomalies. They are constants, woven into the reality of human systems under pressure.

And so, the battlefield will remain littered not only with bullets and broken machines, but with signals. Half-seen, half-understood, moving invisibly through contested air. Each carrying some fragment of operational truth, some shard of intent or vulnerability. The adversaries who endure, who shape conflicts rather than merely reacting to them, will be those who understand that the war for information is fought not once but every moment a device is powered on, every moment a signal leaks into the air.

In the years to come, the definition of what constitutes a "harmless" signal will continue to erode. The operational environment will grow more saturated, not less. Industrial control systems, battlefield logistics, medical telemetry, civilian infrastructure — all will increasingly blur into the contested spectrum, each emission carrying metadata, timing signatures, environmental clues. The side that dismisses these fragments as noise will be the side that wakes to find its movements mapped, its intentions predicted, its vulnerabilities cataloged before the first physical engagement begins.

There will be moments in future conflicts where a signal, meant for no one but its intended recipient, will be captured by patient adversaries. It will not be a dramatic intercept. It will not carry obvious secrets. It will be a maintenance routine, a heartbeat of system status, a brief acknowledgment of receipt. But folded inside that small transmission, in its metadata, its timing, its unintended context, there will be value. Enough value, perhaps, to infer a broader movement. Enough to trigger a defensive realignment, a misplaced offensive, a cascade of consequences rippling outward from a message no one thought mattered enough to shield.

The same impatience that once allowed pagers to blast unencrypted orders across Lebanon's hills still lives in modern systems. It manifests in under-resourced cybersecurity teams, in procurement cycles that prioritize convenience over control, in assumptions that the complexity of new systems will obscure their weaknesses. It manifests in operators who see encryption as an optional overhead rather than as an operational survival mechanism. It manifests in the quiet, deadly space between what is built and what is truly defended.

In this sense, the story of intercepted pagers is not merely historical. It is prophetic. It warns that every advance in connectivity brings with it a commensurate burden of vigilance. That every tool which accelerates communication, coordination, and action simultaneously opens windows of exposure. The last unencrypted message is not an artifact. It is a constant, waiting for the moment when vigilance falters.

And vigilance always falters.

Not everywhere at once. Not catastrophically at first. It erodes in small decisions. It bleeds away through routine. It degrades at the margins, where no alarms sound, where no immediate consequences reinforce the importance of discipline. It is lost when the minor transmission is sent without encryption because "it's just a status check." It is lost when the shortcut is justified because "we'll fix it later." It is lost when the urgent crowds out the important.

This erosion is the true battlefield in the electromagnetic wars of the present and future. It is fought within organizations long before it is fought between them. It is fought in whether cultures value secure practices not merely as technical requirements but as existential imperatives. It is fought in whether leaders understand that risk management is not a checklist but a daily posture of awareness, skepticism, and deliberate action.

When the history of future conflicts is written, many decisive moments will trace their roots back not to missiles launched or battles fought, but to emissions unnoticed. To unencrypted messages shrugged off as too small to matter. To signals treated as background noise until the enemy read them like a map.

There will be no warning when the consequences of such oversight emerge. There will be no flashing indicators or last-minute recoveries. There will only be the sudden realization that the adversary has seen the battlefield differently, moved differently, chosen differently — and that initiative, once lost, cannot easily be regained.

The invisible war, fought in every emission, every signal, every decision to protect or neglect, is no less brutal than the wars fought with conventional arms. Its victories are quieter but no less final. Its defeats are cumulative, compounding until they burst into visibility at the worst possible moment.

In this environment, the final defense is not technology alone. It is mindset. It is organizational culture. It is the relentless practice of assuming that every transmission is a battle fought between exposure and protection. It is the understanding that discipline is not a guarantee of survival, but the only viable foundation for it.

The last unencrypted message will not announce itself. It will not be flagged by alarms. It will slip through because someone, somewhere, at some moment, decided it did not matter enough to be defended.

The adversary will decide otherwise.

The invisible battlefield is not static. It adapts alongside the systems built upon it. Artificial intelligence, once considered a peripheral tool, now sits at the heart of analysis and interception. Machine learning models no longer wait for analysts to comb through harvested signals; they harvest, correlate, and infer vulnerabilities at speeds that human operators cannot match. Every unsecured transmission, every timing anomaly, every minor deviation in signal patterns can be flagged, categorized, and exploited faster than any conventional response cycle allows.

This is the environment modern defenders face. An environment where the adversary's ability to detect and exploit an unguarded signal no longer depends solely on human patience, but on machine-driven persistence. The scale has changed. The speed has changed. But the underlying vulnerabilities — the assumptions about which signals matter and which can be ignored — have not.

The future belongs to those who internalize this reality before it manifests in catastrophe. It belongs to those who abandon the comforting myth of harmless transmissions and who understand that security is not a defensive posture but an operational foundation. It belongs to those who recognize that the electromagnetic battlefield has no neutral ground, no moments off, no areas of lesser importance. Every device is a combatant. Every signal is a risk vector. Every moment of transmission is a moment when survival is negotiated invisibly.

The final warning is not one of inevitability, but of discipline. The battles ahead will not be lost because technology failed. They will be lost because vigilance faltered. Because somewhere along the chain of operations, the idea persisted that some communications were too small to protect, too routine to matter, too isolated to exploit. And that idea, once allowed into the operational bloodstream, will propagate silently until the opportunity it offers is harvested by someone patient enough to wait for it.

The last unencrypted message is not a technical vulnerability. It is a human one. It is a product of assumptions that were once harmless but are no longer tolerable. It is the product of cultures that prioritize speed over security, routine over rigor, assumption over verification. It is the manifestation of every quiet moment when the decision to protect was deferred because the consequences of exposure seemed abstract, distant, or unlikely.

But war has no patience for abstraction. Adversaries have no interest in what was intended. They act on what is available. And every signal offered carelessly into contested air, every fragment of operational posture leaked into the electromagnetic domain, becomes available. It becomes actionable. It becomes part of a broader campaign to degrade initiative, fracture trust, and shape outcomes before conventional battles even unfold.

There is no technological solution that can fully close this vulnerability. No encryption protocol, no access control system, no anomaly detection platform can substitute for a culture that treats every transmission as a strategic decision. The systems may assist, but the mindset must precede them. The understanding must be rooted deep within organizations, reinforced not only through policy but through daily operational practice.

The electromagnetic battlefield is not coming. It is already here. It stretches across every wireless network, every radio transmission, every autonomous system coordinating movements in real time. It moves invisibly, but it shapes outcomes visibly. It determines not just who wins or loses, but who acts and who hesitates, who controls tempo and who reacts, who sees the battlefield clearly and who sees it distorted through the haze of manipulated or missing information.

The adversaries who will dominate this new space are not necessarily those with the most powerful weapons or the largest networks. They are those with the patience to listen longer, to map deeper, to act earlier. They are those who see the space between emissions as contested terrain and who fight there with the same intensity they reserve for conventional fronts.

And so the lesson persists, uncompromising and absolute:
Every signal matters.
Every transmission is a potential battlefield.
Every act of communication is an act of exposure unless treated otherwise.

The last unencrypted message is waiting — not in the past, but in the future.
It will not carry a banner. It will not sound an alarm.
It will move silently, unprotected, into an environment where someone patient, disciplined, and adversarial is always listening.

And when it is heard, it will shape the course of battles long before the first shots are fired.

But even that warning — even the understanding that every transmission carries risk — no longer captures the full danger. In the modern battlefield, information systems are not merely targets for interception or exploitation. They have become vectors for physical destruction. Devices once designed solely for communication, once assumed to be passive participants in the electromagnetic contest, can now betray their users not by leaking information but by detonating in their hands.

The events of 2024 made this clear. Pagers, radios, and communications systems that were once vulnerabilities of exposure became vulnerabilities of survival. Through the quiet infiltration of supply chains and the patient embedding of concealed sabotage, the same devices that once leaked signals into the air without encryption instead released explosives without warning. Trust was not merely eroded. It was weaponized. It was turned inward, against the users themselves.

In this new reality, the concept of operational risk has expanded. It is no longer sufficient to view emissions as the sole battlefield. The device itself — its provenance, its integrity, its hidden layers — has become a contested space.

The silent war for information has evolved into a silent preparation for physical attack, where the first indication of compromise is not an intercepted message but a sudden, lethal detonation.

The progression was inevitable. If information is a battlefield, then the tools that carry it are battlegrounds as well. What can be intercepted can be manipulated. What can be manipulated can be weaponized. And what can be weaponized can be destroyed — not symbolically, but literally, with fire and blood.

The lesson that once centered on the importance of encryption now extends deeper. It demands not only the securing of communications, but the securing of the entire trust chain: the manufacturing, distribution, and fielding of every device entrusted with operational weight. Every radio, every pager, every node in the information architecture must now be treated not merely as a transmitter, but as a potential Trojan horse — silent until it chooses not to be.

The invisible battlefield and the visible battlefield are no longer separate. They are one continuum, blending information, trust, and kinetic power into a single, seamless domain of conflict. Those who treat communications as benign will not merely lose information; they will lose lives. Those who continue to believe that a signal is harmless because it is routine will learn, too late, that in modern war, routine is the perfect camouflage for decisive effects.

The last unencrypted message was never just a leak waiting to happen. It was the first breach in a wall that, once weakened, allowed the enemy to reach through not only with ears but with hands. It was the quiet opening act to a new kind of warfare, where trust is not simply lost, but violently and irreversibly shattered.

And somewhere, even now, in some future conflict already seeded by today's assumptions, another device is waiting.
Not to be overheard.

But to be detonated.

# ABOUT THE AUTHOR

Bill Johns began his journey into the world of computing over 45 years ago, starting as a hobbyist building and upgrading computer hardware. His natural curiosity and technical aptitude soon led him to explore computer networks, and before long, he had built a large Bulletin Board System (BBS) that became a hub for early online communities. At the same time, Bill was applying his growing expertise to building corporate networks, helping businesses navigate the new landscape of interconnected systems.

When the internet began to take shape, Bill adapted his BBS to the online world, delving deep into internet protocols by reading RFCs (Request for Comments) and engaging with fellow tech pioneers on the Undernet, Dalnet, EfNet, and similar forums. His deep understanding of networks and security caught the attention of a major social networking platform, where motivated by relentless attacks, he gained admin privileges on the network's servers through sheer skill and ingenuity. Faced with an ultimatum — explain how he did it and use his knowledge to defend the network, or face the consequences — Bill chose the high road. This decision launched him into several intense years of 24/7 live-fire hacker wars, where he was on the front lines defending critical systems from relentless attacks.

This battle-hardened experience opened the door to high-stakes contracts, including responding to the devastating effects of malware like Code Red and Nimda. Bill was brought in to help recover paralyzed networks that had been written off as lost causes — and he succeeded where others had failed. Once the dust settled from the early 2000s malware wars, Bill shifted his focus to building secure networks for U.S. Department of Defense (DoD) contractors, helping to protect national security infrastructure from emerging cyber threats.

Later in his career, Bill turned his expertise toward securing critical infrastructure, including IT and OT/ICS environments. His work spanned industries such as manufacturing, oil and gas, pharmaceuticals, automotive, water and wastewater systems, electrical power generation, and many years with nuclear power plants. Bill's accumulated knowledge and experience, stretching back to the early days of computer networking and the internet, provide a rare and invaluable perspective on the evolution of cybersecurity. His books reflect the hard-won lessons and insights gained from a career spent not just observing but actively shaping the development of secure digital systems.

www.ingramcontent.com/pod-product-compliance
Lightning Source LLC
Chambersburg PA
CBHW070932050326
40689CB00014B/3169

* 9 7 9 8 2 8 0 3 7 5 3 2 1 *